WITHDRAWN FROM
MACALESTER COLLEGE
LIBRARY

D0073602

Beyond New Testament Theology

BEYOND
NEW TESTAMENT
THEOLOGY

A story and a programme

Heikki Räisänen

SCM PRESS
London

TRINITY PRESS INTERNATIONAL
Philadelphia

First published 1990

SCM Press
26–30 Tottenham Road
London N1 4BZ

Trinity Press International
3725 Chestnut Street
Philadelphia Pa. 19104

All rights reserved. No part of this publication may be
reproduced, stored in a retrieval system, or transmitted,
in any form or by any means, electronic, mechanical,
photocopying, recording or otherwise, without the prior
permission of the publishers, SCM Press and Trinity
Press International.

Copyright © Heikki Räisänen 1990

British Library Cataloguing in Publication Data

Räisänen, Heikki
   Beyond new testament theology.
   1. Bible. N. T. – Critical studies
   I. Title
   225.6

   ISBN 0–334–01907–9

Library of Congress Cataloguing in Publication Data

Räisänen, Heikki.
   Beyond New Testament theology: a story and a programme/
Heikki Räisänen.
      p.   cm.
   Includes bibliographical references.
   ISBN 0–334–01907–9
   1. Bible.   N. T.–Theology–Study and teaching–History.
   2. Bible.   N. T.–Theology–Methodology.   I. Title.
   BS2397.R35 1990
   225.6'09'03–dc20
                                                89–48393

Typeset at The Spartan Press Ltd, Lymington, Hants
and printed in Great Britain by
Billing & Sons Ltd, Worcester

CONTENTS

Preface   ix
Introduction   xi

Part One: From Gabler to Wrede

1 The Dual Programme of Biblical Theology: J. P. Gabler   3

2 Towards a Historical New Testament Theology   6
   (a) Divorcing theology from history: D. F. Strauss   6
   (b) History as revelation: F. C. Baur   8
   (c) The liberal classic: H. J. Holtzmann   9

3 The History-of-Religions Programme of Earliest
      Christianity   13
   (a) Farewell to theology: W. Wrede   13
   (b) A youthful break with dogmas: P. Wernle   18
   (c) The history of religions as preparation for Jesus: H. Weinel   20
   (d) A history of faith in Christ: W. Bousset   21
   (e) Futuristic eschatology versus timeless religion: J. Weiss   22
   (f) Reactions against the history of religions: A. Schlatter,
       P. Feine   24
   (g) A mature synthesis ignored: J. Kaftan   27

4 Summary and Prospect   30

Part Two: From Wrede to the Present

1 New Testament Theology and the Breakthrough of
      Neo-Orthodoxy   35
   (a) Theology in the name of Paul: K. Barth   35
   (b) Dispute over the real message: K. Barth and R. Bultmann   36
   (c) The existentialist self-understanding of Paul and John:
       R. Bultmann   37

2 In the Shadow of Bultmann: Biblical History as Normative   43
   (a) History of revelation: T. Zahn, F. Büchsel   43
   (b) Apocalyptic dogmatics: E. Stauffer   44

(c) Between history and theology: E. G. Gulin, F. C. Grant   45
(d) Taking leave of the Enlightenment: M. Albertz   49
(e) The history of salvation as a universal remedy: O. Cullmann 51
(f) The teachings of an Anglican Jesus: A. Richardson   53
(g) The seed-bed of Catholic doctrine: H. Schlier,
    R. Schnackenburg, K. H. Schelkle   53
(h) Three Nordic contributions: H. Riesenfeld,
    A. T. Nikolainen, R. Kieffer   56
(i) Evangelical harmonies: G. E. Ladd, D. Guthrie, L. Morris   59

3 In the Shadow of Bultmann: Singling out the Normative   62
   (a) The programme of a humanistic theology: H. Braun   62
   (b) Bultmann for a new day: H. Conzelmann, G. Strecker,
       E. Käsemann, E. Lohse   64
   (c) The testimony of the major witnesses: W. G. Kümmel   68
   (d) A strained dialogue: L. Goppelt   71

4 The Unrealized Programme of Separate Tasks: K. Stendahl,
   J. M. Robinson, R. Morgan, K. Berger   74

5 Some Recent Trends   80
   (a) The demand of biblical theology: P. Stuhlmacher   80
   (b) The problem of unity and diversity: J. D. G. Dunn   81
   (c) Discarding the canon: H. Koester   83
   (d) Exegesis as a science of public information: G. Petzke,
       E. Schüssler Fiorenza   85
   (e) The return of experience: L. T. Johnson   86
   (f) The challenge of contextualisms   87

6 Conclusion   89

                 Part Three: Outline of a Programme

1 Historical Interpretation: Principles   93
   (a) The addressees   93
   (b) Proclamation or information?   97
   (c) The New Testament or early Christianity?   100
   (d) The relevance of the 'history of influence'   103
   (e) Religion or religious thought?   104
   (f) Purely historical?   106
   (g) The attitude of the scholar   110
   (h) The prehistory of early Christian thought   112
   (i) Finished products and earlier stages   114
   (j) Historical or thematic structure?   116
   (k) Where to start?   118
   (l) Some relevant emphases in recent research   119
   (m) Conclusion   120

2   Historical Interpretation: A Model   122
    (a) The dialectic between tradition, experience and
             interpretation   122
    (b) Global mystical experience: P. Berger and M. Eliade   124
    (c) Core experiences and the Bible   125
    (d) The biblical experience of the sacred: L. T. Johnson   127
    (e) The symbolic universe and experience   129
    (f) Some biblical examples   131
    (g) On D. Patte's semantic universe   134
    (h) On the problem of 'reductionism'   135

3   Actualizing Interpretation   139

Bibliography   142
Notes   156
Index of modern authors   203

For Risto

PREFACE

For quite some time I have been unhappy with the existing 'New Testament theologies'. At one point I started putting together my thoughts on how I would like to see someone do the job. I thought that I would manage to write an article on the principles and strategies involved quite quickly.

That was not to be. I found the project turning into a full-length book, which began to take up far too much of my time. The area that needs to be covered is so vast that the work could have gone on for ever. I am very much aware that there are all sorts of gaps in my investigation, starting from the fact that not all the syntheses written in recent decades were accessible to me. But I decided that I could not spend the rest of my life on prolegomena, and I can only hope that what is offered here is enough to prompt some further thought on the issues involved.

I bear sole responsibility for the ideas to be found in this book, but it has been a pleasure and a privilege to develop them in an inspiring atmosphere. Conversations with colleagues in our New Testament department – Dr Jarmo Kiilunen, Dr Kari Syreeni and Lic.Matti Myllykoski in particular – have been stimulating. Moreover, I am grateful for helpful and encouraging comments on the penultimate draft by colleagues very familiar with the problems discussed here but who do not share my particular point of view, Professor Georg Strecker and Dr Robert Morgan. The support of Dr John Bowden of SCM Press, extending from general encouragement to painstaking editorial work, has been invaluable.

Most important of all, I should mention a friend and colleague who has been my untiring discussion partner for over two decades. It would certainly have been far more painful than it has to develop (or become aware of) my heresies over the years, let alone publish them, had it not been for the constant support, cheerful humour and impeccable common sense of Dr Risto Lauha, Lecturer in Old Testament Exegesis in the University of Helsinki. I am happy to dedicate this book to him.

Helsinki   H. R.
November 1989

INTRODUCTION

New Testament study is not an end in itself. It is pursued for the sake of some more comprehensive enterprise, although different opinions are possible as to what that enterprise should be. For some, presumably the majority of those interested in such matters, New Testament scholarship should serve the ends of Christian theology and education. For others, its ultimate goal might be the elucidation of the role of religion in our culture. Whatever the particular motivation, there is a pressing need for *synthesizing* accounts of the religious or theological contents of the New Testament and related literature in the light of modern scholarship. Traditionally such accounts have mostly been called 'New Testament theologies'.

Too little is available to satisfy that need today. Rudolf Bultmann's *Theology of the New Testament* still stands as the unrivalled classic in the field. There is hardly a shadow of a challenger in view; New Testament theologies after Bultmann have mostly been textbooks for students with no progress beyond the master either in scope or in method. And yet Bultmann's first volume appeared more than forty years ago. Worse still, the groundwork of his book was laid as early as in the 1920s. Though unsurpassed in the grandeur of its vision, Bultmann's work is, understandably, dated in many of its individual parts, and even the glory of the vision has begun to fade in the course of time. Exegetical scholarship has not stood still in the last generation or two. There is a vast gap to be bridged between special studies and theological syntheses.

No doubt the sheer number of monographs and articles that appear year after year is an important reason for the lack of appropriate syntheses. It seems to be beyond the power of any individual to gain a sufficient overview of what is going on in the numerous sectors of New Testament exegesis, so that only elementary textbooks can be ventured.

Such a situation is, of course, quite intolerable. If a selection of more ambitious syntheses on a larger scale is not available, exegesis may lose its orientation. In any case, it will lose whatever interest it still has in the minds of those not initiated into its mysteries. Synthesizing accounts are particularly needed to provide orientation to those who are not experts in the field. There are many potential users of New Testament scholarship. The systematic and the practical theologian, the historian or phenomenologist of religion, the minister and the priest, the lay person (religious or non-religious) reflecting on questions of world-view and values – each of these groups of people (and others could be added) needs a solid synthesis of what exegetes have discovered as material for their own reflections and constructions.

But it is surely not just the sheer vastness of material to be assimilated that has deterred scholars from trying to vie with Bultmann.[1] There is a gap in content between monographs and syntheses in that many of the more recent exegetical findings have not found their way into the latter. But there is another, more serious gap as well. There is an almost incomprehensible *mental* distance between the bulk of special studies and the available synthesizing accounts. The latter seem to inhabit a different world.

Special studies on the New Testament and early Christianity are quite often conducted in a detached, descriptive, history-of-religions or literary-critical atmosphere.[2] Value-laden theological categories such as 'revelation' or 'inspiration' are seldom used at this level. Considerable theological diversity within the New Testament is taken for granted, and no attempt is made at harmonizing the differences. Biblical ideas are discussed without any sense of obligation to show how they may or may not be relevant to modern men and women in their situation.

All this changes abruptly when one turns from monographs to the synthesizing accounts.[3] The landscape is no longer historical, but overtly theological. We hear a good deal of God revealing himself definitively in Christ and speaking to us through the New Testament texts. Some diversity in the texts is admitted (often reluctantly), but the authors are at pains to show that behind the diversity there nevertheless lies a theological unity. They also make an effort to make the texts speak to modern men and women in their present situation (unless they content themselves with the simple affirmation that such a contemporary appeal is what the texts are all about).

Now it might be argued that it is the *raison d'être* of synthesizing accounts to deal with such issues; that is why they are different from monographs. Nor am I in principle opposed to all attempts at reading ancient texts with modern questions also in mind. The trouble is that the synthesizing accounts bear witness to a mental distance from everyday exegesis, to a gap that they never even attempt to bridge. It seems as if the author of a synthesis would have to deny at the outset the existence of a number of problems which confront any exegete in his or her daily work. The existence of an underlying theological unity in the New Testament is postulated rather than argued. The applicability of at least what are regarded as the central texts to modern situations is taken for granted. Divine revelation is spoken of as if its existence were self-evident. The recourse to theistic God-talk (not just on a descriptive level) is naturally a matter of course.

This is admittedly a somewhat one-sided picture, but I will be concerned to show later on in this book that it is not spun out of thin air. A gap does exist. Occasionally it seems to exist in the minds of scholars themselves. An acute analyst turns into a pious preacher when faced with the task of synthesis. (This situation is even more obvious in the field of 'Old Testament theology'.[4])

Any potential author of a synthesis is faced with a host of problems of principle and method. What exactly should be treated in a synthesis, and from what point of view? To whom should it be addressed? What should be the relation of the author to his or her[5] subject? What kind of attitude should he adopt to theological and ecclesial tradition? What is a meaningful way to organize and emphasize the material?

Not enough energy has been devoted to the resolution of such issues. There have been some laudable recent efforts here, in particular by Robert Morgan and Hendrikus Boers (see the bibliography), but these have not received the amount of discussion they deserve among the guild. It is my aim to call attention to these problems once more.

A reasonable way to tackle the issues is to analyse the history of 'New Testament theology' as a discipline from a methodological perspective.[6] This venture includes a survey of both the actual business of constructing a synthesis and the methodological discussions of how one should go about the job. The first part of this book attempts to sort out the most important features of that story. It goes without saying that I have inevitably concentrated on questions of principle, method and structure. The actual contents of the various works are presented very briefly, and others making a similar survey would surely have chosen the aspects worth mentioning somewhat differently.[7]

All history is a matter of perspective, and my account of the development of the discipline may be taken as a case in point. I have been deliberately selective, highlighting such points as seem important from my own present standpoint (though that is hardly idiosyncratic). So I have paid special attention to the existence (or non-existence) of the following features in the works discussed:

1. Awareness of the problems involved in relating historical study to theology.

2. Recognition of theological diversity within the New Testament.

3. Awareness of the cultural gap between modernity and antiquity and, consequently, of the peril of modernization.

4. As a particularly important aspect of the former, recognition of the centrality of futuristic eschatology in large parts of the New Testament, not least in the message of the historical Jesus.

5. Recognition of the necessity to study the New Testament in a broad context of political, social and religious history.

6. Appreciation of the role of human experience reflected in the religious and theological contents of the New Testament.

7. Willingness also to admit the existence of problematic claims, arguments and standpoints in New Testament texts.

8. Some concern for a fair presentation of competing traditions, notably Judaism.

A presentation from, say, a more ecclesial standpoint would have taken a different shape (as the numerous recent discussions of a 'biblical theology' designed to cover both Testaments amply testify). For instance, I have given relatively little space to Adolf Schlatter or even to Karl Barth. From my perspective, the exegetical merits of these spiritual masters do not justify the amount of attention often paid to them in connection with 'New Testament theology'. By contrast, I have wished to call attention to the merits of some more neglected figures in the field.

I shall devote a fair amount of space to discussing synthesizing works (and programmatic articles) from the turn of the century. The liberal classic of H. J. Holtzmann and the history-of-religions attempts of Wrede, Weiss, Weinel, Bousset, Wernle and Kaftan will receive a good deal of attention – more so than many of their latter-day competitors. This is by no means for the sake of antiquarian completeness. I have not sought to build up a museum of exegesis. In fact I have virtually ignored some contemporaries of those I have just mentioned who might have had a claim to more attention had I wished to give a rounded picture of the currents of the age as a whole.[8] On the contrary, it is my contention that the works of the said scholars contain insights which have been either ignored or unjustly rejected in subsequent New Testament interpretation. My personal experience is that, for all their shortcomings, the theological syntheses of Weinel or Wernle make more refreshing reading than any modern instances of the genre since Bultmann.

I would argue that New Testament scholarship made a fatal mistake when, in the aftermath of the First World War, it turned its back on the liberals and the history-of-religions school and succumbed to the rhetorical-theological appeal of dialectical theology. There is, of course, no point in repristinating the ideas of a century-old school of thought as such. Nevertheless, there is much of value in those old works which has been ignored, or ridiculed, to the detriment of present scholarship. One such feature is the unbending *critical candour* of those older scholars, manifest for instance in their discussions of Pauline theology (an area sacrosanct even to many modern perpetuators of the liberal legacy); another is their willingness to assess religious and theological ideas as secondary theories devised to interpret underlying *experiences* (although they conceived of the nature of these experiences in a one-sided way).

The story I shall try to unfold runs something like this. Two centuries ago, Gabler made a helpful theoretical distinction between historical and theological interpretation of the Bible, assigning the two tasks to two different stages of work. Praise has been lavished on Gabler ever since, but his advice has not been followed. Strauss made a heroic attempt, basically in Gablerian vein, to divorce theology from history. It may have been the radical nature of Gabler's enterprise, too shocking to be palatable at the time, that led New Testament scholars away from his proposal.

Baur and the liberals (the greatest of whom in our field was Holtzmann) fused history and theology together. Baur tried to interpret the total process of history as the revelation of the Spirit; the liberals singled out the (critically established) kernel of Jesus' message as the permanently valid religious and theological norm.

Wrede made a lucid distinction between history and theology, assigning only the former to the domain of the exegete. Unfortunately, he died early, and his proposal was not followed up even among the members of the history-of-religions 'school', whose spokesman he was. Although most of early Christianity was described historically by the history-of-religions scholars, the message of Jesus (interpreted in terms of liberal theology) was still conceived of as a theological norm by which everything else was gauged.

Wrede's proposal was not followed, since the urge of exegetes to act as theologians as well was too deep-seated. In the wake of dialectical theology, New Testament exegesis gave in to the neo-orthodox appeal of Barth. Bultmann made a gigantic attempt to bind the history of religions and theology together. He achieved his goal by a *tour-de-force*: in effect, he limited New Testament theology to the theology of Paul and John (both interpreted in existentialist terms). This move, however, freed him to examine the rest of the material in more objective history-of-religions terms.

All that has happened in the field of New Testament theology ever since has remained in the shadow of Bultmann. His pupils have tried to mediate the legacy of the master to new generations. Others have unrealistically tried to resist Bultmann's influence by describing New Testament thought as in itself normative, as if no problem of application existed. Yet others have tried to single out the normative elements of the New Testament in the course of an allegedly historical presentation. All in all, it is hard to evaluate the subsequent development of the discipline except as an anti-climax to Bultmann's work.

The striking, and disappointing, thing is that so far nobody has realized Wrede's vision. Even more startling is the fact that, except for some theoretical statements, Gabler's idea of distinguishing between historical and theological stages of work has been abandoned as well. The history of the discipline will show, I hope, that the fusion of the two tasks does not make for clarity.

In view of this, a fresh start is needed. I for one am convinced that Gabler's concern, as radicalized in different ways by Strauss and Wrede, needs to be revived. In recent times, some attention has again come to be paid to certain central concerns of the liberal exegetes and the history-of-religions school which need to be reaffirmed. This has happened in related areas of study rather than in 'New Testament theology' proper, but it is clear that the new concerns are pertinent to the future of the latter.

Thus, the existence of theological diversity in the New Testament documents has been taken more seriously than it often was (Dunn). The demand that the New Testament canon should be dismissed altogether in historical study has been revived in the area of 'New Testament introduction', given great dramatic effect by the discoveries in Nag Hammadi (Koester). The claim has also been raised that exegesis should become a public critical science which serves instruction and information in society rather than the proclamation of the church (Petzke). Finally, after so many decades of contempt on the part of the neo-orthodox, attention is again being paid to the religious experiences reflected in the texts (Johnson).

All these concerns will have a role to play in the programme which I shall try to outline in the final part of this book. In addition, I join those exegetes who have recently drawn on the sociology of knowledge as developed and applied to the study of religion by Peter Berger in particular. Berger's (and Thomas Luckmann's) concept of the 'symbolic universe' seems extremely helpful, along with Berger's emphasis on the dialectic between experience and interpretation. However, I shall maintain that 'experience' is to be understood in a much wider sense than it is by Berger, who restricts himself to mystical 'core' experiences.

The bulk of the latter part of this book deals with the principles and approaches of a historical interpretation of early Christian thought. A final chapter hints at the possibility, indeed necessity, that exegetes should also engage in a theological (or philosophical, or some other type of critically actualizing) interpretation of their historical work. The chapter is brief, for the chances of an exegete contributing *qua* exegete to the philosophical-theological quest are, in my view, far more limited than one would guess from reading current New Testament theologies. It is quite impossible to build a theology on the Bible alone. Apart from the other theological disciplines, there are immense other areas that responsible theology must take into account, including history, philosophy, sociology, anthropology and comparative religion. What role the Bible ought to play in a creative theological construction, and how, is not for the biblical scholar to stipulate. What he can do is above all to analyse the ways in which the Bible has been treated in religion, theology and society and relate his findings to what can be said about the original meaning of the relevant passages. This may seem much less than most of us have been accustomed to. And yet precisely this latter task would seem to open up quite new vistas of fruitful research and dialogue.

To summarize the thesis. 'New Testament theology' may be a legitimate part of self-consciously *ecclesial* theology. By contrast, those of us who work in a broader *academic* context should abandon such an enterprise (and, *a fortiori*, any dreams of a 'biblical theology' which would cover both Testaments). More precisely, 'New Testament theology' ought to be replaced, in this context, with two different projects: first, the 'history of early Christian thought' (or theology, if you like), evolving in the context of early Judaism; second, critical philosophical and/or theological 'reflection on the New Testament', as well as on its influence on our history and its significance for contemporary life.

My contention is not that these two tasks ought to be carried out separately, the one first and the other afterwards; that does not seem to be the way the human mind works. Nonetheless, the two tasks ought to be kept distinct (which is possible to a greater degree than some apologetic hermeneuticians claim), and it would be wise to set out the results of each at different stages in the presentation. It is not the scholar's business to make the 'two horizons', past and present, fuse together. Such an assimilation may eventually take place, but that should be left to the readers.

PART ONE

From Gabler to Wrede

I

The Dual Programme of Biblical Theology: J. P. Gabler

Modern exegesis of the Bible is rooted in Deism and Enlightenment.[1] The critical attitude of Deism towards traditional Christianity opened up new vistas in the interpretation of Scripture. Scholars penetrated into the Bible without church spectacles (e.g. John Locke). However, the new approach was no less dogmatic than the old one had been. The inherited ideology was simply replaced with a different one. With the help of philosophical criticism, an attempt was made to uncover beneath the various manifestations of the biblical religion a rational 'natural religion' common to all people.

In the eighteenth century some theologians also called for a critical study of the Bible. An inaugural address by J. P. Gabler in 1787 is usually regarded as the declaration of independence of 'biblical theology'.[2] Gabler demanded that 'biblical' and 'dogmatic' theology be clearly distinguished from each other.

The biblical material had long served as an arsenal of proofs supporting the doctrine of the church (*dicta probantia* or *dicta classica*), organized according to dogmatic points of view. Gabler wanted to distinguish between simple religion and sophisticated theology. The Bible is a document of religion, not of theology. Therefore, a distinction has also to be made between 'biblical theology', which studies the Bible, and 'dogmatic theology', which operates with a much larger body of material. 'Biblical theology' is 'of historical origin, conveying what the holy writers felt about divine things; on the other hand, there is dogmatic theology of didactic origin, teaching what each theologian . . . philosophizes rationally about divine things . . .' (137).[3]

Gabler's address displays a clear realization that the contents of the Bible are not simply identical with the doctrine of the church. Nor is the Bible a homogeneous book (139). Although all of its sacred writers are 'holy men and are armed with divine authority', they do not all have the same religion in mind. Above all, there is a clear difference between the religion of the Old Testament and that of the New Testament. Different parts of the Bible are to be studied in their respective historical contexts. The doctrine of inspiration should be disregarded at this stage of the investigation. The investigation is not to be limited strictly to canonical texts: the apocryphal books ought to be included (140).

Thus, quite a few elements of a genuinely historical study of the Bible are contained in Gabler's programme. In the final analysis, however, his 'historical' biblical theology is firmly made to serve dogmatics.[4] For the most important task of the study of the Bible appears to be the distinction between time-bound and timeless material at a new stage in the work. At this point 'universal' or 'pure' ideas are separated from those which are mixed with 'foreign things' (142). This is an intermediate stage, in which the simple teaching of the Bible is cast into such a form that it can be utilized by 'dogmatic theology' in its subtle constructions. There has to be an investigation into which of the biblical ideas have to do with the permanent form of Christian doctrine and consequently 'pertain directly to us', and which were adapted to the understanding of ancient people and thus apply to them only (141, 142). The Mosaic rites and Paul's advice about women veiling themselves are examples of such obsolete ideas (142). It is noteworthy that the Bible is treated specifically as a body of 'teachings'.[5]

Thus Gabler's programme proves to be another version of the criticism of the Bible by the Enlightenment, which means that it is a modernized version of the dogmatic study of scripture. The notion of a treasury of *dicta classica* is explicitly retained; however, the body of such proof sayings is reduced by way of a process of critical selection to a more modest size (143). Moreover, the investigator appears to know from the start what sort of statements can or cannot be permanently binding. Even though Gabler speaks at length of the accuracy and care needed in making the distinction (140–2), he does not contemplate at all with what sort of criteria that task is carried out. Yet that is the crucial point in his programme. Nor does it become very clear at what stage of the work it ought to be established whether a statement is time-bound or generally valid.[6]

In his later writings, Gabler clarified his position somewhat. The 'pure' biblical theology is to be discovered with the aid of philosophical criticism, according to the principles of 'pure morality'. In contrast to the inaugural address, the philosophical-critical scrutiny now seems to have moved from the realm of exegesis to that of dogmatics.[7] The difference between the historian-exegete and the 'reflective theologian' is given even greater emphasis than before. Exegesis does not need dogmatics. By contrast, dogmatics is dependent on 'pure' biblical theology.[8]

It is Gabler's merit to have distinguished, at least in principle, between historical and normative 'biblical theology'; his own words for that distinction are 'true' and 'pure' biblical theology respectively.[9] Both theologies are needed, but they are not to be mixed up; they belong to different stages in the work. The demand for historical biblical theology has as its consequence that the theology of the Old Testament and of the New Testament respectively must be treated separately. This demand has more far-reaching consequences for Old Testament theology. For even in a purely historical New Testament theology the Old Testament of course, in one way or another, belongs to the historical presuppositions of the subject-matter.

According to Gabler, historical study of the Bible is not sufficient for the needs of Christian theology. Christian theology requires a separate clarification of the yield and significance of the biblical material for dogmatics. This is the concern of pure biblical theology. It seeks the essence of the Bible, which it tries to free from its temporary shell.

2

Towards a Historical New Testament Theology

(a) Divorcing theology from history: D. F. Strauss

A more impressive landmark than Gabler's still rather tentative address is the *Life of Jesus* by David Friedrich Strauss (1835–36). Not only did Strauss demand a historical exegesis independent of traditional dogmatics; he also carried out the task – with ruthless consistency.[1] Strauss's sharp analysis was fatally ahead of his time. The masterpiece of the twenty-seven-year-old author destroyed his career and gave birth to a trauma from which theology has never fully recovered to this day. Nevertheless, today even relatively conservative scholars agree essentially with him.[2] The Gospel of John has lost its position as a source for the life of the historical Jesus. The existence of secondary features and even of wholly unhistorical stories in the Gospels is generally admitted.[3] Strauss also recognized the eschatological nature of Jesus's ministry.[4]

Strauss's main interest, however, was focused on the renewal of philosophical theology, of dogmatics (just like Gabler's). Like Gabler, he did not try to construct a dogmatics on the actual biblical material, but rather on (Hegel's) eternal truths of reason.[5] Dogmatics had to be freed from 'slavery to the letter', i.e. from Gabler's 'true' biblical theology! For this task philosophical criticism was necessary.

Thus Strauss was motivated to historical work by philosophy; by philosophy he was also inwardly liberated to carry out the task without asking what the consequences might be (I, xii). Thus he actually came to do pioneering work for the historical interpretation of the New Testament. Yet he himself had no interest in historical syntheses. It is no coincidence that, after the analytical destruction, he made no effort at putting together a picture of the historical Jesus from those elements that had withstood his criticism.[6] Strauss was interested in historical research only as a means to philosophical theology. Historical study liberated theology from taking the biblical sources too seriously. The case of Strauss shows that in terms of content a biblical theology keen on serving philosophical theology can have any relation whatsoever to traditional theology.[7] Exegesis can serve, or at least intend to serve, theology even if its results happen to be purely 'negative'.

Strauss, then, did two things. First, he provided the historical study of the New Testament with a wealth of material and motivated his teacher Baur to create a synthesis in which he himself was not interested. Second, he devoted his attention to a philosophical-theological assessment of the Gospels. In this process, however, most of the New Testament turned out to be irrelevant. Strauss continued Gabler's search for timeless truth, but his net was so fine that the result amounted to virtually nothing.

The relationship of philosophical speculation to historical work bent on objectivity in Strauss's book is interesting.[8] Speculation appears in the framework – in the introduction and in the concluding christological sketch. The main body of the text is free from such speculation; in it, the normal immanent criteria of historical study are operative.

Thus philosophical assumptions do affect Strauss's way of framing his questions as a historical critic, even crucially. In this sense he is not 'free from presuppositions' (although that is what he himself claims).[9] But the actual historical-critical analysis is independent of speculative philosophy. True enough, a philosophical standpoint (though not necessarily Hegel's philosophy) is needed to define one's attitude to the supernatural. Strauss does assume a closed system of natural laws.[10] Yet he by no means rejects 'miracles' *en bloc* on this score. On the contrary, he admits those which have analogies.[11]

The fact is that even if the interpreter declines the notion of an airtight law of causality (as today he must), he still has a tough time in coming to terms with Strauss's thorough analysis of the miracle stories. This analysis tends to dissolve the

testimony of these stories even before one gets to the 'miracle'
itself. Strauss's analytical results can be linked with quite
different philosophies.

Strauss's chief effort failed. His historical criticism was experienced by others to be more of an enemy of speculative dialectics
than an ally.[12]

Like Gabler, Strauss 'knew' beforehand what true dogmatics
had to look like. But if one takes historical work seriously,
aprioristic dogmatic constructions tend to explode. The failure of
Strauss's theological endeavour serves to underline the importance of Gabler's innermost intention: dogmatics has to be built
on historical results. Or at least it has to be so constructed that
historical results do not militate against it. In a way Strauss
represented the latter solution in separating historical truths
from eternal ones altogether. But such a complete separation was
not, and generally is not, felt to be persuasive, because of the
traditional connection of theology with history or the traditional
claims of theology concerning history.

(b) History as revelation: F. C. Baur

The first New Testament theology that can be regarded as
essentially historical was composed by Ferdinand Christian
Baur. His lectures on this subject were published posthumously
in 1864. Baur begins by stating that 'unlike dogmatics . . . ,
biblical theology ought to be a purely historical science' (1).[13]
New Testament theology is part of this science. Its task is to
present both 'the doctrine of Jesus' and 'the doctrinal concepts
that are based on it' as elements of a historical process of
development (28). Baur attaches great importance to demonstrating differences between doctrinal concepts. In a programmatic and pioneering way he describes the history of the early
church as a history impelled by conflicts.[14]

It is important to Baur that the content of the New Testament
be depicted specifically as 'doctrinal concepts'.[15] New Testament theology is in fact already part of the history of dogma (33).
New Testament theology does not ask whether the doctrines
described by it are 'true'; it only asks 'what was taught'.

Baur's historical New Testament theology betrays the influence of Hegel's philosophy.[16] Baur portrays the history of early
Christianity and the doctrinal concepts of the different New

Testament writers as a process in which the Spirit realizes itself dialectically. Although his commitment to Hegel was a liability in that Baur interpreted the history of the early church too schematically from the viewpoint of the conflict between Jewish and Gentile Christianity, Hegel's philosophy helped him to recognize a problem which had not been clearly seen before.[17] Conflicts over the interpretation of the Jewish legacy of the early church do play an important part in the life and thought of that church. This insight is not irrevocably bound up with any particular philosophy.

In Baur's historical theology there are clearly normative elements as well. The doctrine of Jesus is not only the basis and presupposition of further development (45), but also the real core of Christianity, indeed the 'whole of Christianity' (64–5). The simple teaching of Jesus is not yet 'theology'; it is 'religion'. His new religion is not a dogmatic system; it only comprises 'basic convictions, principles and injunctions as immediate expressions of religious consciousness' (45–6). Baur has to eliminate eschatology from the teaching of Jesus and to interpret the reign of God immanently as a 'divine principle implanted in humanity' (74). The moral religion of Jesus becomes the norm; when later dogmatic development is gauged by it, this development appears to be a process of degeneration. Yet Paul has only made explicit what was implicit in the message of Jesus, namely the break with Judaism (128); and the doctrinal concepts of John amount to the highest stage of New Testament theology and its most perfect form (351ff.).

Baur attempted to describe the 'true' New Testament theology as defined by Gabler. By contrast, he did not undertake Gabler's normative task at all, the separate presentation of 'pure' biblical theology. Unlike Gabler, Baur felt no need to separate time-bound elements from permanent ones, since for him ultimately history itself was 'revelation'.[18] As a result, however, normative elements invaded his historical work.[19]

(c) The liberal classic: H. J. Holtzmann

In due course Hegel's philosophy of history lost its hold on New Testament study, when metaphysical speculation was supplanted by the Neo-Kantian theology of Albrecht Ritschl. Nevertheless, essential features of Baur's construction long persisted in presentations of New Testament theology. The notion that in the background of the New Testament stood a process of theological development had come to stay. Liberal exegetes continued to analyse the 'doctrinal concepts' of the New Testament and their relationship to each other. The teaching of Jesus was modernized; eschatology was eliminated. The simple morality of Jesus and his consciousness of God amounted to a norm with which one could assess later developments.

Historical research had to a great extent become independent of traditional dogmatics. At the crucial point, however, in interpreting Jesus it held fast to the habit of making normative-theological statements. As exegetical results were considered decisive for dogmatics, a new stage of work – which Gabler had demanded – was not felt to be necessary. Then, however, liberal dogmatics surreptitiously invaded the historical account.

All these features appear in Heinrich Julius Holtzmann's great textbook of New Testament theology (1897; the following references are to the second edition of 1911), the representative great work of the period, 'a model of critical conscientiousness',[20] to this day unsurpassed in thoroughness. Holtzmann considers the task of New Testament theology to be the reconstruction of the religious-ethical thought-world of the New Testament. He underlines the difference between the New Testament world-view and ours: New Testament ideas cannot as such be made part of our thinking about God and the world (1,XIII). The temptation to modernization has to be resisted.[21] Holtzmann ensures, however, that his work will also pave the way for a contemporizing theological interpretation: in the future, 'New Testament religion ought to be proclaimed without preaching doctrinal concepts of the New Testament' (1,XIV). Recognition of the distance between biblical ideas and our own gives rise to the freedom of religious thought (2,117). Yet the contemporizing task is implicitly there even in the work of the historian when he identifies what is new and unheard-of in the New Testament (1,XIV–XV).

Although New Testament theology aims at setting out the 'biblical teaching' (1,20), Holtzmann emphasizes, especially in the case of Jesus and Paul, the crucial significance of inward life and inner experience as the background and presupposition of the 'doctrines'. New Testament theology is largely an interpretation of the mystery of the great personalities in the New Testament, above all the religious genius of Jesus (cf. e.g. 1,175,341,347), but also of Paul (cf. e.g. 2,4; 2,32). The influence of romanticism is obvious.[22] However, Holtzmann embeds such reflections in the solid framework of history-of-religions research. Unlike his predecessors, he begins his New Testament theology with an extended presentation of Judaism.[23]

The background of Jesus' proclamation is his filial consciousness which cannot be derived from anything else, being the simplest and purest expression of religious perfection and also the most efficient impulse to the accomplishments of Christianity in world history (1,414). To be sure, the new and creative features here are embedded in a nationally limited framework. Much is taken over from Judaism, including the notion of a supernatural future Kingdom, but that is not the centre of Jesus' message (1,409). The filial consciousness just had to be clothed in a contemporary form; even so, a pressure towards universalism tends to break apart the historically conditioned shell (1,283). Thus the permanent gift of biblical theology to science (!) and life consists in the demonstration that 'the pure fire brought by Jesus to the altar' is totally independent of national Jewish messianism (1,409).[24] The self-consciousness of Jesus is even discussed by Holtzmann under such headings as 'Time-bound and timeless elements' or 'Measurable and eternal elements' (1.413–20).

Thus normative-theological questions and answers make their presence felt. Yet Holtzmann does not weave them so inextricably into his historical presentation that it would be impossible for the reader to separate the actualizing interpretation from the historical. Holtzmann does acknowledge a strong messianic and futuristic-eschatological element in the teaching of Jesus and he explicitly says that only we can distinguish, in retrospect, between the kernel and the husk.[25]

Paul's theology, too, is based on experience. His whole teaching is fundamentally an explication of the contents of his conversion experience, a 'systematization of the christophany' (2,238).[26] Paul's doctrinal construction, quite different from Jesus's simple religion, is animated by experience-based talk about the Spirit as the moral principle indwelling in the believer. If this 'life-giving soul' were removed, only a rather fantastic 'Gnostic construction of thought' would remain. If Paul's theology is taken as a mere system of doctrinal concepts – which often contradict each other[27] – it is a history-of-religions fossil which cannot be made the object of preaching (2.260–1).

Paul's way of generalizing his own very individual experience[28] is also open to criticism. Its other side is the anathema flung by him at anybody who teaches another doctrine (2,253–54). The Pastorals and the Johannine letters go further along the same intolerant line; not to mention the later church, which could deduce its exclusiveness from Pauline premisses.[29]

Thus Holtzmann's monumental work, in which doctrinal constructions are described in minute detail,[30] simultaneously points to the relativity of all doctrinal concepts.[31] The gift of New Testament theology to science is the analysis of these concepts. Its gift to religious life, however, consists in its pointing to what lies behind the doctrinal concepts (2,262). Such staements indicate that normative theology is not altogether absent from the picture. Indirectly it puts its stamp especially on the section on Jesus, in which Holtzmann distinguishes between permanently significant and time-bound features.

3

The History-of-Religions Programme of Earliest Christianity

(a) Farewell to theology: W. Wrede

William Wrede's lecture on 'The Task and Method of So-called New Testament Theology' in 1897 can be regarded as the declaration of the programme of.the history-of-religions school, which was just beginning.[1] Wrede's programme was based on the detailed work of critical exegetes like Holtzmann. At important points, however, he wished to shift the emphasis.

Wrede thought that since Gabler's days New Testament theology had only seemingly become 'a purely historical discipline'.[2] In reality, too close a relationship to dogmatics had prevented the discipline from becoming truly historical (69). 'Like every other real science, New Testament theology has its goal simply in itself.' It tries to grasp its object 'as objectively, correctly and sharply as possible', and that is all. How the systematic theologian gets on with the exegetical results is his affair. New Testament theology is very reserved towards dogma and systematic theology (69).[3]

Gabler had already made the point that the Apocrypha ought not to be despised in 'true biblical theology'. Wrede stresses that the boundaries of the canon must not have any significance at all in New Testament theology.[4] Canon is a dogmatic concept: 'no New Testament writing was born with the predicate "canonical" attached'. Anyone who treats these writings as such in historical work places himself under the authority of the bishops and theologians of the second to fourth centuries.[5] Certainly the church would like to see New Testament theology concentrate on the canonical writings to which the church has a special relationship. But Wrede emphasizes that, contrary to Schleiermacher, it is not the task of theology to serve the church. Even if a theologian engaged in historical work were personally anxious to serve the church with his work, it is not in his power to do so. He cannot adapt his results to the needs of the church, and the manner of handling the subject depends on the nature of the latter. According to Wrede, even the setting of the tasks comes mainly from the subject-matter; the needs of the church can affect it only in a very limited sense. At this point, more recent hermeneutics would undoubtedly protest: it always depends on the scholar himself what sort of questions he puts to his sources.

According to Wrede, New Testament theology has to deal with everything that belongs together historically. The writings of the second-century apologists signal a turning-point and can with good reason be omitted from New Testament theology (73).[6] In practice such a widening of scope would not cause a shift of emphasis in the presentation. Jesus, Paul and John would remain the peaks of New Testament theology. A shift would only become visible as regards the rest of the New Testament, since the Apostolic Fathers would be put alongside with James, Hebrews and Peter.[7]

The total picture will indeed be changed only if the anti-Pauline opposition or John's Gnostic background is taken seriously, and that is not even on Wrede's horizon.

Down to Holtzmann, New Testament theology had been tantamount to an analysis of the 'doctrinal concepts' of the various writers. Wrede demanded a complete change of perspective. The New Testament, and other early Christian literature, consists only to a very small degree of 'doctrine', let alone of 'theology'. Most authors do not attempt to 'teach' their readers; their aims are of a practical nature (75). The New Testament is a document, not of theology, but of religion.[8]

Even though Wrede's criticisms are directed specifically at Holtzmann, he does not altogether break with the latter's approach.[9] One should remember that Holtzmann had clearly stated that doctrinal concepts are secondary in religion. It was he, moreover, who had started his presentation with a description of Judaism, i.e. in terms of the history of religions.

The abandonment of the 'book by book' method is linked in

Wrede's programme with the abandonment of the method of doctrinal concepts (84ff.). In neither case is this a merely technical change. For the concentration on doctrinal concepts had, according to Wrede, been motivated by an interest in the possibility of using the concepts in dogmatics (79). And from the ecclesial point of view it would no doubt seem important that every New Testament writing be treated independently and exhaustively (94). Wrede warns, however, that scholarship should not be too closely tied to practical needs. An analysis of the individual writings belongs to detailed exegesis, not to a synthesis.

Most New Testament writings are too brief to deserve a separate analysis of their ideas in a synthesis (74). Nor are most writers outstanding enough to merit individual treatment; most writings contain simply average Christianity (85–6). Individual treatment should be given only to those who clearly stand out from the mass: Jesus, Paul, John and – Ignatius. In the case of Paul, it would even be hard to draw a line between religion and theology, though 'Paul is not, of course, a theologian or systematician in the modern sense' (76).

Wrede recommends the drawing of tradition-historical lines of development (79–81).[10] One has to pay attention above all not to the documents, but rather to what lies behind them.[11] Only in this way can the woods be seen from the trees. Wrede bitingly calls the New Testament theology of his time an arid and boring 'science of minutiae and of insignificant nuances' (78), or 'micrology' (81).[12] One has to get rid of the writings in order to find one's way to their subject-matter. 'In the last resort, what we want to know is what was believed, thought, taught, hoped, required and striven for in the earliest period of Christianity; not what certain writings say about faith, doctrine, hope, etc.' (84–5).[13] After all, we do not expect a history of doctrine to lay out 'the content of the relevant literature'!

Wrede criticizes 'the usual discussions of biblical theology' for giving the impression that early Christian views were 'produced purely by the power of thought, as though the world of ideas hovered above external history as a world of its own'. Yet the early Christian world of thought is 'very strongly conditioned by external history', and this must be made quite clear in New Testament theology (100). Wrede states that Paul's characteristic doctrine of justification by faith is inseparably linked to his experience in the mission among Gentiles.[14] His experiences in his Pharisaic past, or his conversion experience on the road to Damascus, do not suffice to account for its rise.[15]

Wrede admits that a 'New Testament theology' understood in his way in no respect differs from a history of religion. This fact, however, he does not regard as a weakness but as an advantage. A specifically theological type of treatment would amount to a mere disturbance, in that it would result in a mixture of the personal view of the scholar with the object of research (70). Thus, the traditional name of the discipline is wrong in both its terms. It is not a question of *New Testament* theology, since the subject-matter covers all chronologically relevant material. Nor is *theology* alone the studied object, but rather religion. The appropriate name would then be either *'early Christian history of religion'* or – in view of such germs of 'theology' as do occur, in Paul at least – 'the history of early Christian religion and theology' (116).

From the viewpoint of today's hermeneutics one might express amazement at the ease with which Wrede speaks of the objectivity and lack of bias of historical research. He does not reflect on the presuppositions of historical understanding.[16] It would be very unwise, however, to dismiss him on the score of positivistic historicism or the like. Even hermeneuticians ought to judge a tree according to its fruits and not merely according to cultivation handbooks.

The historical results reached by Wrede in his own reconstruction almost a hundred years ago have proved epoch-making and have withstood the critical scrutiny of several generations almost incredibly well. Thus his analysis of the 'Messianic secret' which appeared in 1901 paved the way for form-critical research and is still the outstanding classic in Markan studies.[17] With this work Wrede – along with Johannes Weiss – destroyed the foundations of the liberal portrait of Jesus.[18] The reconstruction of the message of the 'historical Jesus' was to prove a much more uncertain enterprise than was still assumed by Holtzmann.

Wrede's book on Paul (1904) is also a work to which today's Pauline research must return, despite its popular presentation.[19]

Therefore Georg Strecker, himself deeply involved in the hermeneutical task as a full-blooded representative of the Bultmann school, states that the necessary hermeneutical critique could diminish Wrede's significance for New Testament research only to a small extent. 'It remains undisputed that his historical-critical work led to new insights which determine research even today.'[20]

An early death at the age of forty-seven prevented Wrede from carrying out his programme. However, his studies prove that he would have been capable of doing that. In his programmatic essay he presents a sketch of the contents of a history of early Christian religion (101–15).[21]

Wrede, then, was moving toward Gabler's 'true New Testament theology' in a splendid way.[22] By contrast, Gabler's 'pure New Testament theology' remained beyond his ken. Wrede broke the bond which connected the object of his research with the present.[23] He did consider it necessary that New Testament study and dogmatics stand in relation to each other, but it is the duty of dogmatics to see to it that such a connection is established. This question is treated by Wrede briefly in one footnote (!). There he rejects the notion that New Testament theology ought to presuppose the normative revelatory nature of the New Testament writings (thus B. Weiss and W. Beyschlag).[24] Biblical theology will first investigate the biblical religion 'without presuppositions'. Then afterwards a judgment is made by dogmatics about what is discovered: it is revelation in such and such a sense, if at all.[25]

Undoubtedly Wrede dealt with the relationship between biblical theology and dogmatics in a rather incidental way. He gives to understand, however, that he does not deny Gabler's demand for the right to exist of a theological interpretation of the New Testament either. In fact his view of the relation of exegesis to dogmatics is rather similar to that of Gabler: dogmatics must build on exegesis, not vice versa; the exegetical work has to be done in a purely historical way; philosophical (dogmatic) criticism is to be used when the exegetical results are utilized by dogmatics.

The difference lies above all in the fact that actual historical work had made a huge advance since Gabler. Wrede was free to leave any actualizing reflections to the dogmaticians, for in his day dogmatics was the discipline which had been put on the defensive[26] and was anxious to find a *modus vivendi* with historical research.[27] It can therefore be considered to be only a minor shortcoming, if it is a shortcoming at all, that Wrede did not provide a clearly marked place for actualizing New Testament interpretation within the theological enterprise as a whole.[28] Robert Morgan, himself a much more theologically orientated scholar, states that Wrede's 'atheological' enterprise might well have a useful (though negative) theological function in providing 'a criterion against which all theological interpretations must be tested'.[29]

Gerd Lüdemann justly claims that 'Wrede's programme has never been refuted, nor has it – which is equally strange – ever been really carried out'.[30] However, the syntheses written by Paul Wernle and Heinrich Weinel move along the road marked by Wrede. Again, Wilhelm Bousset virtually realized the programme as far as christology is concerned. Yet in my opinion the unfinished presentation of earliest Christianity by Johannes Weiss comes closest to Wrede's intentions.

(b) A youthful break with dogmas: P. Wernle

Wernle's account of the 'beginnings of our religion', written with youthful enthusiasm at the age of twenty-eight, is a thrilling story of the rise of Christian faith and theology.[31] It corresponds to Wrede's demands in that Wernle dispenses with 'micrology', restricting himself to a few dominant features.[32] The book opens in history-of-religions manner with a presentation of ancient folk beliefs and their influence and goes on to a depiction of Judaism. Unlike Wrede, however, Wernle does not strive at all for a 'purely historical' account. He wants to come forward with a polemic book (vi) which endeavours to lead Christians from the fetters of theology and dogmas to the original freedom of the gospel of Jesus.

Wernle's image of Jesus is fully in accordance with the classical liberal view. He does realize the thoroughly eschatological nature of Jesus' message (49). But although Jesus' proclamation is clothed in the form of Jewish hopes for the future, his real message consists in the promise that an unmediated union with God is possible (41). Wernle distinguishes in a very straightforward fashion between what Jesus said and what he meant, and it is only the latter that is important. Wernle's historiography thus receives a heavy theological accent. The message of Jesus, stripped of its Jewish garments in a modernizing way, becomes the norm by which all later developments are judged. Wernle does not notice that this norm is a mere abstraction.

The theology of the early community was based on powerful experiences. Yet the early Christians, according to Wernle, lacked a language of their own which would have enabled them to express their experiences in a genuine way. They therefore resorted to familiar Jewish categories, squeezing the ineffable into the stereotypes provided by Jewish language (104). Earliest christology arose out of love for Jesus and enthusiasm, yet the result was a 'bizarre and fanciful' picture. Jesus' new and liberating message was embalmed in Jewish thoughts (105). The 'Judaizing' movement in the early church receives no sympathy whatsoever from Wernle (111).

In a manner typical of the whole era Wernle draws a caricature of Judaism. Yet he admits that even the best aspects of the preaching of Jesus have points of contact in Judaism. Jesus was a reformer who 'crystallized all that was sound, profound and authentic in the Jewish religion and removed what was artificial and morbid'. He brought to his disciples redemption, the freedom of the children of God, but the early church remained at the level of a sect (113).

Paul is praised for severing Jesus from Judaism and rescuing him for humanity (113). Without Paul we would not have Jesus either. On the other hand Wernle directs severe criticisms at Paul's theoretical theology. To be sure, Paul's theology has its basis in genuine experiences,[33] but Paul has generalized them in a sweeping manner. He has also apologetically created theories the starting-point of which is how things ought to be.[34] Thus Paul's pessimistic view of man arises from an apologetic need: as Jesus alone is the Redeemer, humanity outside the dominion of Christ *must* be so totally corrupt and lost that no other way remains open (164, 214).

Wernle produced a normative account in which he severely criticizes all belief in dogmas and sacraments since the earliest church. The doctrines of expiation and justification are condemned in the light of Jesus' simple gospel. Theology is

significant in so far as it is based on genuine experience. Wernle
represents a phase in the history of research which Wrede had
already by-passed, although the centrality of religion and
experience is common to both scholars. Nevertheless, Wernle's
book still makes a fresh impression because of his acute
observations and bold criticisms.[35]

(c) The history of religions as preparation for Jesus: H. Weinel

Heinrich Weinel's *Biblische Theologie des Neuen Testaments* is to a great extent reminiscent of Wernle's book.[36] The
title is misleading; in accordance with his sub-title Weinel
actually discusses 'the religion of Jesus and the early Christians'. He programmatically places Christianity in a broad
history-of-religions framework (14–37). The history of religions,
however, is portrayed theologically as a preparation for the
account of the author's own religion. Christianity is the answer
to the religious longing that had arisen in other religions,
especially in Judaism.[37]

Weinel, too, gauges later developments by the religion of
Jesus.[38] He, too, adopts the traditional liberal image of Jesus.
He does realize that a number of things in the message of
Jesus do not fit this picture, e.g. the eschatological expectation and the idea of reward. But this is a matter of tension
between inherited Jewish materials and the peculiar new
message; all emphasis is put on the new. The recourse of
Jesus to traditional views which do not really fit his new
religion is often due e.g. to the vehemence of his fight with
his opponents.[39] Instead of presenting a true history-of-religions analysis. Weinel tries to identify the essence of Christianity in the New Testament. As for his historical aims, he is
most successful in the third part of his work, which is devoted to the time after Jesus and Paul, i.e. in the section
which is of least existential value to him.[40]

Weinel emphasizes the significance of experiences and feelings as the background of early Christian thought. Jesus felt
always and everywhere that he was surrounded by the living
goodness of God. 'All is experience here' (156). Jesus experienced God directly in everyday life (159,166). The immediacy of
the experience of God is common to him and to later 'simple

Christians', even though what was later listened to was not the song of the birds but ecstatic speech (166).

The enthusiastic piety of the early church is vividly depicted (197ff.). The experiential side of Paul's faith is underlined as well. Paul's 'Christ mysticism' bespeaks strong feelings (242). What really counts for Paul as evidence for the truth of Christianity is experience (286f.). Whenever on occasion he pursues other routes (such as using proof-texts from the Bible), 'the religion of contemplation (*Innerlichkeit*)' is immediately endangered (287). Again, in John's mysticism, 'feeling is every-thing' (448).

Weinel describes Christianity on the way to becoming a church in rather negative terms as a religion of law and sacraments, which he gauges by the norm of 'an ethical religion of redemption' (342ff.). But although the nature of piety is altered, Weinel still discovers behind it a genuine experience: humanity torn asunder finds rest in the idea of one flock and one shepherd. Man feels at home in the worldwide catholic com-munity (507).

(d) A history of faith in Christ: W. Bousset

Wilhelm Bousset conceived his task in similar terms to Wrede.[41] The New Testament is to be interpreted in a broad history-of religions framework from Alexander the Great to Irenaeus.[42] Bousset's *Kyrios Christos* attempts to present a history of the faith in Christ from the earliest stages to Irenaeus; thus he goes chronologically even beyond the borderline suggested by Wrede. The development of faith in Christ is depicted as the development of a religion which finds a concrete shape in the *cult* rather than as a history of intellectual constructions. To capture the atmosphere is more important than to put forward a conceptual analysis.[43]

The title 'Kyrios' was adopted in the exalted atmosphere of the living cult spontaneously and subconsciously, as a designa-tion of Jesus who was felt to be present (99). Once the title had been adopted, it was easy to read Old Testament references to the Kyrios with it in mind, and in this way the interpretation of the OT served in turn as a catalyst for the adoration of the Kyrios.

Many of Bousset's individual ideas do not stand up to

scrutiny, but as a whole his work presents an impressive overall picture with regard to one central theme. A shortcoming is the exclusion of the historical Jesus from the investigation. At this point Bousset's critical research has apologetic traits. In essence, we are once again confronted with a theological history of religion which regards the scholar's own religion as the climax of that history.[44] The negative counterpart of the idealization of the religion of Jesus was the denigration of Judaism as an inadequate religion.[45]

Bousset was also still under the spell of the liberal picture of Jesus; he severely criticized the eschatological interpretation of Jesus by Johannes Weiss. He described the religious development of the early church in terms of a historical interpretation. By contrast, he searched for a permanently valid theology in the religion and ethics of *Jesus*. The same criticism applies to Wernle and Weinel, but not to Wrede (at least not to the same extent). The latter's programme of presenting the general lines of the development of the tradition in 'purely historical' terms still awaits its realization.

(e) Futuristic eschatology versus timeless religion: J. Weiss

The work that comes closest to Wrede's ideal is Johannes Weiss's *Earliest Christianity*.[46] It was conceived as a history of the early church, but to a great extent it also deals with early Christian thought. Weiss was in close contact with the history-of-religions school, even though his approach is at some points more conservative than e.g. that of Bousset.[47] The *magnum opus* remained unfinished because of the early death of the author; as it is, it is far too much dominated by Paul.[48]

The part which was to deal with Jesus never appeared. This is not fatal, however, for Weiss's understanding of Jesus is well known.[49] In a pioneering study he had argued that Jesus' preaching of the kingdom of God was inextricably involved with eschatological-apocalyptic views. The 'kingdom of God' was not a this-worldly phenomenon but something supernatural that could be brought about only by God.[50] On the exegetical level this was tantamount to a break with Albrecht Ritschl's interpretation of the kingdom of God, on which the liberal picture of Jesus had been based. However, Weiss distinguished clearly between historical and actualizing interpretation. In historical terms, Ritschl's concept of the kingdom of God was very different from the kingdom proclaimed by Jesus. Yet the calm theological conclusion Weiss drew from this was that the kingdom of God as preached by Jesus was not a viable concept in modern systematic theology, whereas the concept as used by Ritschl was viable.[51] Thus Weiss's view comes quite close to that of Strauss, who had pleaded for a liberation of Christian theology from the fetters of history, but it is established through a solid historical interpretation.

Weiss's way of dealing with Jesus nonetheless partly conforms to standard liberal practice in that he, too, distinguishes between Jesus' eschatological and non-eschatological proclamation (141). He, too, regards the latter as the more important; it alone is of lasting religious value. But unlike most liberals, Weiss is conscious of the fact that this is a value judgment of his own and that in making it he is actually emphasizing one side in the message of the historical Jesus more than the other.[52] Consequently, unlike other liberals, he abstains from elevating a 'core' abstracted from the preaching of Jesus to the status of a norm by which he could evaluate the development after Jesus.

Correspondingly, Weiss discovers in Paul, alongside the dramatico-mythological eschatological layer, another layer which is independent of eschatology: God's inmost being which is attuned to grace and love has at last been revealed. This of course implies belittling the Jewish religion, as if God's grace and love had been unknown in it before Jesus and Paul; in this Weiss is a child of his time.[53] But since he does not make his theological decision the scarlet thread of his historical presentation, he nevertheless succeeds in sketching a historically satisfactory overall picture of the rise and development of early Christian theology.[54]

In his synthesis Weiss aims at a historical reconstruction, but now and then he expresses his point of view in theological matters as well. Thus the 'imperishable heritage' left to the church by Paul consists in his disclosing faith as the soul of religion, in his heroic faith-experience and in his 'glowing exaltation' of that love which necessarily radiates from faith (651). By contrast, Paul's doctrinal thoughts are not of lasting significance.

Unlike Wrede, Weiss writes in a church context.[55] It is typical of his approach, however, that when leaving historical reconstruction he shows interest in the Christian life of his time as it is actually lived rather than in church dogmas.

Indeed, Weiss makes an emphatic distinction between experiences and doctrines (e.g. 83ff.). The notion that doctrine or mythology stands at the very centre of religion is an intellectualistic misunderstanding; what matter are the emotional values attached to the various conceptions. The peculiarity of Christianity can only be understood if one recognizes the differences in emotion and atmosphere between it and mystery cults.[56]

To be sure, Paul does not distinguish between faith and thought; in his person the two belong inseparably together (422).[57] Yet for Paul theology always stands in the service of practice. In the open manner of liberal theologians, Weiss admits a large number of contradictions even in central areas of Paul's thought. Mostly he puts forward a traditio-historical explanation: different traditions clash in Paul's thought-world (e.g. 539). For instance, as has already been noted, Paul's mysticism stands in tension with his eschatology.

Weiss in no way blackens the development of Christianity at the end of the first century and onwards. He even criticizes the customary denigration of the Jewish religion.[58] Later layers of the New Testament are more akin to 'post-apostolic literature' than has been thought (655f.). Weiss draws a very favourable picture of the Gospel of John, emphasizing that it is based on the profound mystical experience of the evangelist (e.g. 793, 803).[59] One looks in vain for anything resembling Wernle's sharp criticism of the docetic trend in John's christology.[60] Weiss's book closes in an impressive way with an extensive presentation, free from all polemic, of I Clement, which forms a bridge to the future development of the church, led by Rome (849–63).

(f) Reactions against the history of religions: A. Schlatter, P. Feine

At the turn of the century conservative church exegesis tried to overcome history-of-religions work either by rejecting its results or by trying to make them serve a conservative viewpoint in a modified form. The former strategy found a representative in Schlatter, the latter in Feine.

Schlatter often receives a fair amount of attention when the history of New Testament theology is outlined, not only from the more conservative side,[61] which is understandable, but also from other quarters.[62] This is a little surprising, for obviously Schlatter's actual New Testament theology remains in the fetters of dogmatics.[63] A certain existential touch, in that Schlatter connects the thoughts of the men of the New Testament closely with their life, is not enough to establish congeniality with Bultmann,[64] much less to make him a peer of the latter as a biblical theologian.[65] Some of his presuppositions alone – e.g., he uses the Gospel of John as a source for the preaching of Jesus without the slightest reserve – mark Schlatter unmistakeably as a figure from a bygone era. So does his insistence on the theological unity of the New Testament.

Schlatter distinguishes in principle between historical and dogmatic work and defends this distinction against a still more conservative view.[66] The prime virtue of a historian is the capacity for 'sight', the ability to observe objectively the given facts in the texts (127, 136, etc.). A complete separation of history from dogmatics is, however, impossible; the historian must give room for the dogmatician in himself too. It is only the 'dogmatician in us' who 'supplies the historian with the capacity for making judgments through which he distinguishes between what is possible and what is not, and between what in the outline of history produces effects and what is dead' (126).[67]

This is a valid hermeneutical insight, and the demand that scholars ought not to overlook their own presuppositions (127) is justified. But in Schlatter's actual working out of his New Testament theology, the dialectical relationship he posits between the historical and the dogmatic approach tends to lead to the clear preponderance of the latter. The scholar's own faith is considered to be a presupposition of true objectivity.[68] Indeed, Schlatter argues for his historical way of conceiving the task on thoroughly biblicist grounds: such a viewpoint secures us (though not infallibly, of course) 'against producing a mixture of what scripture says and what the church teaches,[69] or a mixture of the Bible and our own religious opinions' (128).

Schlatter defends the limitation of New Testament theology to the canonical writings. He tries to substantiate this decision historically, but writes as if the old church had unanimously arrived at the present form of the canon (145ff.).[70] He goes so far as to claim that presentations 'in which quotations from the epistles of James and Ignatius, the Didache and the Pastoral Epistles are all mixed up together' cannot 'give us genuine knowledge'; if a scholar does not understand this, it is 'because the notion of the Christ is without significance for him' (147f.).

Schlatter indeed adopts a very polemical attitude to liberals and to the history-of-religions school, accusing these scholars of the writing of fiction (135), and of combining a historical presentation with polemic against New Testament Christianity (1909, 5). Yet his own presentation of New Testament theology contains much that can only be regarded as fanciful.[71] The dogmatician in this particular historian and advocate of impartial observation makes him capable of 'seeing' some strange things and of not seeing some obvious ones. Schlatter's New Testament theology is, in essence, his (systematic) theology, opaque in the construction of its argument and often presented in a rather meditative manner. If the work is understood in this way, it can even be appreciated.[72]

What appealed to Bultmann in Schlatter's enterprise was above all the latter's contention that the men of the New Testament 'frustrate the attempt to separate the act of thinking from the act of living'.[73] Here indeed is a salutary emphasis on the non-intellectual aspects reflected in the New Testament. New Testament theology certainly has to do with 'knowledge' obtained from the New Testament, but this knowledge is associated, both as cause and as effect, with the 'Christian experience' of its authors (163). Schlatter is actually in agreement with liberal and history-of-religions scholars when he asserts that the 'impulses' which drove Paul 'are far more important than the formulae which he invented about the purpose of the law, the death of Christ and the justification of believers' and that 'the power of the men of the New Testament did not consist solely in their thoughts' (163). But he proceeds to the warning that insistence on this easily leads to 'free constructions of the imagination' (an allusion to the work of more radical contemporary scholars), as we cannot perceive other people's wills except indirectly, through their ideas (164).

Schlatter does put forward some worthwhile ideas when speaking of the task of New Testament theology, but these are so general that they could just as well be used in criticizing his own way of putting the theory into practice.[74] His case therefore serves to underline once more the importance of judging a tree above all from its actual scholarly fruits rather than from merely theoretical prolegomena.

According to Paul Feine (1910; my references are to the 1936 edition), the task of New Testament theology is historical in character. Yet he openly states that he is carrying out that task as a theologian, convinced that he is dealing with unique writings, documents of revelation that are still normative (1), and that from the start Christianity was superior to other religions – for has it not remained victorious over other cults of late antiquity (10)? A practical result of this approach is the elimination of differences within the New Testament.[75] At the centre of New Testament theology stands the historical person of Jesus (3); in dealing with this centre, Feine makes no significant distinction between the historical Jesus and the kerygmatic Christ (cf. 12). Feine does engage in discussions with history-of-religions research, which he regards as justified in a certain sense. Yet what New Testament writers such as Paul and John have borrowed from Hellenism is *terminology* and nothing else.

The comment that in the works of Schlatter and Feine 'hardly any difference between New Testament theology and ecclesial dogmatics can be detected' is not far off the mark.[76] Each aims at a historical interpretation. In practice, this aim is marred by an actualizing tendency, which is especially clear in the case of Schlatter.

(g) A mature synthesis ignored: J. Kaftan

Julius Kaftan's New Testament theology is written from a judicious history-of-religions point of view. The posthumous 'concise and spirited'[77] book of the old systematic theologian seems to have been overrun by the ascent of Barthianism. Yet undoubtedly its exegetical merits far outweigh those of Schlatter or Feine. It is apposite to comment on it at this juncture as the closing point of an era.[78]

According to Kaftan, the task of New Testament theology is a purely historical one. A theologian's personal interest in the message (*Sache*) of the New Testament does not affect this point at all. On the contrary, whenever such an interest lures one to read texts in a strained way from the viewpoint of traditional church conceptions, it is detrimental.[79] Kaftan demands objectivity of historical study, even though it is impossible to prescribe how the ideal should be carried out (7).

Kaftan agrees with Wrede's demand that the presentation should focus on faith and religion rather than on 'doctrinal concepts'. This in fact amounts to none other than a demand to penetrate into the roots of the *Sache* itself (8): the New Testament contains little reflection that could be called theology.

By contrast, Kaftan declines Wrede's other demand that New Testament theology be replaced with a religious history of early Christianity. He wants to substantiate his limitation to the canon with reference to the history of its effect: it is as a canonical collection of writings that the New Testament has become important for the cultural life of humanity in the first place. It would mean a loss for the humanities if New Testament theology were replaced with just a piece of religious history (9, 209).

Kaftan notes that the limitation to the canon makes little difference to the first part of a synthesis, since extra-canonical sources are by and large lacking for the time before Paul. By contrast, the issue is important as regards John and Hebrews. It is wrong to treat these writings merely as documents of early second-century piety. Both because of their canonicity and in particular because of their content these writings are among the original waymarks of our religion and still exert influence as such. They are thus to be treated just as thoroughly as the gospel of Jesus and as Paul.

By contrast, Kaftan omits from his presentation e.g. the Pastorals, since in them early Christianity has already become a holy tradition (18). One would have thought, however, that in an account which focuses on religion and takes its cue from the subsequent influence of the writings in question, the Pastorals in particular would be given an important place. They may lack theological depth and originality, but surely they are representative of a form of religion and piety to which, from the second century on, the future was to belong.[80]

Kaftan chooses eschatology as his starting-point. In so doing he is actually the first author of a New Testament theology to do justice to a central insight of latter-day exegesis. To be sure,

Kaftan puts a great emphasis on the shift of eschatology in a present direction. So great a significance is attached to the sayings relating to the present, which are undoubtedly to be found in the preaching of Jesus, that in the final analysis even John only seems to realize the deepest intentions of Jesus himself (209). Kaftan contends that the development from Jesus through the early community and Paul to John was consistent and inevitable. He finds more continuity in it than did the history-of-religions school (or than average scholarship does today). But Kaftan tries to argue on historical grounds.[81] At many points indeed he shows that such dogmatic ideas as had been read into the New Testament even by critical scholars are in fact lacking in it.[82]

In the manner of the historians of religion, Kaftan stresses the importance of experience as the basis of the statements of the New Testament. He distinguishes between interpretations embedded immediately in experience and logical theological reflection. The former are represented by the preaching of Jesus and most of the message of the early church. Beginnings of the latter are found in Paul and in Hebrews, whereas the Fourth Gospel is more clearly a document of religion than of theology. Unlike Wernle and others, Kaftan does not blame Paul for his attempts at theologizing. Yet he makes it clear that what Paul produces is not a system but thoughts moving spontaneously, so that contradictions are a commonplace.[83]

Kaftan is the first author to have written a synthesis that can be regarded as a relatively successful historical account of the theological thought-world of the New Testament. The choice of eschatology as a starting-point is a bold step forward. The shortcomings of Kaftan's synthesis – the overemphasis on continuity in the first place – can be overcome with the aid of an even more careful historical argumentation. It is a pity that this book, written by an outsider, has been almost totally ignored by the guild of New Testament scholars.[84]

4

Summary and Prospect

Gabler's question about the relationship between historical and systematical-normative 'biblical theology' has proved crucial. Often the distinction has been made in principle, and historical study of the Bible has been pursued, yet a normative element has intruded into the historical work. This is what happened both to Baur and to the liberals (Holtzmann, Wernle), and even to history-of-religions exegetes (Weinel), in whose constructions the historical Jesus, interpreted in a modernizing way, in actual practice represents Gabler's normative biblical theology. In particular, the danger of latent normativity lurked in those cases when no clear distinction was made between exegetical and systematic stages of work. On the other hand, precisely those scholars who did distinguish between them were pioneers of New Testament scholarship. They dared to analyse Jesus or Paul without being discouraged by any difficulties their results might cause to a theological enterprise which regards Jesus and Paul as norms (Strauss, J. Weiss, Wrede).

Wrede pointed the way in the direction of a historical synthesis, but let the question of the consequences for normative theology rest on the shoulders of dogmatics.

The distinction between theology and religion, already pointed out by Gabler, was emphasized in the works of the liberals and the historians of religion. Baur had already focused on a description of early Christian religion as a process of development. Thanks to the history-of-religions school, New Testament theology ceased to consist in an analysis of doctrinal concepts and changed more clearly into a treatment of experiences and their interpretations. The interpretations were often assessed critically.

Wrede demanded a history of early Christian religion with no concern for the boundaries of the canon; in this regard his programme was carried out by Wernle and Weinel. Kaftan, however, tried to argue for a limitation to the canonical writings in terms of their subsequent influence.

The history-of-religions school had confronted New Testament theology with challenging new tasks. The challenge was met in specialized studies. By contrast, the synthesis outlined by Wrede awaited its realization.

It still does. The First World War put an end both to the dominion of liberal theology and to any wider interest in the history of religions. The massive rhetoric of dialectical theology which called for a return to the traditional truths met a need of the time. Even those exegetes of the younger generation with a history-of-religions orientation took the theological road marked by Karl Barth. So did the greatest of them, Rudolf Bultmann. Bultmann's thought combines Bousset's view of the early church and Weiss's picture of Jesus; he was also among the first to accept in essence Wrede's interpretation of the 'Messianic secret' as a construction of the community. Nevertheless, Bultmann's *Theology of the New Testament*, which is still the classical synthesis, with no serious rival in sight, came to be anything but a summary of the history-of-religions research into the New Testament.

PART TWO

From Wrede to the Present

I

New Testament Theology and the Breakthrough of Neo-Orthodoxy

(a) Theology in the name of Paul: K. Barth

Karl Barth's *Commentary on the Romans* (1919)[1] inaugurated a new era in theology which has profoundly affected the development of 'New Testament theology' as well. In his parish ministry Barth felt that academic theology had left him at a loss. With massive force he called for a fresh theological interpretation that would take Scripture seriously as God's word. He denied that he rejected historical study of the Bible, but he only conceded to it the status of a preparatory stage of work. As regards the real subject-matter or message (*Sache*) of the Bible, critical exegetes had understood next to nothing of it.

Barth applied the text of the Bible directly to the situation of the modern reader. It was his starting-point that our problems are those of Paul, and Paul's answers ought to be ours too. The differences between bygone situations and our situation are purely trivial (1).

In the second edition Barth claims that as an expositor of Scripture he has to wrestle with the text, until he so internalizes it that he can almost speak in the name of the author. The commentator almost has to forget that he did not write the letter to the Romans himself (8)!

Clearly theology is a purely church science to Barth; the task of theology is identical with that of proclamation.[2] For this identification he was sharply censured by critical exegetes such as von Harnack.[3]

Both editions of *Romans* were severely castigated by exegetes.[4] Adolf Jülicher would have greatly appreciated the book if only its author had been content with presenting it as an applied homiletic exposition.[5] Offered as a scholarly commentary, however, it amounted to a violation of the sacred documents, rooted in the hybris of a pneumatic.[6] The book would in future contribute to the understanding of the period in which it arose; by contrast, it contributed nothing new to the understanding of Paul.[7] Even the conservative Schlatter, to whom Barth had appealed as one of his precursors, commented that, in the hands of Barth, Romans ceases to be a letter to *the Romans*.[8]

(b) Dispute over the real message: K. Barth and R. Bultmann

All the more surprising was the support given to the enterprise by one exegete. In 1921 Rudolf Bultmann had published his *History of the Synoptic Tradition*, a ruthless form-critical analysis which delivered a severe blow to the study of the historical Jesus. As a historian, Bultmann had proved to be a radical sceptic. Yet he fully acknowledged Barth's theological aspiration. He accepted Barth's starting-point: only those interpreters are capable of expounding a text who have an inner relationship to the 'real subject-matter' (*Sache*) of the text. Even Barth's injunction to forget that the expositor is not the author of the text was endorsed by Bultmann![9]

Nevertheless even Bultmann points out that Paul's text is violated by Barth. Bultmann's critique has to do precisely with the 'real subject-matter' of the text which Barth had emphasized. Bultmann blames Barth for interpreting the whole of Romans as a hundred per cent expression of the *Sache* itself. Such an assumption is impossible, unless one wishes to establish a modern dogma of inspiration. Even the letter to the Romans must be assessed critically with the gauge of the *Sache*, with the result that some sections are peak passages and others are not.[10]

Both Barth and Bultmann are interested in actualizing biblical theology, in what the Bible offers modern man as the Word of God. There was nothing new in the demand to return to the 'real subject-matter' (*Sache*) of scripture. The same intention had permeated e.g. Wernle's vigorous book.[11] It was just that Wernle and company understood the subject-matter of scripture in a different way from Barth. It is in the understanding of the *Sache*, too, that Barth and Bultmann part company. Each perceives the nature of actualizing biblical theology quite differently from the other.

For Barth, e.g. Romans as a whole amounts to normative revelation. He states that Bultmann requires him to mix fire with water and admits that he does in fact represent a sort of modern doctrine of inspiration.[12] Barth is the mirror-image of Strauss, as it were. Both have their respective starting-points in dogmatics; but whereas Strauss accepts no New Testament material as such into dogmatics, Barth accepts nearly everything. Bultmann's starting-point resembles that of Gabler: the material has to be sifted; one has to keep what stands the test. His sieve is, however, so fine that his actual attitude to scripture – the difference in tone notwithstanding – comes close to that of Strauss.

(c) The existentialist self-understanding of Paul and John: R. Bultmann

Jülicher made the point that Barth is a man of two worlds, in whose breast two souls wrestle with each other.[13] The comment would fit Bultmann even better. Bultmann is on the one hand a critic who has made the intentions of the history-of-religions school his own; on the other hand he is an edifying theologian and preacher.[14] A tension between historical and actualizing biblical interpretation runs through his whole work. Barth was unable to offer biblical scholarship a concrete programme capable of realization.[15] Therefore dialectical theology, with its interest in normative biblical theology, conquered continental biblical scholarship mostly in a Bultmannian version.

Bultmann aims at a clear distinction between his own theological exegesis and that of liberal and history-of-religions scholars, which he calls history-orientated (*zeitgeschicht-lich*).[16] He himself distinguishes between 'what is said' and 'what is meant'. The real task of exegesis is to penetrate to the real subject-matter which the text expresses. The significance of that message *for me* must be clarified; one must not remain at a distance from the text as a detached observer.[17]

Against Bultmann the point has to be made, however, that precisely this was what the scholars criticized by him intended to do. In the preaching of Jesus in particular a clear distinction was made between what was said and what was meant. What Jesus was believed to have meant was of crucial existential significance to the scholar himself. It is very difficult to see any structural difference between Bultmann's theological exegesis and that of the scholars criticized by him.[18] It is just that he defines the *Sache* in a slightly different way from them: it is a matter of the human self-understanding manifested in the texts.[19] By contrast, Bultmann is clearly averse to putting experience in focus; this he rejects as psychologizing.[20] The text is more important than the person of its author.[21]

Bultmann emphasizes that there is no such thing as neutral exegesis: every statement on history by an interpreter is always also a statement on the interpreter himself. Exegesis is 'objective' when it causes the text to influence the interpreter so that he lets the text speak as an authority.[22] Bultmann regards exegesis fundamentally as a task of the church which presupposes faith on the part of the interpreter, even though such faith cannot in any way be controlled or even required in practice. He dismisses the question whether one should apply to the New Testament interpretative principles different from those applied to the interpretation of, say, Augustine or the Bhagavadgita, asserting that the question is artificial.

But this very dismissal reveals the actual narrowness of Bultmann's view. He is not interested in taking alien traditions seriously on their own terms. This fact is given striking expression in Bultmann's account of Judaism, which amounts to a vicious caricature and causes his New Testament theology to be incurably lop-sided.[23]

An interpreter, Bultmann claims, always stands in a certain tradition by which his interpretation is determined; for Bultmann this is the tradition of the 'church of the Word', however free his attitude to the actual shape of this tradition may be.[24] Although theology and proclamation are not identical, they are very close to each other.[25] Even the tasks of exegesis and systematic theology overlap in principle.[26]

Thus the real task of New Testament theology does not consist in the reconstruction of past thoughts and situations. The real task consists in translating the message of the texts into modern language.[27] The self-understanding of man which is reflected in the texts is to be so explicated that the possibility is opened up for modern man to understand himself in a similar way.[28] The carrying out of this task presupposes a strictly 'content-critical' (*sachkritisch*) approach which distinguishes between what the texts basically mean and what they actually say.

Thus, what Bultmann aims at is a normative biblical theology. On the face of it, large parts of his *Theology of the New Testament* resemble a history-of-religions presentation.[29] By contrast, the sections on the theology of Paul and John, which amount to the actual core of the work, approximate to a normative interpretation. In them Bultmann emphatically distinguishes between what is said and what is meant. Yet a similar approach is also found in the initial chapter on Jesus.

Moreover, both in assessing the kerygma of the earliest church[30] and in describing 'the development toward the ancient church', Bultmann is engaged in serious criticism of the writings in question, using as criterion that which Paul and John really meant, according to his modernizing interpretation.[31] Thus Bultmann's theology bears a structural resemblance to those very theologies of the New Testament from which he tries to distance himself. It is just that the criterion of the liberals in *their* criticism of the church (and of Paul) was a different one (the core abstracted from Jesus' proclamation). In both cases the criterion is equally abstract and unhistorical.[32] Even in Bultmann's book those parts in particular are affected by modernization which are of greatest existential importance to the scholar.

Bultmann defines New Testament theology as 'the unfolding of those ideas by means of which Christian faith makes sure of its own object, basis, and consequences' (I, 3), or, as the interpretation of the theological thoughts of the New Testament, 'as explication of believing self-understanding' (II, 251). Where earlier scholars distinguished between a theological interpretation and the experience behind it, Bultmann makes a distinction, in principle at least, between 'theological propositions' and the 'faith' or believing self-understanding on which they are based (II, 237f.). He also talks of distinguishing between 'theological' and 'kerygmatic' statements (II, 240). In practice a sharp distinction is not possible, yet it is important in principle to Bultmann.

Christian faith presupposes a Christian kerygma which proclaims Jesus Christ as God's eschatological act of salvation (I, 3). This means that there can be no New Testament theology until after Easter. Thus the message of Jesus cannot belong to New Testament theology; it belongs to the presuppositions of the latter.[33]

This decision is of a piece with Bultmann's definition of theology. The initial chapter on Jesus is very brief, in particular in comparison with previous New Testament theologies. Acknowledging the insight of Weiss, Bultmann starts with the eschatology of Jesus, which still belongs to the context of Jewish apocalyptic (I,4).[34] The 'essential thing' in Jesus' eschatological proclamation is, however, 'the idea of God that operates in it and the idea of human existence that it contains' (I,23).

Thus Bultmann's interpretation of Jesus closely resembles the liberal view of Jesus which likewise first acknowledged eschatology as a historical phenomenon and then denied it theologically. Bultmann's Jesus, too, teaches simple ethics; only the references to feeling and experience which were emphasized in previous scholarship have been stripped off. In accordance with the fundamental emphases of dialectical theology the term 'religion' does not appear at all.

Yet the 'presuppositions' of New Testament theology include both 'the kerygma of the earliest church' and 'the kerygma of the Hellenistic church aside from Paul'. Even this decision follows logically from Bultmann's definition of concepts. The remarkable result is that most of his book deals with something other than New Testament theology! The earliest church in Jerusalem did not 'explicitly' understand the person and fate of Jesus as the eschatological occurrence (as Paul and John did later on); on the contrary, it was 'in danger' of remaining a Jewish sect (I, 36f.).

According to Bultmann, New Testament theology in the real sense consists only of the theology of Paul and John. In these sections Bultmann's approach changes visibly: the historian of religion (who does ask sharp content-critical questions and is anxious to perceive dangers in the development of the church also in that capacity) turns into a proclaiming theologian. Bultmann presents the theology of Paul as a coherent logical system – in a way that contradicts what he himself says about Paul as a theologian.[35] In actual fact, on the basis of indications found in Paul's letters,[36] Bultmann has developed a system which has anthropology as its core and which has been constructed with tools provided by Heidegger's existentialist philosophy.[37] The highly selective nature of his procedure is evident e.g. from the fact that the passage Romans 9–11, in which Paul wrestles with the salvation-historical problem of Israel, is wholly ignored.[38]

Bultmann continually distinguishes between Paul's words and his real intention. The talk of the eschatological battle between the spirit powers and Christ (I Cor. 15.24–26) is 'naive mythology' which is 'in reality' only 'expressing a certain understanding of existence' (I, 259).[39] In Paul's real intention the question whether a man will acknowledge Jesus Christ as the Son of God and Lord is identical with the question whether he is 'willing to give up his old understanding of himself and henceforth understand himself only from the grace of God' (I, 300f.). The statements about Christ's pre-existence and incarnation are mythological talk which as such neither challenges the hearer nor expresses the nature of faith (304). The mythological statements express the 'fact' that 'there exists a divinely authorized proclamation of the prevenient grace and love of God' (305).

Bultmann detaches Paul's theology from its concrete historical context.[40] In a similar vein he asserts that in the Gospel of John, 'Jesus is not presented in literal seriousness as a pre-existent divine being who came in human form to earth to reveal unprecedented secrets. Rather, the mythological terminology is intended to express the absolute and decisive significance of his (Jesus') word – the mythological notion of pre-existence is made to serve the idea of the Revelation' (II, 62).

In Bultmann's book the boundaries of the canon are, time and again, freely transcended. He moves well beyond the New Testament. The apostolic fathers enter the picture not only in the account of the 'development toward the ancient church' but already in the reconstruction of the Hellenistic kerygma aside from Paul. In this sense Bultmann's approach is broad-mindedly based on the history-of-religions approach. Gnosticism, too, is described extensively and not without a certain sympathy. But then those parts in which non-canonical literature enters the picture do not belong to 'New Testament theology' proper, but only to its presuppositions or consequences.[41] In fact the material of New Testament theology consists, in Bultmann's view, only of a canon within the canon, of Paul and John existentialistically interpreted![42] He thus perceives his task more narrowly than anybody before (or after!) him. One is struck in particular by the total exclusion of the synoptic Gospels from New Testament theology.[43]

Bultmann's great work is paradoxical in many ways. On one hand it sums up in its historical-exegetical opinions the critical and history-of-religions results of the previous generation, continuing the work of Wrede, Weiss and Bousset in the spirit of these men. Bultmann even develops the history-of-religions interpretation of the New Testament in a more radical direction by adopting the (dubious) theory of an existing Gnostic myth of salvation used by both Paul and John. The whole of the work, however, bears essentially the stamp of an almost homiletical 'content-critical' effort to challenge the present-day reader through the message of Paul and John. Thus Bultmann's programme after all comes to present an opposite pole to that of Wrede.[44] Historical understanding is overwhelmed by actualizing interpretation.[45]

In the Shadow of Bultmann: Biblical History as Normative

Barth was interested in normative theology, but in his conception historical exegesis was assimilated to the task of actualization. Bultmann depicted most of the New Testament from the viewpoint of the history of religion, but presented the thought of Paul and John as if it were normative theology. A survey of the conceptions born in the shadow of Bultmann's great work – either shortly before it[1] or after it – will demonstrate to how great an extent the concern for actualizing, normative theology has dominated the exegetical scene down to the present day.

In many conceptions of New Testament theology, New Testament ideas are simply presented as normative, as if the problem of time-bound and timeless material (Gabler), or myth and history (Strauss), or the shell and the kernel (the liberals), had never come up, not to mention the dilemmas produced by history-of-religions or eschatological studies.

(a) History of revelation: T. Zahn, F. Büchsel

Zahn's brief outline from 1928 is guided by salvation-historical concerns. New Testament theology has to be 'a historical presentation of the development of Christian doctrine in its initial period, documented in the New Testament' (2). The 'doctrine of the Bible reveals religious truths which are to be proclaimed, but these truths are always connected with divine acts of revelation' (1). Zahn treats New Testament ideas throughout as 'teachings'.[2] It is not appropriate, however, to deal separately with the teachings of different authors, for their individuality is not important. What are important are 'historical facts' such as the person, death and resurrection of Jesus, the pouring out of the Spirit and the entrance of Gentiles into the church (1f.).

Zahn harmonizes the New Testament into a theological unity.[3] For instance he omits a separate treatment of John (except for the Logos concept) and uses the Fourth Gospel straightforwardly as a source for the preaching of Jesus. He does however, realize that if the teaching of the New Testament is organized according to the doctrinal concepts of the various writers, the logical consequence is to abstain from presenting the doctrine of Jesus (who is not a New Testament author!) (1). At this point his methodological insight is more acute than that of most subsequent writers. A reconstruction of the message of Jesus only belongs to a synthesis if this is orientated on history, be it the history of religion or even – as in the case of Zahn – 'salvation history'.

Büchsel's (1937) 'revelation-historical' conception resembles Zahn's view. New Testament theology is 'a history of God's word in the New Testament' (thus the sub-title). God does not reveal himself all at once, but in a series of separate, if connected, revelations (4). It follows that the apostles could not be content with merely repeating the teaching of Jesus; it was their task to connect God's new revelation (in the Easter event and later) with the revelation that took place in the historical Jesus. Thus Büchsel's approach is conservative throughout. New Testament theology is a proclamatory 'science of the church' (173). Büchsel also harmonizes different New Testament teachings with one another. For instance, there is no difference worth mentioning between John and the Synoptics.[4]

(b) Apocalyptic dogmatics: E. Stauffer

Stauffer never says in so many words whether his peculiar New Testament theology of 1941 (ET 1955, the references are to the latter) should be understood as being purely descriptive, or also as a normative account. It is possible to read the book just as a historical interpretation, although readers have often construed it differently.[5] As Stauffer does not comment on the relation of historical interpretation to actualization, his work generates the erroneous impression that we still live in the pre-Gablerian state of innocence.

Stauffer's conception is certainly original. His starting-point is the history of religions. The New Testament material is arranged in an apocalyptic framework extracted from the Pseudepigrapha, and from the Old Testament interpreted in the light of the former.[6] Stauffer draws broad lines from Babylon and Iran, in passing touching even on Buddhism (e.g. 103f.), to the New Testament and even to later writings. The boundaries of the canon play no part. Stauffer even treats Jewish apocalyptic and early Christian material without further ado as parts of the same overall view without reflecting at all on the methodological justification of such a procedure.

For Stauffer, all of the New Testament represents one and the same 'apocalyptic' total view. The New Testament is emphatically a document of 'teaching'. Having briefly surveyed the 'development of primitive Christian theology', in the main part of his book Stauffer gives an account of the 'Christocentric theology of history in the New Testament'. Jesus, Paul, etc. are given a separate treatment within a systematically organized framework, but each represents the same teaching.[7] The themes of this teaching are, however, selected in a peculiarly eclectic way.[8]

Thus Stauffer's work, despite its history-of-religions starting-point and its descriptive presentation, resembles a dogmatics organized by *loci*. Stauffer begins with what was before the beginning of time and closes with eschatology.[9] The result is a system which was represented by no one in the early church. Justice is not done to any New Testament writer.[10] The relationship of New Testament theology to systematic theology or to present-day concerns is not reflected on, nor are any questions of principle or method. The reader is led to think that the New Testament 'theology of history' also amounts to normative Christian theology.[11] Stauffer does not make this claim in so many words, and the book can also be read as a purely descriptive account.[12]

The English translation of Stauffer's work appeared in 1955. Ironically, in the next few years the author himself produced a trilogy on Jesus in which he entered on a quite different path.[13]

(c) Between history and theology: E. G. Gulin, F. C. Grant

In 1940 Eelis Gulin, Professor in Helsinki (later Bishop in Tampere, Finland), produced the first Nordic New Testament theology. It would surely have attracted international attention had it not been written in Finnish.[14] Gulin's book opens in a pronouncedly theological fashion. 'When we speak of New Testament theology we start from the fundamental fact of Christian faith that the New Testament message about Jesus Christ is the final truth about God's work for the salvation of mankind' (1940b, 9). Therefore a scholar must have an 'existential relationship' to the truth he is exploring (10). This starting-point accounts for Gulin's limitation of his discussion to the texts of the New Testament, which he does not justify in so many words.

New Testament theology is a historical discipline, but nevertheless akin to systematic theology, for it has to 'present the religious content of the New Testament in a systematic form'. As a 'classical monument' of the proclamation that created the church, the New Testament is a document which is normative for systematic theology; New Testament theology wishes to aid systematic theology to carry out its task. But an exegete can best guarantee the authority of the New Testament by adopting a 'purely historical' attitude to his task. He will ask, 'What is the message of the New Testament itself concerning the basic truths of our religion, and how is this message to be understood when applied to the circumstances of that time?' Modern applications belong elsewhere (10f.). Gulin thus defines his task just as Gabler did: a distinction is made between the historical and the theological task, and because of this very distinction the former can best serve the latter.

Gulin thus perceives the task of New Testament theology to be a systematic (but not a dogmatic) one. This emphasis is visible in his presentation, which resembles Holtzmann's method of 'doctrinal concepts'. To be sure, Gulin strongly stresses the fact that the New Testament texts have been born in the midst of life, and that the presentation should therefore do justice to the 'rhythm of life' characteristic of the New Testament message. For this reason, his book is structured historically rather than thematically.[15] Within the main sections, however, he resorts to a doctrinal-systematic treatment which is especially clear in his interpretation of Paul.[16] Gulin reports on what Paul 'teaches', not on how he interprets his experiences or on what kind of self-understanding lies behind his theology. The content of Paul's faith makes up a 'tight organic whole' (124). There is no talk of contradictions or other problematic features.[17]

Thus Gulin's presentation differs from liberal New Testament theologies. Throughout he also keeps his distance from the history-of-religions school.[18] The influence of Hellenistic syncretism extends only to Paul's language, not to his message. Yet although Gulin shares this view with Feine, on the other hand he states that in the works of Feine, Schlatter, and (for the most part) Büchsel 'hardly any difference can be discerned between New Testament theology and church dogmatics' (15).

Like Kaftan, Gulin starts with eschatology, for the correct interpretation of which the foundation was laid by Johannes Weiss (28). He stresses the 'dual prospect' of Jesus' eschatology: the kingdom of God is imminent, but it is also already present (e.g. 37). In actual fact, the emphasis in Gulin's presentation is put – as it was in Kaftan's – on the presence of the kingdom. He fails to wrestle with the problem that 'the burning eschatological expectation of the original gospel of Jesus' did not materialize (94), even though it is the 'historical gospel' that is said to be normative for theology (11).

There is no significant difference between Paul and Jesus. Paul is Jesus' 'ingenious interpreter, who faithfully translates the message of his master into a new language'. This assertion presupposes certain interpretations of both Jesus and Paul. Jesus regarded himself as the eschatological Son of Man and understood his death as vicarious (45). Paul for his part inherited his view of Jesus' pre-existence from Jesus himself!

Interpreting Paul, Gulin stresses the importance of present eschatology: the cosmic shift has taken place (126). The imminent expectation is alive and well, but the real battle is already over (130).

The problem inherent in Gulin's theological position is crystallized in the chapter on John. He notes a difference in content between the Synoptics and John (202f.); even John's difference from Paul is 'immense' (203). The problems facing the interpreter are enhanced, due to the 'internal contradictions' in the Fourth Gospel (204). How do these statements relate to the assertion that the New Testament is a unity in which 'Paul is duplicated in John and John appears already in Paul', and 'the Synoptic doctrinal tradition is akin to both as far as its motifs are concerned' (13)?

The answer seems to be that John acted in a new historical and theological situation, in which 'the immediate clarity of the earliest times has already given way to deepening meditation' (204). John is 'immensely more christocentric' than the Synoptic Gospels (207). Instead of seeing here a problem over the unity of the New Testament revelation, Gulin states that 'in this Gospel (John) the biblical revelational religion appears at its brightest' (210).

Gulin's account is meant to be, and within certain limits is, a historical one. The treatment is, however, coloured by a theological pressure to achieve a certain kind of historical result: Gulin does observe differences between New Testament writings, but he glosses over them to emphasize unity. Yet the claim of unity is not based on a careful analysis of the differences.

Gulin rejects a 'content-critical' theological task as not belonging to the realm of exegesis. Yet he assumes that exegesis will reach results which are normative for systematic theology. This seems to be the reason why he does not take up the problems which the New Testament raises in the mind of a present-day reader, although he is not unaware of them. He thus evades the hermeneutical problem.

Grant's *Introduction to New Testament Thought* of 1950 does not claim to be a New Testament theology, but it deserves to be discussed in this connection. Grant, who subsequently edited an English translation of Johannes Weiss's *Earliest Christianity*, moves freely over history-of-religions territory. Like scholars at the turn of the century he stresses the significance of experience as the background to early Christian thought.[19] Unlike his early predecessors, however, Grant does not put his observations on this relationship at the service of a relativizing of theological interpretations.[20] He is prevented from this by his pronouncedly church-centred point-of-view. Grant posits a basic unity between the New Testament and the subsequent formation of doctrine; what is developed in the latter is found implicitly in the former.[21] Not only does Grant unabashedly use the category of 'revelation' in speaking of the Bible (28, 41f.), but he also speaks of the guidance of the Holy Spirit in the emergence of doctrine (27). Thus Grant's presentation is put into a strongly theological framework reminiscent of Catholic exegesis.

Grant limits himself to canonical writings; the history of religions only serves to illustrate them.[22] As for the New Testament, the focus is on the final form of the documents (47).[23] Grant chooses a thematic approach, since the extant material is far too limited for a historical treatment. To describe the rise of the Christian doctrine satisfactorily one would probably need ten times more material than the five hundred pages of the New Testament (22)!

Grant talks a great deal about the problem of unity and diversity in the New Testament.[24] In principle he accepts a great variety (30–42), but on theological grounds he postulates a crucial unity behind it (42, 45f.). The admission of variety has no specific consequences.[25] For instance, Grant observes that there is no unanimity in the New Testament over the conception of sin (172, 175, 180, 182). He draws no conclusions whatsoever from this statement. However, since he thinks that Christian theology ought to be based on biblical consensus (72) and presupposes that later theology has been developed harmoniously from the germs found in the Bible, his conception is beset with a considerable internal tension.[26]

Grant's book is written in an impressionist and essayistic style which is both an asset and a liability. As it contains a great number of stimulating details and points of view, in any case it is still fresh. Parts of it appear more interesting than the whole. Grant's view of the Jewish religion deserves special attention; in abstaining from all caricatures he is ahead of his time (101f., 310). It is also praiseworthy that he recognizes eschatology as the starting-point of all New Testament thought, even though in his actual interpretation the stress lies too heavily on present, 'realized' eschatology.[27]

(d) Taking leave of the Enlightenment: Martin Albertz

The last two volumes of Albertz's idiosyncratic four-volume work (1947–1957) cover what is usually called New Testament theology. Albertz talks instead of its 'message'. He is concerned to detach himself from the legacy of the Enlightenment and wants to return to the Reformation principle that the Bible is its own interpreter (II/1, 15). Although Albertz states that his task will be the description of historical reality 'as it was' (I/1, 9), his account bears a strong proclamatory stamp reminiscent of Karl Barth. Like Barth's, Albertz's view was conceived in parish ministry, initially independently of the Swiss theologian (II/1, 12f.).

Albertz regards it as his task to present the message of the New Testament rather than, for instance, the 'religion of the New Testament which never existed' (II/1, 21). Albertz shares with Barth a negative attitude to 'religion'. The message is unitary; the various witnesses bear testimony to one and the same gospel (II/1, 17). Thus it comes as no surprise that Albertz chooses a thematic structure; even the sub-units of the different sections mostly follow a thematic order.

The outline is strange enough. It is based on the triadic formula II Cor. 13. 13, the main sections being 'The Grace of our Lord Jesus Christ', 'The Love of God' and 'The Community of the Holy Spirit'. Eschatology is vigorously stressed as the scope of the whole message (esp. II/1, 194f.). Even New Testament ethics is presented within the framework of eschatology under the title 'Preparation for the Parousia'. Despite such merits the outline as a whole appears arbitrary. Thus the ethical chapter closes with a long section on fulfilling the law of Christ; this section is sub-divided into parts dealing with the different commandments of the Decalogue, and rather surprising topics come up for comment in connection with various commandments. This section resembles Luther's Catechism more than a historical essay on the New Testament.

Albertz joins different parts of the New Testament together into harmonious wholes, failing to do justice to the historical variety of the texts.[28] The problem of reconstruction and actualization is covered up with proclamatory solemnity. The reader gets the impression that there are no problems at all in translating the message of the New Testament into modern terms.[29] Yet what Barth succeeded in doing after World War I was no longer possible for Albertz in the aftermath of the new crisis. His construction has gone largely unnoticed, and rightly so.[30]

(e) The history of salvation as a universal remedy: Oscar Cullmann

Cullmann's books on the New Testament conception of time, christology and salvation history together come close to a total presentation of New Testament theology.[31] Cullmann regards his work as history of religions which differs from the dogmatically orientated research of the Bultmannians.[32] He sees more disadvantages than advantages in the present emphasis on hermeneutical questions and the rejection of the subject-object-scheme (1967, 66f.). The exegete must be careful not to read the content of his own faith into his texts, the faith-world of which may be rather different (67). 'My personal experience' is not just an exegetical asset, but can also be a source of error (67). A text can also be appropriately understood and interpreted by someone who does not believe in it; otherwise history of religion as a whole would be an impossibility (71).

Nevertheless Cullmann thinks that a biblical scholar is carrying out a normative task. He presupposes without further ado that what is central in the New Testament is central in Christian proclamation as well (1962, xi-xii). The 'essence' of the New Testament message is the essence of Christianity (1967, 19). The most basic task of exegesis is in fact to find the core common to all New Testament writings (1967, 19). One of the tasks of scholarly exegesis is to promote faith (95); in the final analysis, the salvation-historical proclamation of the New Testament can be understood in appropriate depth only by a believing Christian in a Christian community (323f., cf. 189). A penetration into the interpretation of the faith of the New Testament writers will be possible for one whose own faith has been 'purified from everything extraneous to the New Testament witnesses' (72). Demythologizing is justified to the extent that it is carried out within the Bible, i.e. as historicizing of myths (139).[33] Obviously, Cullmann's interest as documented in the works mentioned is confined to the canonical writings (although in another connection he has done pioneering work on non-canonical sources such as the Pseudo-Clementines).

Cullmann finds fundamentally in the writings of the Old and the New Testament a common salvation-historical view. The Bible is an account of events interpreted by faith, and these events constitute a series with a teleological progression. Christ is the centre of the history of salvation.

On a descriptive level, Cullmann's critical attitude to existentialist interpretation is no doubt justified: historically speaking, the thought-world of the New Testament writers was not dominated merely by a 'call to decision'. It is another matter to what extent different New Testament writers really represent such an overall view as Cullmann has constructed in a harmonizing way.[34] In this regard he has been criticized even by many rather 'moderate' scholars.[35]

Add to this that the concept of 'salvation history' as used by Cullmann is rather diffuse. Cullmann has a tendency to interpret any emphasis on continuity (1967, 55) or utilization of the Old Testament (129) as manifestations of a salvation-historical view.[36] Now it is clear that Paul wanted to show that there was continuity between the message he proclaimed and the classical tradition of Israel. It is equally clear, however, that he was not always very successful in demonstrating continuity.[37] Romans 9–11 is less a salvation-historical interpretation of the events of Paul's missionary work (249) than an expression of his struggle to find an answer to a burning social and theological problem.

Following modern Old Testament study (von Rad in particular), Cullmann rightly stresses that traditions were reinterpreted in Israel in the light of new events (e.g. 35f.) and that a similar process went on in the early church (e.g. 107). But this is a modern phenomenological insight which is very different from the notion, held by the New Testament writers, of a divine plan that stands behind all events. Cullmann confuses these two points of view with each other.[38] He fuses two quite different notions of 'salvation history': on the one hand, von Rad's Old Testament interpretation in terms of a 'history of testimonies' (which is not without intrinsic problems of its own);[39] on the other, the view of the New Testament writers concerning 'God's plan'.

Cullmann gives no answer whatsoever to the questions of those who find a 'translation' of the New Testament message into the language of modern thought inevitable.[40] It is enough for him to know that it was not revealed to the men of the Bible how they were to 'understand themselves' (102f.). For Cullmann, too, the thoughts of the New Testament writers are normative as such.[41]

(f) The teachings of an Anglican Jesus: A. Richardson

Richardson's 1958 book starts from the hypothesis that the apostolic church had a common theology which can be reconstructed from the New Testament (9). This common theology goes back to Jesus (12). Richardson states that in good scientific fashion in his book he will test these hypotheses which, in his opinion, best account for the material. He thus starts in a way that looks very much descriptive and historical. Yet he expressly dissociates himself from such research as aims at objectivity (12), stating that the starting-point of his interpretation will be 'historic Christian faith' (13). In his view Christian origins can only be understood with the help of an insight mediated through Christian faith (13). New Testament theology has an apologetic task.

Despite his announcement of the task ahead, Richardson does not in fact proceed by testing his basic thesis. On the contrary, he simply assumes the common theology of the early church.[42] He describes it in the framework of a thematic structure but omits to explain how the (idiosyncratic) organization chosen might be justified on the basis of this assumed theology.[43] The thoughts of different writings and writers are put together off-hand, Jesus himself being the author of 'the brilliant re-interpretation of the OT scheme of salvation' in the NT (12).[44] But as L. E. Keck puts it, a Jesus who teaches everything ascribed to him by Richardson is 'a Christian theologian, probably an Anglican'.[45] Richardson's is a 'completely unhistorical' presentation; a New Testament theology such as he depicts never existed.[46]

Richardson's speculative-apologetic attempt to outline a normative New Testament theology did not take scholarship forward. Its 'almost enthusiastic' reception in the Anglo-Saxon world a generation ago is hardly a compliment to the state of biblical scholarship in that world at that time.[47]

(g) The seed-bed of Catholic doctrine: H. Schlier, R. Schnackenburg, K. H. Schelkle

Of course, the assimilation of historical and actualizing accounts of New Testament theology normally takes place in a subtler way. In a couple of articles Bultmann's pupil Heinrich Schlier, who was converted to Catholicism, perceptively elucidates the ecclesial nature of Catholic New Testament theology. The limitation to New Testament writings is recognized as a decision which can only be justified on theological grounds. From a historical point of view the New Testament writings make up a 'rather strange formation', a fairly fragmentary 'collection of different theologies' (1975, 326, cf. 430f.).

Wrede was right: New Testament theology must be sharply distinguished from a history of early Christian religion. Schlier chooses New Testament theology. Not only does such an enterprise limit itself to the canon, but it also aims (without denying the existing diversity) at presenting one common theology (328). That such a theology exists is a postulate of faith; New Testament theology indeed demands faith of its practitioners (329). Accordingly, Schlier assumes that New Testament theology is to concentrate on the final form of the canonical writings (430) and that the preaching of the historical Jesus does not belong to New Testament theology, being rather its presupposition (330–2). Finally, Schlier notes that a complete New Testament theology should also indicate how New Testament theology combines into a unity with Old Testament theology in terms of content (340).

Other Catholic exegetes, too, have adopted a theological and church-centred stance in questions of principle. According to Rudolf Schnackenburg, dogmatic theology and New Testament theology cannot contradict each other in terms of content, since the same revelation is studied and illuminated by both. Subsequent theology is found in a germinal form in the New Testament (14). Bultmann is right in that New Testament theology must be interpreted theologically.[48] Schnackenburg postulates a unity behind the actual diversity of the New Testament, but to recognize this unity, theological insight is required.[49] Formally the unity finds expression in the fact that all theologies in the New Testament are based on the common primitive apostolic faith.[50] But Schnackenburg realizes that the message about Jesus is only found in the New Testament in an already interpreted form; therefore, the best starting-point is the earliest Christian tradition (22f.).

The only Catholic synthesis so far with a modern approach is written by K. H. Schelkle.[51] The four-volume work appeared in 1968–1976.[52] Not surprisingly the work is theological and orientated on the church; a historical account of New Testament theology goes with a striving for normativeness. Theology is a believing science, reflection on revelation (III, 11); the Bible contains the word of God (III, 14); exegesis serves the church (III, 15).

Although there are internal differences and lines of development within the New Testament, it is appropriate to speak of one New Testament theology. However, Schelkle defines the nature of the unity rather vaguely: all writers bear witness to Jesus Christ, and the witnessing takes place in the church (III, 16).[53] The New Testament is normative for the church, just as 'in any intellectual or spiritual movement the beginning is normative for all future' (III, 23).[54] Thus historical and normative New Testament theology in principle coincide.

Schelkle structures his presentation thematically; yet the sub-division is according to writings or groups of writings (the Synoptics – Paul – John – the rest of the New Testament). Schelkle is unwilling to organize his work according to dogmatic loci, but his outline bears traces of dogmatics too.[55]

In treating the various themes Schelkle starts from the Old Testament, and in general early Judaism, and the writings of Qumran in particular, are also paid some attention.[56] Thus Schelkle manages to draw traditio-historical lines concerning different themes and concepts. His starting-point must be regarded as fruitful.[57] A shortcoming in the actual treatment is the lack of sufficient differentiation between the different writings.[58] This deficiency is not, however, due to the thematic method itself, but to the particular manner in which it has been carried out.

The unclear relationship between the historical and actualizing tasks brings about problems. If the New Testament is normative for the church, what should one make of subsequent developments in the church or of modern thought in general? Too much is left open by Schelkle in this area. He does allude to a number of problems, but is mostly careful not to give a clear opinion on them.[59]

(h) Three Nordic contributions: H. Riesenfeld, A. T. Nikolainen, R. Kieffer

In his short Swedish outline Riesenfeld distances himself from those scholars (Käsemann is mentioned as an example) who find themselves capable of telling what constitutes a genuine version of early Christianity and what is mistaken. They act 'less as scholars than as teachers of the church'. 'A scholar has to clarify lines of development and to recognize connections. A teacher of the church is animated by the zeal to decide what in the New Testament is normatively valid today' (365). Thus Riesenfeld takes sides with a historical New Testament theology, the task of which is to 'structure the beliefs which appear in the New Testament in a way which is appropriate to the material' (364).

However, the way Riesenfeld carries out his task does not correspond to these principles. The 'appropriateness' just mentioned turns out to be identical with a decision of faith based on Christian experience. The diversity of the four Gospels is no problem, since experience has shown that in practice and in individual devotion they can intuitively be fused into a total picture of Jesus (367).[60] Both the Synoptics and the Fourth Gospel present a true picture of Jesus (372). Either the Johannine tradition has openly drawn the conclusions from hints given by Jesus or else it is based on teachings communicated to a close circle in which Jesus spoke more openly of his person and mission (374, 419, 427). His pre-existence is also mentioned in Mark 10.45 (377).

The birth narratives of Matthew and Luke are based on the stories of Joseph and Mary respectively (411). The internal differences between the Synoptic Gospels are so small that they can be ignored in a presentation of this size (419). The section on the Synoptics which takes some forty per cent of the whole, in fact deals with Jesus alone. John is treated as a sequel to that section – before Paul.

Riesenfeld structures the material according to writings which makes a historical perspective possible. The net result, however, is a harmonized ecclesial picture in which the internal differences within the New Testament have been eliminated. Thus despite his principles Riesenfeld appears as a 'teacher of the church'. No answer is given to the question 'In what sense can New Testament theology be normative?' Riesenfeld simply writes as if the picture drawn by an historian could be 'intuitively' appropriated as such as a norm by a present-day believer.

Nikolainen's Finnish textbook – the first full-scale Nordic theology of the New Testament since Gulin's – appeared in 1971, a year before the author was nominated Bishop of Helsinki. Nikolainen (best known to the international community of scholars for his much earlier work on the resurrection faith)[61] does reflect on questions of structure[62] but not on those of principle. In accordance with the church-theological starting-point of the author, the work limits itself to the canonical writings. This time, too, the historical and the normative task coincide:

> The New Testament is the common point of departure for the Christian churches in the light of which – according to our confession – decisions must be sought to present-day problems too. Since the whole Bible is God's normative revelation, a total representation of New Testament theology must attempt, using the methods of scientific investigation, to do justice to each writer and each pericope. (VI)

Thus my teacher's programme turns out to be, point after point, the exact opposite of the programme of Wrede (who is not referred to) – down to the principle of including each and every pericope (which Wrede rejected as 'micrology').

The question of normativeness is, of course, closely connected with the question of unity. Nikolainen admits the diversity of the New Testament, but he evades the problem caused by it. Of two versions of Jesus' teaching, both are 'naturally' normative (17). No conclusions are drawn by Nikolainen from the facts (which he expressly recognizes) that Matthew 5.17–20 represents a theology other than Paul's (29) or that James's concept of faith differs from Paul's (230). Nor does anything follow from the fact that 'Luke regarded the unbelief of the Jews as final, whereas Paul expected that Israel would still be converted to faith in Jesus' (182).

In an epilogue the author skilfully identifies a large number of different christologies and eschatologies in the New Testament. But although the christological material makes a variegated impression, this is only a matter of different emphases (312f.). As regards eschatology, Nikolainen isolates no less than twelve different conceptions, yet they are not 'incompatible alternatives' (316). But in the light of the material presented by the author himself, the compatibility looks rather like a mere postulate (one is reminded here of the similar cases of Gulin and Grant).[63]

Nikolainen organizes his theology according to groups of writings. The inclusion of the preaching of Jesus in a New Testament theology presents no problem for him.[64] The separate treatment of the theology of each Synoptic Gospel (a strategy chosen before him only by Conzelmann) deserves special mention. The 'post-apostolic' writings receive more attention than usual. Different post-apostolic writings are dealt with separately, and they are not branded as 'representatives of a lower, degenerate understanding of Christianity'.[65]

As regards details of the organization, pride of place is given to christology, paraenesis and soteriology. Eschatology is highlighted as well. The words 'teaching' and 'doctrine' figure conspicuously in the table of contents. Nikolainen's approach indeed comes rather close to the traditional method of 'doctrinal concepts'.

It is peculiar to this work that Paul's teachings on various topics are gleaned from each letter separately. The author is taking seriously his principle that justice should be done to each pericope of the New Testament.[66]

The first non-Finnish Nordic theology of the New Testament saw the light of day in 1977 when René Kieffer's Swedish textbook appeared.[67] Ten years later the book appeared in a German translation, to which the following page numbers refer. Kieffer thinks that New Testament theology has a scientific task but that this cannot be defined in purely scientific terms. For the limitation of the textual corpus to be examined to the twenty-seven canonical writings, which is an 'absurdity' from a 'purely historical standpoint' (1987, 23), amounts to the acknowledgement of the decision of the Christian churches.

Thus it is a question of research which 'in one way or another already accepts Christian faith'. Kieffer asks, 'Can a theology which studies such a corpus be scientific?' His answer: yes and no. The analysis itself can be controlled by anyone, whether a believer or not. But the very starting-point, namely, that the New Testament writings constitute a meaningful objective of study, is a 'postulate which can only be verified from inside by a believer' (19). Thus the principle sharply stated by Wrede and Schlier (see above, pp. 13,54) is confirmed by Kieffer.

Kieffer's reflections on the structure of a New Testament theology are informed by linguistics, an area in which much of his other work has been done.[68] Should the presentation be organized diachronically or synchronically? Kieffer rejects a structure based on a diachronic sketch of the 'historical lines of development',[69] appealing above all to the hypothetical and subjective nature of any such sketch (20f.).[70] He defines the task as a synchronic study of the textual 'corpus' that the New Testament is.

In practice Kieffer deals with each writer separately, so that the difference between New Testament theology and New Testament introduction is diminished. He surveys the Gospels, Acts, letters and Revelation, in that order. In each section he first treats the 'main structure and function' of the writings, which in practice means roughly the traditional issues dealt with in Introduction.[71] Then follows a 'detailed theological analysis', thematic in nature and reminiscent of the traditional method of 'doctrinal concepts'. The result is a series of individual pictures.[72]

As regards its theological content, Kieffer's book is conventional.[73] By contrast, the methodological decision invites interest and testifies to more reflection than is found in most of the recent syntheses.

(i) Evangelical harmonies: G. E. Ladd, D. Guthrie, L. Morris

Ladd's lengthy 1974 textbook[74] is self-consciously 'conservative-evangelical' (25). All letters of the Pauline corpus as well as Jude and II Peter are treated as authentic. Although Ladd does call the Synoptists theologians, he nowhere treats the theology of their Gospels: Matthew, Mark and Luke are only given space as sources for the message of Jesus.[75] Even the Fourth Gospel, which is said to complement the Synoptics, is dealt with as a witness to the authentic teaching of Jesus. Indeed John makes his appearance in Ladd's book before the primitive church and Paul. Even though Ladd admits in principle the rich variety of the New Testament which 'must not be sacrificed' (33), in practice he harmonizes everything into a unified teaching.[76]

Ladd describes his task in a symptomatically unclear way: biblical theology is a descriptive discipline – 'primarily' (25).[77] The author clearly transgresses the limits of description when he speaks of the normative revelational character of the Bible (32) or identifies himself with the salvation-historical perspective of the Bible as he understands it (27). Ladd justifies his limitation to the canonical writings with the very special plea that these writings 'are conscious of participating in redemptive history while the noncanonical writings lack this sense of redemptive history' (32)![78]

Guthrie's thousand pages (1981) are characterized by a purely fundamentalist approach. Despite the erudition of the author, the book is an anachronism.[79] Guthrie himself states that he must discover the unifying factors behind the diversity because he 'knows that revelation cannot be contradictory' (30). But instead of searching for unifying factors, he is often content with simply by-passing the differences, say, between the different Synoptic versions of a certain event. Passages which represent unfulfilled eschatological expectation are given a particularly strained exegesis.

Morris's volume (1986) is written from a somewhat less extreme conservative perspective. His approach is theological and ecclesial. True, he is 'striving hard to find out what the New Testament authors meant' (10); however, this is done not merely 'as the necessary prelude to our understanding of what their writings mean for us today' (which might indicate a two-stage process of interpretation), but on the supposition that a normative account will ensue. No critical discrimination within the New Testament is appropriate; on the contrary, the author will 'resist the temptation to discard passages or books that we see as of inferior importance' (10).[80]

Morris contests Wrede's rejection of the notion of the canon. But he actually confirms Wrede's point in establishing the ecclesial nature of the concept of canon yet once more.[81] 'If we take seriously the idea that God guides his church', we must see in the way the canon came into being 'an indication that these are the books that he means his people to have' (12).

Morris treats the New Testament as 'teachings' (14). It is not his task to trace the history of early Christian religion, or even the history of how the New Testament teachings received their present form; that history is less important than the teachings, and in addition it is impossible to recover (13f.). Morris stipulates a basic theological unity in all New Testament writings with the very general argument that the writers were 'all recognized as Christians' (which writers of early non-canonical books were not?) and that the various books would not have been accepted into the one canon 'if there had not been some (!) kind of unity' (16). The existing variety is, in the final analysis, a difference in the idioms or categories of thought used to express the common conviction; there is no other difference between e.g. Jesus' proclamation of the nearness of the kingdom and John's talk of the incarnation (16). No wonder that the imminent expectation is explained away (e.g. 88f., 107f.), and the sections on Paul and John are organized in trinitarian terms.

While the work itself is conventional, Morris's choice of outline is of some methodological interest. He resorts to structuring the book according to groups of writings, for too little is known of history and chronology to support a chronological structure.[82] While Morris' outline is thus the exact opposite of what Wrede had in mind, he actually concurs with Bultmann in not devoting a chapter to the historical Jesus. Of course, his reasons are quite different: he thinks that the teachings of Jesus come through accurately enough even when the four Gospels are presented separately. But his decision points to the obvious fact that if you restrict yourself to the canon, you should take seriously the fact that the teaching of Jesus as reconstructed with critical methods is not an issue there.

3

In the Shadow of Bultmann: Singling out the Normative

The attempt of the liberals, the history-of-religions school and of Bultmann to filter out from the material that which is permanently valid and normative, i.e. 'content criticism', is alive and well too. In the vein of the liberals and Bultmann, but in contrast to Wrede's programme, the separation of the normative material from the rest takes place in the works of these scholars at one and the same stage, indeed at the only existing stage, which might be called (as some of them call it) 'historical-theological'. Braun, Conzelmann and Käsemann – all representatives of the Bultmann school – make clear theological distinctions within the New Testament. By contrast, Kümmel and Goppelt, who do make some distinctions, also tend to harmonize a number of differences within the canon.[1] Lohse represents a middle path between more radical and more ecclesial conceptions.

(a) The programme of a humanistic theology: H. Braun

Braun has not written an account of New Testament theology, but he has reflected on the problems connected with such an enterprise in a provocative article. He carries on Bultmann's theological and philosophical content criticism consistently, applying it relentlessly also to the notion of the existence of a 'reified' God 'in himself'.

The views of the New Testament writers of man's relation to God are contradictory even on central points. Braun demonstrates this in connection with five themes: the portrait of Jesus, salvation, Torah, eschatology, sacraments (405–11).[2] From the viewpoint of actualizing theology, Braun then concludes: the

very existence of contradictions between New Testament statements in itself shows that the real concern of these statements
cannot possibly consist in what they say, contradicting each
other (405). The interpreter has to penetrate deeper.

A closer examination shows that all different New Testament
positions on the five topics concerned are, in one way or another,
problematic from the perspective of a modern world- view (412–
16). Therefore the interpreter cannot choose one New Testament
view and by-pass the others; rather, he has to penetrate behind all
the views in question.

Braun thinks, however, that in the treatment of all five themes
in the New Testament some critical germs can be detected
which, in principle at least, break through that naive reified
notion of God which is presupposed in most texts. Below the
christology, for instance, glimpses can be caught of an old 'non-
christological' layer (e.g. Luke 6.46): Jesus points out to man his
radical obligation and puts him under God who grants his gifts in
a sovereign way (Matt. 20.15: 416f.). Behind the imminent
expectation of the end lies the insight into the unique importance
of the present moment (421f.), etc. Although the New Testament
as a whole is in need of severe philosophical criticism, in its
different parts germs exist which can be consistently developed
so that a theologically satisfactory result ensues. Braun admits
that these germs are not reflected on in the New Testament itself
(e.g. 420); no consequences are drawn from them. Yet – somewhat surprisingly – he ends up by asserting that they represent
'the real trend of the New Testament' (423).

Braun considers the key question of New Testament theology
to be: 'What is God ultimately, within the meaning of the New
Testament?' His answer: 'God' is 'the whence of my being taken
care of and of my being obliged, which comes to me from my
fellow man', the fact that 'I may' and 'I ought'. God is 'a definite
type of relation with one's fellow man' (423f.).[3]

The answer reveals that Braun may have shown what 'God'
means 'ultimately', but not what 'God' means 'within the
meaning of the New Testament'. He exaggerates the significance
of such critical germs as he has discovered in the totality of the
New Testament.

Nevertheless it has to be said that Braun has made a meaningful attempt to penetrate into normative biblical theology in

Gabler's sense. With the aid of 'philosophical criticism' (Gabler) he has tried to winnow from the New Testament grains out of which one might develop a theology which is possible for us. The fact that the New Testament offers a very limited number of such germs is part of the larger problem, a self-evident fact which does not in itself rule out Braun's enterprise.

It is no answer to Braun for his critics, typically enough, usually to claim that he goes too far and 'dissolves theology into anthropology' or reduces Christianity to a version of humanism.[4] The question is unavoidable: is not Braun simply progressing with methodological consistency down the road on which Bultmann came to a premature halt?[5] To appeal to confessional viewpoints is to evade the real issue. The real problem with Braun's view is, rather, the extent to which he undoubtedly modernizes parts of the New Testament in an effort to find some biblical basis for his humanistic reinterpretation.

Braun is less interested in a historical account of New Testament theology. Still, his actualizing theology is based on history-of-religions work in which he compares New Testament notions with the religious views of antiquity in general. Braun finds that a 'reified' view of god(s) is common to the whole religious world of antiquity. By contrast, those segments of the New Testament which (in Braun's view) make God a type of one's relation with fellow men amount to something new.[6] Thus one might conceive of Braun's scholarly enterprise as a whole as a two-stage project: the first stage is history of religion; the second one, to which, according to Braun, all of 'New Testament theology' belongs, is philosophical and theological.

(b) Bultmann for a new day: H. Conzelmann, G. Strecker, E. Käsemann, E. Lohse

Conzelmann wants to offer students of theology a slightly amended version of Bultmann's New Testament theology (1969, XV).[7] He fights for the basic intentions of dialectical theology (XIII. 7).[8] Conzelmann defines New Testament theology in a way similar to Bultmann, but he is more specific: theology interprets not only the 'faith' but also the original *texts* of faith, i.e. the oldest formulations of the *creed* (XV).

Conzelmann seems, however, to identify the creed with the much more extensive concept of 'kerygma', and this is bound to cause confusion.[9] He wants to organize his theology in terms of the history of tradition (XV), starting 'where the themes of New Testament theology first become perceptible: in the kerygma of the primitive community' (9). Hence, quite logically, the historical Jesus does not belong to New Testament theology but to its presuppositions.[10]

But Conzelmann's first main section on 'the kerygma of the primitive community and (!) the Hellenistic community'[11] covers an astonishingly wide and variegated field, if it is supposed to describe that 'creed' which is then interpreted by New Testament theology proper. Although Conzelmann does not consistently distinguish between the views of the early church and the Hellenistic community, his talk of an early kerygma in the singular appears strange.[12]

In the vein of Bultmann, Conzelmann makes a clear distinction between what is said and what is meant. He tries, however, more carefully than his mentor to discover in Paul's own texts traces of an awareness of such a difference on the part of the apostle himself.[13] The difference between what is said and what is meant is carried to extremes in the section on Paul's theology of the law. If Paul's talk of the law is 'objectivized' to a salvation-historical view, it appears absurd in many ways. But when it is taken as a 'theological interpretation' which reveals human origins and destiny it becomes comprehensible (225, 227f.).

Conzelmann thinks that Bultmann's readers are tempted to 'sip' the latter's interpretations 'as a pure distillation'; hence he himself wants to stress the historical components somewhat more (XV). Thus he does for instance deal with Romans 9–11 in connection with Paul's theology. The result, however, is meagre. For instance, Paul's talk of the conversion of Israel in the end-time is basically designed only to spell out that 'faith cannot be derivative, that it only arises from preaching' (251). Conzelmann portrays Paul as a reflective theologian who 'works out' the kerygma into a conceptual form (e.g. 202). Correspondingly John 'works out' the Jesus tradition into conceptual theology (9). Nevertheless Conzelmann, consciously modifying Bultmann, also speaks of a theology of the Synoptic Gospels and gives a (far too) brief[14] survey of the theologies of Mark, Matthew and Luke.[15]

The liberal scholars and the history-of-religions school distinguished between religious experience and the theological theories designed to interpret it, regarding the former as the more essential part. In the existential interpretation of Bultmann and Conzelmann a corresponding distinction is made between the real 'subject-matter' (*Sache*) and the deficient means of expression used in voicing it. Structurally there is little difference between the two models of interpretation. The essential difference is, to my mind, the fact that the existential model, especially as applied by Conzelmann, divorces Paul from social reality. He is depicted as a professor of systematic theology who self-consciously 'works out' various aspects in his materials, as if he were aware of the weaknesses of his 'means of expression'. At crucial points historical interpretation is overrun by the actualizing application. It is symptomatic that Conzelmann constantly resorts to using the first-person pronoun: Paul is speaking of God's demand on 'me' (228 and passim).

Strecker, who has edited an important volume on the history of the subject, defines the task of New Testament theology in the vein of Bultmann. The historical and theological approaches are combined; Strecker speaks of a historical-eschatological dialectic (1975, 18–31). New Testament theology has to make Christian faith understandable (23f.) in a way that keeps open the possibility of a confession of it (31). Content-criticism has a place in New Testament theology; what a text says and what it means are questions that can be distinguished (26). It is a special task of the discipline to search for a unity behind the differences (25).

Strecker puts forward the interesting idea that New Testament theology ought to start with Paul (29) – an idea subsequently put into practice independently of him by Morris, though in a very different conceptual framework. Jesus is counted by Strecker, as by Bultmann, among the presuppositions of New Testament theology. Strecker claims that the discipline ought to focus on the final form of the New Testament writings. A logical consequence of this is that not just the reconstruction of the preaching of Jesus must be left to the periphery, but other reconstructions as well – both the kerygma of the earliest community (still described at length by Bultmann) and the apostolic creed (important to Conzelmann).[16] Within a Bultmannian framework, Strecker has taken the methodological discussion one step forward.

*   *   *

Käsemann has been one of the most influential figures in contemporary New Testament studies. He sums up his view of New Testament theology in a brief programmatic paper (1972/73). Right at the beginning, this scholar, whose career has been beset with severe conflicts with the church, states that New Testament theology ought to serve the church (235f.)! Scholarship must not detach itself from life – and Käsemann thinks here of the life of the church in particular. Without any relationship to the life of the church, 'the discipline loses its distinctive character, its concrete roots, and it ceases, too, to be indispensable and binding' (236).

Thus Käsemann's position is diametrically opposed to that of Wrede, though he also praises Wrede lavishly (237). Käsemann rejects Wrede's programme, not because it is incompatible with the church but because the fragmentary nature of the sources makes it impossible to write the history of the early Christian religion that Wrede had in mind.[17] Käsemann states that the New Testament is a fragmentary collection of documents from the earliest period with 'by and large . . . no internal coherence' (242). Nevertheless he never raises the question whether or not New Testament theology should restrict itself to the canonical writings (it seems that it should). New Testament theology is 'a historical discipline' which should strongly stress 'the nuances, biases, divergences and contradictions as and when they occur' (242). Its themes should be treated in terms of a history of the traditions with an eye to what future developments are foreshadowed in the New Testament documents. Thus New Testament theology can in a very broad sense be regarded as the beginning of the history of dogma (243).

A dominant aspect should be eschatology (243f.). Yet an even more central place belongs to christology. 'The revelation of Christ in its progress and varied interpretation' is the real clue to the New Testament. Käsemann rejects Bultmann's decision to move the historical Jesus from New Testament theology to its presuppositions. What he fails to see is that this move was a necessary consequence of Bultmann's way of defining 'theology'. Käsemann himself offers no clear definition. He simply states that 'the discipline of New Testament study' (sic!) has to do not only with theologians (which Jesus was not) but 'with early Christian preaching in general' (244). But in that case, does the preaching of Jesus belong to early *Christian* preaching?

New Testament theology should make clear what it means to follow the Nazarene who came to the cross 'to break in God's name through pious taboos and conventional religiosity' – a fact largely suppressed by established Christianity (244f.). Thus biblical study 'has always to exercise a critical function against existing taboos, and the continued rediscovery of the biblical message is for the Church danger and hope alike' (243).

Clearly, through his work Käsemann has made a massive contribution to New Testament study in general. By contrast, his comments on the task of New Testament theology in particular hardly take the methodological discussion forward. The relation between the historical and the theological tasks remains confusing.[18]

Bishop Lohse puts forward a slightly more ecclesiastical version of Bultmann's New Testament theology.[19] The advance of the exegetical work on Bultmann is manifest e.g. in the fact that the theologies of the Synoptic Gospels are treated in a separate chapter between Paul and John. Nor does the presentation of Paul's theology start with anthropology, as in Bultmann, but with christology.[20] But Lohse delineates the nature of New Testament theology without Bultmann's methodological acumen. He defines the task simultaneously in both historical and systematic terms (9f.). New Testament theology must 'describe how the kerygma about the crucified and resurrected Christ has been elaborated in the preaching recorded in the New Testament which is fundamental for the church'. At the same time one has to ask whether the kerygma has been expressed 'appropriately' in the various writings. Lohse does not reflect on either why an extensive account of the historical Jesus should belong to an exposition of 'the theological thoughts of the New Testament writings'[21] or why he restricts the exposition to the canonical material. His answer to the content-critical question culminates in a reference to Christ crucified (I Cor. 2.2) in classical Lutheran vein.[22]

Lohse's book is a useful summary of basic exegetical knowledge, but it does not further the discussion of the principles and methods of New Testament theology.

(c) The testimony of the major witnesses: W. G. Kümmel

Kümmel's 1969 textbook (ET 1974) offers the reader an iron

ration of historical New Testament theology which is, however, at crucial points coloured by the interests of normative theology. The approach is, by and large, historical but the starting-point is that the scholarship is pursued in the context of the church by believing Christians (1974, 16, 322). The New Testament cannot be examined with methods that differ from those applied to other ancient writings, but it is important that the scholar be inwardly moved by his work.

Kümmel restricts himself to the 'major witnesses' of New Testament theology, a group which consists of Jesus (!), Paul and John. The treatment of Jesus in a 'New Testament theology' is justified by Kümmel on purely theological grounds:[23] a Christian has 'a burning interest' in whether his faith has a sound foundation and wants to know to what extent the picture of Jesus given by the apostolic proclamation agrees with his 'historical actuality' (25). Kümmel's theological question thus resembles that of Strauss, although the answers are rather different.[24]

Similarly, it is purely theological reasons that require Kümmel to ponder at the end of his book whether the New Testament 'witnesses' ultimately put forward one and the same message. He is confronted with this question precisely as a Christian who is convinced that he encounters in the New Testament writings 'the knowledge of God's revelation in Christ'. The question of a common message 'does *not* thrust itself upon us from the involvement with the proclamation of these witnesses themselves, who stand in no direct connection with one another, but from the awareness of their common membership in the canon' (322f.). Thus Kümmel's perspective is essentially different from that of Wrede.

Kümmel in fact states frankly that the New Testament has a normative significance. This is due to the fact that 'it stands in a more or less close relationship temporally and substantively to the historical revelation in Christ'. Hence one can reasonably expect to find the witness in its purest form in those forms of proclamation 'which stand closest in point of time to the historical Christ event'. These include, first, the message and figure of Jesus as perceptible in the earliest strata of the Synoptic Gospels; second, the proclamation of the primitive community; third, Paul, who was the first to think through this proclamation theologically. In spite of all differences, these three forms of proclamation permit us to see a common message which can be called 'foundational' and by which the message of the rest of the New Testament can be 'measured' (324).[25]

Thus Kümmel represents a version of normative historiography structurally similar to that cherished before him by Baur, the liberals and Bultmann. It is only that the norm has been established differently in the different cases. Baur and the liberals found the norm in the ethical message of the historical Jesus, Bultmann again in a definite type of self-understanding. Kümmel thinks he has found the norm in what is common to Jesus, the primitive comunity and Paul. His approach amounts to a step backwards in the direction of the old method of 'doctrinal concepts'. A peculiarity is that Jesus becomes a witness among others to the Christ event.[26]

As regards the structure of the book, it strikes one that John, who is counted among the 'major witnesses', does not belong to those parts of the New Testament which constitute the norm. Rather, John belongs to those who are to be measured by the norm. The inclusion of the Johannine literature in Kümmel's book is due mainly to the fact that in the Fourth Gospel Jesus is interpreted consistently 'from the perspective of the faith of the primitive (sic!) community after Easter and Pentecost'; hence the question arises whether the original message has been appropriately developed or not (324).[27]

Kümmel comes to the conclusion that Jesus, the primitive community, Paul and John all agree on crucial points. The common core consists on one hand in the conviction that the salvation brought by Jesus is to all both a present and a future reality; on the other hand (and this is the most important point), in the conviction that in Jesus God has 'condescended' to bring salvation to men (325–33). But surely the question must be asked: 'How meaningful is it to claim that the historical and the Johannine Jesus represent one and the same message in this regard?' Kümmel has a strong interpretation of Jesus' talk of the Son of Man (assuming that Jesus identified himself with the eschatological 'Man'): 'in Jesus the coming kingdom of God becomes present, because in Jesus as the "Man" of the end-time God stoops and himself achieves the deliverance' (330). Paul's proclamation of salvation is 'a direct (!) continuation of the message of Jesus and the primitive community' (331).[28]

Since Kümmel strives to attain a normative biblical theology by means of a historical reconstruction (the earliest testimony), he has to harmonize the differences found in that testimony. He also fails to pay attention to the fact that in the earliest church there were a number of Christians who, at least 'in point of time', had as close a relation to the 'historical revelation in Christ' as Paul (or closer). Actually here Kümmel lands in a methodological dilemma, for how can one establish a historical reconstruction merely on selected material (the 'main witnesses')?[29]

Kümmel's conception, which stresses continuity among the witnesses, resembles that put forward by Kaftan four decades earlier, yet an explicitly theological emphasis is more pronounced in Kümmel's work than in that of the liberal systematician.[30] Kümmel's talk about the normativeness of the New Testament remains quite vague. The normativeness of the central message for modern Christianity is assumed, but Kümmel does not clarify what this means e.g. as far as 'mythical' statements are concerned.[31]

From the point of view of normative biblical theology Kümmel's presentation is unsatisfactory. Again, as a historical account it suffers from the fact that the interests of actualizing theology affect so clearly both the structure of the book and the questions asked in it. As a careful compendium of basic exegetical knowledge the book is useful.

(d) A strained dialogue: L. Goppelt

Goppelt's synthesis, which appeared posthumously in 1975 and 1976, remained unfinished.[32] Nevertheless, the intentions of the author sufficiently come to light. His approach is reminiscent of Kümmel's, but the presentation is not always so clear, mainly due to a still heavier theological emphasis. Goppelt wants to combine historical analysis and theological understanding. The 'presuppositions of modern thought' and the 'principles of historical analysis' must be brought to a critical dialogue with the claim of the New Testament to revelation.[33] This aim is linked with a thorough-going polemic against 'purely historical' exegesis.

Goppelt joins the 'salvation-historical' position, as he calls it (represented by von Hofmann, Zahn, Schlatter and Cullmann). However, he replaces 'salvation history'[34] with the 'promise/fulfilment' scheme (I, 280). But in the context of the critical dialogue mentioned above, one must ask: Can we still maintain the idea that Jesus is the conclusive revelation of the God of the Old Testament (28of.)? It is important for exegetes to join in discussion with systematic theologians. Only in this way can New Testament statements become intelligible as 'ultimate claim and ultimate affirmation'. Thus the idea of the normative character of New Testament theology clearly lies behind Goppelt's work. New Testament theology 'assumes the decisive position for Christian theology in its entirety' (I, xxvi).[35]

There is nonetheless little in Goppelt's work directly to answer modern questions.[36] Cautious content criticism is, however, put forward regarding one-sided emphases in Matthew and James (II, 235) and statements on pre-existence. Goppelt thinks that these are 'intended more or less[37] as visual aids' for Paul himself (II, 77f.).

Goppelt limits himself in practice to the canonical writings. To justify this, on the one hand he appeals to their particular 'history of influence' on society (*Wirkungsgeschichte*) (I, 271f.) and on the other claims that the New Testament writings distinguish themselves theologically from contemporaneous non-canonical writings (II, 158f.).

The preaching of Jesus cannot possibly be excluded from New Testament theology. Apart from the discussion of principles, the whole first volume is devoted to an analysis of the proclamation and mission of Jesus.[38] To be sure, the starting point of New Testament theology is the Easter kerygma (I, 5). Nevertheless, in Goppelt's view the intrinsic structure of New Testament theology demands that the mission of Jesus be examined first (I, 7). He does not manage to make clear, however, why the goal should be a historical reconstruction rather than a clarification of how Jesus was seen in different traditions and by different writers.[39] Goppelt's presentation is methodologically unclear in other regards, too. For instance, he often constructs his picture of Jesus on Matthew's editorial sentences (e.g. Matt. 5.17–20: I, 103–5).[40]

Indeed, Goppelt deems the crucial question to be whether Jesus' earthly ministry is 'the essential – and not something like the psychological – basis of the Easter kerygma' (I, 10). The justification for the treatment of Jesus' mission is thus basically the same as in Kümmel's case. For Goppelt, too, it is important to point up a continuity between the mission of Jesus and the message of the early church. By its very nature, the mission of Jesus leads up to the passion and resurrection. In the resurrection this ministry was brought to its goal: the total eschatological renewal of the human being. Thus Jesus' ministry and resurrection together amount to God's final self-revelation (I, 247).

Goppelt admits Jesus' imminent expectation, but in practice reduces his eschatology to the present coming of the kingdom in the renewal of man's relationship to God (I, 61, 71).[41] Jesus eschatologically suspends the law which Goppelt understands in the traditional way as a manifestation of a 'principle of achievement' (I, 123). It was Jesus' attitude to the law that led to his death (I, 224). He was rejected by people because he wanted to transform them through his eschatological demands, but they wanted to remain unchanged (I, 227). Thus Goppelt's 'salvation-historical' approach leads to a markedly theological explanation for a problem which appears rather different in a historical light.[42] Jesus also expected his own death and already during his lifetime gave his disciples the key to its interpretation (I, 191f.).

In trying to demonstrate the continuity between Jesus and the church Goppelt interprets the concept of 'faith' in the miracle stories of the Jesus tradition in an overly theological way.[43] He also thinks he can find in Jesus' criticism of the scribes and the Pharisees the anthropology of Romans 7.15–24 (I, 86). Nor does the fact that Jesus did not want to gather together a community around himself amount to discontinuity. For salvation was not connected with an acceptance of the teaching of Jesus, but with adherence to his person alone. During his earthly mission this possibility was open only to a few. Thus the ministry of Jesus actually points beyond itself to a time in which 'it would be possible for all people to be connected to his person' (I, 210)!

Throughout, Goppelt's endeavour to demonstrate continuity engenders problematical constructions.[44] The same holds true for his effort to show Jesus to be the fulfilment of the Old Testament promises.[45] Goppelt solves the problems raised by historical criticism by inventing 'better' historical interpretations. Their artificiality becomes a stumbling stone for the dialogue he envisages between criticism and a normative theological interpretation.[46]

4

The Unrealized Programme of Separate Tasks: K. Stendahl, J. M. Robinson, R. Morgan, K. Berger

Wrede separated the historical work from the theological task. He did not argue that an actualizing theological interpretation of the New Testament was completely unjustified, but he wanted to leave it to systematic theologians. Another possibility would have been a clear distinction in the biblical scholar's agenda between a historical and an actualizing stage, i.e. a return to Gabler's programme. However, no theology of the New Testament or a corresponding synthesis has been written from either this point of view or from that of Wrede.[1] The ideal of clearly separating the historical task from the theological has so far only been put forward in programmatic declarations – and even that has fairly seldom been the case.[2] This is so despite the fact that in everyday exegetical work such a distinction is a commonplace.[3]

In a programmatic article in the *Interpreter's Dictionary of the Bible* of 1962, Stendahl stressed the importance of a two-stage interpretation of a biblical text. First one has to make out descriptively 'what it meant' when it was written. Only after that has been established one may go on to ask tentatively 'what it means', what its significance is to us. Between these two stages of work a clarification of the hermeneutical principles involved is to be included (1984, 12–22). Stendahl thus invites biblical theologians to work in strictly inductive terms.

The separation of the tasks is by no means intended to paralyse the role of the Bible in modern life, but on the contrary to enhance it: '. . . where these three stages become intermingled, there is little hope for the Bible to exert the maximum of influence on theology, church life, and culture' (21). How much of the last two stages should belong to the discipline of biblical studies is purely a practical question (21). In descriptive work the canon can have no crucial significance; at the actualizing stage it will (37f.).

It is the lasting merit of the history-of-religions school that it demonstrated the gulf which separates the question about the historical meaning of a text from that concerning its actual significance (12–14). Following a Scandinavian tradition of research Stendahl thus takes up Gabler's way of putting the question in a modern form. He criticizes existentialist interpreters for confusing the historical question with the actualizing one, and 'salvation-historical' theologians (Cullmann, Stauffer) for not telling us how their historical reconstructions relate to the theological questions proper (16–20).

Robinson accepts the 'ingenious' programme once laid out by Wrede. The concept of a 'New Testament' is misleading, for the process of canonization has separated things which belonged together and joined others which did not belong together. The objective of New Testament research therefore ought to be 'early Christian religion'; New Testament theology as a historical discipline ought to yield to a history-of-religions perspective (1973, 388). The principal representatives of the genre – Bultmann's and Conzelmann's works are discussed[4] – actually amount, despite their titles, to histories of early Christian religion (388–95). Scholarship either has to accept this state of things and become even more consistently historical, or 'New Testament theology' must change altogether (387).

The starting point for a renewed 'New Testament theology' is Bultmann's recognition that New Testament thoughts cannot be repristinated; as such they can have no serious claim to normativeness today (395). If interpreters wish to communicate the once-binding contents of these texts in such a way that they can again be encountered as a genuine alternative, to be either accepted or rejected, they have to go behind the texts. This step, which is to be strictly separated from the historical work, corresponds to Bultmann's hermeneutics as expressed in his programme of demythologizing, rather than to what he called 'New Testament theology' (390). One might also claim that it corresponds roughly to Gabler's 'pure biblical theology'.

Robinson recommends that New Testament theology so conceived focus on the linguistic intentions (*Sprachbewegungen*) that can be uncovered in New Testament texts. These should be translated into modern idioms, e.g. into socio-ethical or political language (395–400).

Robinson thus distinguishes very clearly between the history of early Christianity and New Testament theology. However, a more appropriate designation for what he understands by the latter would be 'critical assessment of the New Testament' or something like that.

In the area of the history of religions Robinson has worked widely, in particular with the Gnostic texts from Nag Hammadi, consciously trying to break down all boundaries between canonical and non-canonical material.[5] Together with Helmut Koester he has attempted to carry out Wrede's programme radically.[6] But he has also reserved a place for actualizing biblical theology in the agenda of the exegete. It is interesting that such a pronounced demand for a clear distinction between the two tasks, the historical and the theological, comes from a scholar known for the depth of his hermeneutical understanding. For while there may be some (limited) justification in blaming Wrede for historicism, such an accusation would be singularly out of place when Wrede's methodological distinction is taken up by a leading figure of the 'New Quest'.

Robert Morgan of Oxford has made the German methodological discussion known in the Anglo-Saxon world, among other things by translating the programmatic articles of Wrede and Schlatter. He has also developed his own view in a series of publications (esp. 1977 and 1988a). Morgan criticizes theological historiography (which has been practised in different ways by scholars as different as Bultmann and Kümmel) and confronts the exegetes with the challenge of D. F. Strauss.[7] In the vein of Strauss, historical and theological questions ought to be separated even today – 'not in the hope that New Testament studies might become less theological but that the theological interpretation of the New Testament should be set free from the obligation to be simply a historical discipline' (1977, 244). Theology cannot be built on historical work, but theological constructions can be assessed and criticized from a historical perspective (1977, 244, 265; 1988a, 182f.).

In saying this, Morgan is deeply concerned to secure church-orientated study of the Bible a place in the exegetical enterprise, which he considers largely secularized, and to bridge the gulf between critical scholarship and faith (1988a, 25). He wishes to encourage believing scholars to a religious reading of scripture along with (but not in contradiction to) their rational critical work. If someone does not want to expound the New Testament in such terms, that is a respectable choice. Secular biblical study is quite justified in a secular academic context (e.g. 1988a, 179). Yet most people read the Bible for religious reasons, and it would be a serious drawback for the religious community if biblical scholarship were to abandon such a vision altogether.

Morgan's distinction between the different tasks, then, is connected with the separation of different aims on the part of the interpreters and, even more basically, with the existence of 'two different interpretative communities': 'the rational community of historians and the religious community of God- worshippers'. These different communities approach the texts with different aims (1988a, 184, etc.).

Scholars with religious or theological aims belong to both of the communities mentioned above. They should fearlessly ask theological questions, or fuse historical and theological inter-ests, in their work. A believing scholar chooses as his interpreta-tive framework such a theory of religion which does not require him to deny the reality of the transcendent (1988a, 187–9, etc.). Unlike Stendahl, Morgan thus proposes a deductive strategy. The believing scholar knows at the outset where he stands.[8] His reticence about the Bible as the Word of God is not because of uncertainty in this matter; it is an expedient which is necessary, since 'to start out with that claim would be to break off communication' with the secular and pluralist world outside (278f.).[9] Morgan does not endorse Stendahl's idea of two separate stages (1988a, 184f.). But how exactly he would keep the two tasks apart, while fusing the two interests, does not become very clear.[10]

*   *   *

Klaus Berger has worked widely in the history-of-religions area, trying to elucidate the New Testament from that perspective. He has also devoted a great deal of attention to methodological and hermeneutical questions. In his recent book on hermeneutics (1988a) he presents, over against Bultmann, the programmatic thesis that exegesis is to be separated from application as much as possible (19).[11] But this separation is not at all due to lack of interest in application (as was the case with Wrede). On the contrary, Berger puts forward a number of stimulating (if somewhat loosely connected) reflections on the problem of application.

He presents these reflections in a church context, meditating on the path that leads from exegesis to preaching. However, he also points out that when scholarship aids the church, it does this in its own way; it cannot be controlled by the church in any way. Nor is preaching the only area in which the church needs the help of a biblical scholar: it is also in need of its own critical stocktaking (104f.).

Berger's point of departure for application is not the text, but the actual human situation (22, 25). The point is not how to make ancient writings understood, but how to find in them some help and consolation in human misery. In this, a deliberately selective attitude to scripture is a necessity (18f.), and it has always been so (41). Exegesis cannot bring about binding statements; historical reconstructions cannot in themselves be normative today (113).[12] Historical-critical exegesis shows (against, e.g., traditionalist or existentialist interpretations) that there are no general truths apart from concrete historical reality (117f.).

Historical exegesis reveals the inevitable risk implied in any application. Exegesis can never confirm the correctness of any application. What it can do is to assess the *degree* to which a given application deviates from the original meaning of the text (120f.). Exegesis will also have to make clear the strangeness of the texts from a modern point of view; only thus can innovation (instead of mere confirmation of one's existing stance) take place in encounter with the texts (125ff.).

On the exegetical level, Berger is currently working on a 'history of theology' in early Christianity (1987, 190).[13] We can therefore expect that at last a truly historical synthesis will see the light of day. Berger has given a (tantalizingly brief) sketch of his approach (1987, 186–202) in a programmatic book on 'New form criticism'. His plan is highly original, and it is impossible to assess it before the work has appeared. However, some features can be noted.

Berger regards the problem of unity and diversity as the basic problem of 'New Testament theology'. Attempts of systematically inclined interpreters to posit a fundamental unity behind the obvious diversity (either by ranking certain theological notions as the centre of scripture, or by speaking of a consistent understanding of human existence, or else by identifying primitive kerygmatic formulae) have failed (1987, 188f.). Berger does accept the task of establishing connecting links between the various 'theologies', but it is to be pursued philologically and historically. He finds his clue in the 'numerous and interesting cross connections' (189) of a lexical and conceptual nature, established largely by way of word statistics (192ff.).[14] Berger assumes a number of common traditions, historically mediated through contacts between persons and groups, which were received and reinterpreted in various ways by different authors. In this overall picture, geographical centres receive a central place.[15]

5

Some Recent Trends

(a) The demand of biblical theology: P. Stuhlmacher

In recent times, a growing interest in a theology of the whole Bible which covers both Testaments, mentioned as a desideratum by Schlier, has been detectable.[1] Old Testament scholars have in general been more prone to move in this direction.[2] Of New Testament scholars it is Peter Stuhlmacher who has been most determined to go forward in this direction, in close cooperation with his Old Testament colleague in Tübingen, Hartmut Gese.[3] In his church-orientated hermeneutical reflections Stuhlmacher complains about the alleged lop-sidedness of the historical-critical method and demands that it be complemented with the principle of 'agreement' (1979, 206ff.). On the other hand he wants to preserve an open mind before the text; the interpreter only has to accept the witness of the text when it convinces him (1979, 221). Stuhlmacher indeed brings forward clear theological criticisms of such New Testament writings as the letter of James (1979, 234), Hebrews (237) or the Gospel of Matthew (239). Thus his conception is beset with an internal tension: the attitude to the text fluctuates between agreement and disagreement, as the case may be.

The tension is enhanced, because Stuhlmacher, while emphasizing (in accordance with Schlatter) the importance of 'listening' to the text, in fact claims that the notion of 'atonement' is the centre of biblical theology (1979, 225ff.). Yet this notion is only rarely mentioned in, say, the Synoptic Gospels or Acts. Thus the alleged centre is far from central in many parts of the documents. Obviously, dogmatic reasons have affected the choice.

A theology of the whole Bible as envisaged by Stuhlmacher would have to be constructed in terms of the history of tradition. Stuhlmacher has illustrated this approach by dealing with some central themes, such as the law, along the lines of biblical tradition history.[4] While the starting-point is promising, the actual treatment of the theme of the law is biased by a tendency to demonstrate a continuity at all costs, even by artificial means.[5]

Stuhlmacher also stresses the history of the influence of the texts as well as the experiences reflected in them. In both cases he again gives a fruitful starting-point an ecclesiastical bias. His history of influence is less interested in all the influences the texts may have exerted than in the fact that they had an influence on the rise of the creeds of the church (221). Stuhlmacher infers that the texts therefore ought to be read in the framework of those creeds (methodologically, a *non sequitur*).[6] In an analogous way, he regards the experience that gave rise to the texts as guidance for Christians (1982, 78). The reference to experience serves as an argument for adopting the language which has been traditionally used in interpreting that experience (1982, 74f.). At this point Stuhlmacher parts company with liberal and history-of-religions exegetes, who also stressed the experience but used it to relativize the interpretations.

Thus the problem with Stuhlmacher's biblical theology is that he pays too little attention to the internal differences in the New Testament on one hand and those between the Testaments on the other.[7]

(b) The problem of unity and diversity: J. D. G. Dunn

James Dunn's book on unity and diversity in the New Testament comes close to a 'New Testament theology'.[8] The question of unity or diversity is, of course, one of the central questions of principle in any New Testament theology. Dunn starts from a theological problem: 'Is there a final expression of Christian truth whose meaning is unequivocal? (2)'. The problem that provides the agenda of his study is, however, the historical question, once raised by Walter Bauer, 'Was there ever a single orthodoxy within primitive Christianity? (5)'. Dunn deals with this issue in the bulk of the book, in what might well be called history-of-religion terms. In the last section of the

book he returns to the theological and ecclesial question: 'What
continuing value has the canon? (374)'. What can the actual
diversity of the canonical writings teach the church which uses
the Bible? The answer is that the New Testament canonizes a
far-reaching diversity (376–7), but it also marks out the limits of
acceptable diversity (378). Thus, without explicitly addressing
himself to the methodological issue,[9] Dunn has produced
something like a 'Gablerian' two-stage work: an account of
early Christian religion in all its diversity followed by a succinct
theological consideration of what the Christian churches can
learn from that history.[10]

Dunn deals with the problem of variety both thematically (in
a way reminiscent of Braun) and in a section dealing with the
early history of Christianity. He concludes that the only
unifying factor between all different writings and layers of
tradition is the conviction of the 'unity between the historical
Jesus and the exalted Christ' (369). Once this basic conviction is
given a concrete shape, differences also appear. Dunn endorses
Käsemann's thesis that the New Testament constitutes the
foundation, not of the unity of the churches, but of the variety of
confessions (376, cf. 122). But he agrees rather with Kümmel in
finding the lasting norm in what is taken to be common to the
different witnesses.[11]

What makes Dunn's book particularly interesting is its place
in the present field of exegetical study. The author comes from a
'conservative evangelical' background.[12] And yet all New
Testament theologies written after World War I outside the
Bultmann school, including that of Kümmel, display a good deal
more harmonization than this work. Dunn's book has also been
well received by the scholarly community.[13] This indicates that
if New Testament theology is to remain on – or rather to rise to!
– the level of today's monograph research, there is no return to
syntheses which by-pass such internal differences within the
New Testament as have been demonstrated by Dunn.

It is another matter that the strength of the unifying thread as
defined by Dunn is disputable. His construction stands or falls
with the claim that 'the kerygma of Jesus and the kerygma of the
first Christians are ultimately one and the same' (31), an
affirmation which is hardly supported by Dunn's actual
findings.[14] It stretches credibility to hold that the adoptionist

christology of the Jerusalem church (see 19–20, 216–19) which, in Dunn's own words, 'contrasts markedly with the cosmic view of Christ which we find particularly in the later Paulines and in Revelation' (20), is 'ultimately one and the same' as John's incarnational theology.[15] Dunn resorts to special pleading in defending the development that led to the canonizing of John on one hand and the rejection of Ebionitism on the other – even though he himself stresses that the latter was much closer to the faith of the earliest believers (242–4).[16] It is difficult not to agree with Meeks: Dunn's '"unifying centre" is almost as elusive as the Bultmannian kerygma'.[17] But he has done scholarship a great service in emphatically drawing attention to the issue of diversity.

(c) Discarding the canon: H. Koester

Helmut Koester has treated early Christian literature from the viewpoint of literary history rather than the history of religion. Just as Wrede rejected 'New Testament theology' as an independent discipline, so Koester demands that 'New Testament introduction' be replaced with a history of early Christian literature (1971, 270). He has realized this programme in a two-volume work (1980/1982) which – inconsistently! – bears the title 'Introduction to the New Testament'. In fact it is an attempt to write the 'history of the earliest Christian churches' during the first 150 years (1982, xix).[18] Although the work is not directly connected with the discussion of 'New Testament theology', it does have indirect importance for this discussion, too.

Koester efficiently transcends the limits of the canon in that he uses some sixty non-canonical writings or fragments in his work. The texts from Nag Hammadi have a conspicuous place. The distinction between 'orthodox' and 'heretical' writings is regarded as obsolete. Hypothetical sources of various documents are accorded a place in their own right in Koester's discussion; apart from Q, he also deals with e.g. the Synoptic Apocalypse and the collection of parables in Mark 4 as independent documents of Palestinian Christianity (149f.). The development of Christianity is described as 'a complex process, full of controversies and difficult decisions' (xx). Koester dedicates his work to Bultmann's memory; he it was who encour-

aged his pupil to deal extensively with non-canonical materials
(xxiii).[19] In fact, however, Koester is even more clearly following
'Bultmann's liberal *religionsgeschichtlich* teachers'.[20] He is
adamant in his demand that early Christian literature be
considered in close conjunction with Jewish, Hellenistic and
Gnostic literature.

Earlier Koester had demanded that the renewed 'introduction'
be also a theological discipline which would criticize inherited
prejudices hidden in the religious and cultural world of the
Christians and provide criteria for evaluating new cultural
developments (1975, 7). As the subject-matter of the research
consists of texts which once 'spearheaded a religious revolution'
(7), this fact should affect the approach used in their study. We
can learn from history, i.e. from the complex and difficult
decisions taken by man as a historical being (1971, 270). The
texts would have to be allowed to 'give their critical judgments
about our thoughts' (1975, 9). Yet the relation of the theological
task to the historical one does not become very clear in
Koester's programme.[21] In his great work he leaves questions of
actualizing theology open.

Indirectly it can be observed that Koester's chapter on Jesus
(73–86) looks more like an existential than a historical interpretation.[22] Moreover, he seems to appreciate the Gnostics a
great deal more than early Catholics. It would be helpful if he
expressed the grounds for his theological stance more
clearly.[23]

Koester also goes his own way in stressing the significance
which each writing has had in the ongoing development, i.e. its
history of influence, more than its traditional theological
evaluation. Thus, Romans, Ephesians and Colossians each
receive roughly as much space as the Gospel of Thomas and the
Shepherd of Hermas, and much less than Revelation, the
Pastorals or Ignatius.[24] Koester's judgments on the dating and
assessment of various writings can often be regarded as one-
sided.[25] Nevertheless, his contribution is a massive challenge to
New Testament study. It makes the contribution of the
history-of-religions school topical once more,[26] even though the
author's intellectualism, reminiscent of Bultmann,[27] deviates
from the cultic-experiential emphasis of Bousset and company –
hardly to its advantage.

(d) Exegesis as a science of public information: G. Petzke, E. Schüssler Fiorenza

In 1975 Gerd Petzke, a pupil of Braun, published an article which has thus far received too little attention, although indirectly it has great significance for our problem.[28] In a post-Christian society, in which Christianity is only one orientation system among others,[29] exegesis as a normative science is dead. It ought to develop from an apologetic discipline[30] to an 'informative science' (8). This has nothing to do with positivist antiquarianism. The legitimate function of exegesis consists in its providing a basis for a social critique of religious conceptions and institutions.[31] In showing the social presuppositions of the rise of the Christian tradition, biblical study necessarily relativizes its contents. For example, the Deutero-Pauline social ethics has proved to be a historical power which still gives 'popular morality' its stamp. Knowledge of the situation of the birth and background of this morality – e.g. of the household codes – promotes its emancipatory critique. It is also important to know the history of the influence of the tradition, e.g. of the household codes. The boundaries of the canon then have no significance; Christian tradition constitutes a unitary process that has not yet come to an end. Thus the task of exegesis coincides with that of church history (15).

As informative exegesis demonstrates the existence of different theological systems within the New Testament and in subsequent church history, it can contribute to contemporary theological efforts to seek 'such ways as correspond to the social situation' (17).

Petzke's standpoint resembles that of Wrede in that he wants to divorce exegetes from the service of the church. To promote preaching is a task far too narrowly conceived. On the other hand, the task of exegesis is not 'purely historical' either. Rather, with his critique of the tradition the exegete must serve a community larger than the church, society as a whole. In fact Petzke's position resembles that of Gabler, already radicalized by Strauss. Historical criticism must be coupled with philosophical criticism, in this case a criticism based on an empirical-critical social theory (19).[32]

In its relentless consistency Petzke's position is reminiscent

of that of his mentor, Braun. Yet – as in Robinson's case, too –
the latter's individualist existentialism has been replaced with a
social emphasis. Petzke draws heavily on sociology of religion
and on sociology of knowledge. The stress placed on the social
influence of the texts in subsequent history calls for attention.
From this point of view the Pastoral letters have been a force
greater than either Jesus or Paul (16).

In a somewhat similar vein, Elisabeth Schüssler Fiorenza,
objecting to alleged 'value-free objectivism' (4), argues for 'a
paradigm shift in the ethos and rhetorical practices of biblical
scholarship'. Biblical studies ought to accept public-political
responsibility (4) to develop into 'a critical reflection on the
rhetorical practice encoded in the literatures of the biblical
world and their social or ecclesial functions today'. This
programme does not abandon the distinction between two
stages of work, or at least that between two different foci.
Biblical study is to 'continue its descriptive analytic work,
utilizing all the critical methods available for illuminating our
understanding of ancient texts and their historical location'. But
this study should also include 'a hermeneutic-evaluative practice exploring the power/knowledge relations inscribed in
contemporary biblical discourse and in the biblical texts themselves'. A scholarly community thus engaged in public discourse could be 'a significant participant in the global discourse
seeking justice and well-being for all' (16–17).

(e) The return of experience: L. T. Johnson

At the turn of the century New Testament scholars stressed
the centrality of the religious experience that underlies the
texts; theological theories (e.g. of Paul) were described as
interpretations of those experiences, and often assessed rather
critically. I noted above that in recent times Stuhlmacher, too,
has emphasized the significance of the experiences behind the
texts, although within a rather different hermeneutical framework. It is the recent work of Luke T. Johnson, however, which
especially commands our interest in this respect.

In its structure Johnson's 1986 book resembles a traditional
New Testament introduction. In this case, too, the difference
between New Testament introduction and theology is diminished, for Johnson programmatically pays special attention to the

religious experiences reflected in the texts and to their interpretations. Taking up the programme of the history-of-religions school, the promise of which 'has never been fulfilled' (7), Johnson bases his presentation on the 'dialectic between experience and interpretation' (16). He thereby utilizes, as did Petzke (terminology apart), the concept of 'symbolic world' (symbolic universe) provided by the sociology of knowledge (12–18).[33]

Johnson rejects 'New Testament theology' in all its forms as 'simply another attempt to reduce the many to the one by the discovery of some abstract and unifying principle' (546). In itself, nothing would prevent one from interpreting early Christian texts in the way suggested by Johnson (taking the standpoint of the dialectic between experience and interpretation, doing justice to the diversity) in a history-of-religions framework. However, Johnson deliberately chooses an ecclesial framework, stressing the significance of the canon (10f., 544–7). In accordance with his canonical starting-point, Johnson consistently concentrates on the final form of the documents and omits e.g. to deal with the historical Jesus at all. The lesson of the canonical texts for today's church could be that Christians learn to read the canon 'in a living conversation with all the writings in all their diversity and divergence', analogous to the Talmud, as it were. Only so can these writings 'continue to speak' (548).

In focusing on religious experience Johnson follows Otto and Eliade. His approach shares the strengths and weaknesses of his mentors. The latter include a too narrow conception of the experiences reflected in the texts as 'numinous' peak experiences of the inner self which ignores their social context. In fact, the New Testament speaks much more of social experiences (e.g. conflicts) than of 'numinous' ones.[34]

(f) The challenge of contextualisms

Johnson wants to do away with all New Testament theologies, because they are based on abstract principles. The point can be made even more sharply. Robin Scroggs has called attention to the threat of 'contextualisms' to New Testament theology. In recent biblical study, questions that were earlier suppressed in the interest of the history of ideas have become uppermost: social stratification, economic dynamics, political situation, family structures and social mores, psychological dynamics, literary and rhetorical conventions (18). Scroggs, for one, fears that 'in all of these approaches, New Testament theology as it has traditionally been conceived is . . . seriously called into question' (19). For instance, narrative criticism of the Gospels presupposes that parts of the narrative have no meaning independently of the whole; presumed theological statements cannot be lifted out from the narrative context and made into abstract structures (21). Scroggs, concerned to counteract this tendency, quotes a letter from D. M. Rhoads: we no longer see a story as the vehicle for an idea. Therefore we can no longer extract from the Gospels an abstract theology or christology in the traditional sense (22).

The point can be made, however, that we might still be able to discover in rough outline what sort of convictions *underlie* each story.[35] A story, like anything else, can be examined from any number of viewpoints, even against its 'nature', as it were. Science can never be content with mere re-telling; it has the right to squeeze from its sources any information that these can be made to yield, however reluctantly or 'against their will'. While we certainly cannot convert every statement in a Gospel narrative to a 'doctrinal' statement, we might well be able to discern *some* convictions that may be called theological or ideological. The world of the text is important, but so are two other 'worlds': the ideologically constructed symbolic universe of the author and the concrete world of his everyday reality. An interpreter does well to take all three into account when dealing with a text.[36]

However dangerous, then, the 'contextualisms' may look from the viewpoint of old-style 'doctrinal concept'-theology, they are no threat whatsoever to a history of early Christian thought, for the simple reason that the latter is by definition directed to a different problem than are these other approaches. As history of thought does not consist of a study of the texts as *texts*, but rather tries to penetrate to what lies *behind* the texts, it is immune to new methods that may diminish the usefulness of the texts as 'theological' statements. It is not rendered futile by these methods. By contrast, it can – and indeed must – learn from these approaches to weigh ever more carefully how it can or cannot extract information from the texts.

6

Conclusion

Our century has not produced the history of early Christian religion and theology which was envisaged by Wrede as early as 1897. Stauffer started in that direction, but turned the faith of the early church into a system of a unitary theology of history. Bultmann and Conzelmann drew many historical lines of development, but gave the most central parts in the process a modernizing treatment. Except for Conzelmann, authors of syntheses have no longer even considered it necessary to give an account of Hellenistic or Jewish religion. The religious experience once stressed by liberal and history-of-religions scholarship has been put on one side in the shadow of neo-orthodoxy; only quite recently has experience been allowed to re-enter, but not yet in syntheses of New Testament theology. Bultmann and his followers have sought in the New Testament the self-understanding of faith; others have looked for teachings or revealed truths. Thus New Testament interpretation has once more gained an intellectualistic stamp.

Even such authors of a New Testament theology as wished to take a historical attitude to the task actually charged their picture of the faith of the early church theologically. They mostly restricted themselves without further ado to the canonical writings and they continue to talk of the biblical revelation. It has been thought that a historical presentation as such will produce normative results. Therefore scholars have felt constrained to assert that behind the diversity a unity will be found, even when the actual analysis would seem to point in a different direction.

Gabler already demanded that the historical stage of work be

separated from the actualizing one. Stendahl has renewed this
demand, and Robinson also pleads for a distinction between
history-of-religions and theological work. In the existing syntheses, however, this distinction is hardly made, although it is
quite usual elsewhere in exegetical work. Nevertheless, the
intermingling of the tasks, in whatever way, has been detrimental to the syntheses. An author of early Christian religious
history or of New Testament theology would do well to keep
them apart. As the era of neo-orthodoxy draws toward a close,
biblical scholars have before them a return to the insights of the
turn of the century, which in the meantime have been buried
under theological rhetoric. After Barth and Bultmann led the
guild to a by-way which proved a dead end, Wrede's vision still
awaits its realization. What this might involve in practice will
be considered in the next part.

PART THREE

Outline of a Programme

I

Historical Interpretation: Principles

(a) The addressees

Some of the most important choices facing anyone who plans a synthesis of the religious contents of the New Testament are the questions: Whom is the synthesis supposed to serve? Who are its hoped-for 'consumers'? Am I speaking primarily to fellow scholars (the 'academy'), to the church,[1] or to a wider audience?[2] Ultimately, the options are reduced to two, for although in practice fellow scholars are often the first audience, addressing them can hardly be taken as the *final* goal. Behind them, either a church or a secular community is discernible as the audience to which the message, directed in a more technical dress to colleagues, can be communicated in simpler terms.

Most often New Testament theology has been understood to be ultimately a function of the church.[3] This function is still taken for granted e.g. in a recent introduction to exegetical methods in which the statement is made: 'The application of historical-critical methods to the New Testament . . . has as its ultimate goal the believing appropriation and actualization [of the text] in the proclamation of the church.'[4] Even relatively radical exegetes who have encountered much opposition from their churches have wanted to work in a church context (J. Weiss, Bultmann, Conzelmann, Käsemann). Wrede's idea that historical exegesis should not look beyond itself, that 'New Testament theology has its goal simply in itself' (69), has not had much response lately. While specialists increasingly work without necessarily paying any attention at all to theological questions in the strict sense,[5] all syntheses and most of the reflection on principles connected with them – or even short general statements on what the discipline is all about – have been governed by the conviction that New Testament study has an ecclesial-theological task. Here a remarkable hiatus between special studies and the syntheses makes itself felt. Synthesizing seems to possess a philosophy of its own, distinct from that which governs monograph production.

Ernst Käsemann, in his programmatic essay, wrote that

> there can be no separation between learning and life. No one can work in a vacuum . . . each discipline is continually being asked whether it enriches our own experience and is of use to others . . . Scientific thought will always have some connection with practice, albeit in varying degrees . . . (236)

So far, so good. But then, with astonishing ease, 'life' is simply narrowed down to 'Christian life' or 'life in the church':

> So too the history and exegesis of the New Testament, whether we like it or not, exercise a function in the life of the Church and relate to the community within which Christians live . . . were my work of no possible help to (Dom Helder Camara) in his troubles, I would not want to remain a New Testament scholar. No real service is rendered to the Spirit by one who is unable to assist men under trial. New Testament theology gives an overall direction to all specialist skill and puts this discipline of ours, whatever the tensions, in relation to the Church. Without this relation the discipline loses its distinctive character, its concrete roots, and it ceases to be indispensable and binding.

Is there then no life *extra ecclesiam* in Western 'post-Christian' societies? One may well agree with Käsemann in his contention that learning must not be separated from life. But 'life' can – and should – be understood in much wider terms even when one is talking about the Bible. It is true that the roots of the exegetical discipline are in the church (but so are those of almost any Western branch of scholarship). Certainly, if one wants to do 'binding' research, as Käsemann puts it, one should address the church – although one may find that that particular addressee is very reluctant to let herself be 'bound' by critical exegesis.[6] But concern for life (as opposed to research just for the sake of research, out of mere curiosity as it were) does not in itself necessarily lead a scholar to an *ecclesial* path.

If one is free to choose one's course,[7] it seems natural to take a broader view. Exegesis, as well as social sciences or medical science, can be pursued with the aim of providing people with means of coping with life – in this case, with their cultural and religious heritage.[8]

To confine oneself to serving a church is – to exaggerate only slightly – comparable to a social scientist's or a historian's confining himself to serve a certain political party (or a certain nation) with his research. It is hard to see much difference in principle between a historian committed to a party and an exegete committed to a church. In both cases a broader perspective seems desirable.[9] A synthesis directed to the wider society, to people interested in the findings of New Testament study independently of their relationship to a church, seems preferable to a church-orientated way of conceiving the task.[10] In the context of a state university such a solution is especially natural.[11]

The point that in a post-Christian society exegesis should be orientated on the concerns of society rather than those of the church has been made forcefully by Gerd Petzke (above, p. 85).[12] But this starting-point also resembles that of Wrede, with a slight modification. Wrede pointed out that it is not possible for an exegete to serve the church in particular even if he would like to do so. For obviously he cannot change any of his results in accordance with some wishes of the church. On the other hand, contrary to Wrede, it is possible to take even church interests into account without jeopardizing strictly scholarly methodology, when asking questions and choosing tasks (consider Luke Johnson's enterprise: above, p. 87). While I am personally quite happy to engage now and then in applied studies in a church context[13] (which in principle I deem comparable to research projects ordered and paid by non-academic bodies such as governments or industrial enterprises), I would not adopt such a stance permanently, nor when outlining a synthesis of my field.

It is, of course, perfectly possible to opt for a different strategy and pursue exegesis and New Testament theology in a church context. In that case many other methodological choices will –

indeed must – be different, if the path chosen is followed consistently. It is not my intention to try to do away with church-theological study of the Bible. My point is simply that we may not have always realized how very different such a task is from a historical interpretation of the material. The question is whether such compromising attempts to combine both tasks as currently govern the synthesizing market are methodologically defensible. I for one plead for a sharp distinction and opt for the non-ecclesiastical path.

However, an orientation towards (one's own) society is no more than a first step. The truly appropriate horizon today for biblical study (or any other discipline, for that matter) is humankind as a whole. Theology and exegesis need a global perspective, an 'ecumenical' horizon, in the original sense of the word.[14] The future of humankind depends on the capacity of different nations and cultures – which to a considerable degree means different religions – to get along with one another. 'These days, nobody would seriously dispute the fact that peace in the world very much depends on peace among the various religions.'[15] Therefore it is an important task even with regard to world peace to study the rise of Christianity and also to make it understandable to representatives of *other traditions*. Even more important may be the task of enhancing the understanding of Christianity in its relation to other traditions among its adherents and its cultural heirs (see below, 99). Of course, this does not mean that the results of such study should or could be made to correspond to any global needs, as if the old church framework were simply replaced with a wider but no less dogmatic framework. I am only speaking of the scope and the ethos of the enterprise.

Now Christian churches and their members are part of humankind; they thus very much belong to the potential users of the kind of research I have in mind. In fact many members of the churches welcome a broad perspective or are engaged in pursuing it themselves. My point is simply that the traditional interests of the churches, which are still often assumed in an authoritarian and aprioristic way, cannot provide the orientation for a synthesis.[16] A non-ecclesial synthesis has to be comprehensible and to give clues to understanding to anybody, independently of faith and world-view. If traditional systematic theology and church leaders (or laymen) are reluctant to cope with such scholarship, recipients are to be sought elsewhere. In any case, close co-operation with comparative religion is necessary.

(b) Proclamation or information?

The answer to this next question is implied in the previous decision. Exegesis orientated on a world society cannot aim at a kerygmatic goal. Saying this amounts to a break with the tradition, cherished by neo-orthodoxy, in which New Testament theology and Christian proclamation are closely intertwined (Bultmann, Conzelmann, etc.). As far as syntheses (as distinct from special studies) are concerned, this decision amounts to a new step in the history of New Testament research.

In fact, this decision is a great deal more crucial than the previous one. The boundary between exegesis orientated on society and exegesis orientated on the church is not a hard-and-fast one, and it is undoubtedly possible to pursue candid research in a church context as well if one is not afraid of some pain and pressure. It all depends on one's working ethos. Is the historical work ultimately designed to appeal to people in the interests of a given community (an outsider would speak of propagandistic aims), or does its goal consist in the clarification of the issues at hand?[17]

Put in other words: the decision to work in a church context still leaves the scholar plenty of room to move in. But if he also works with the firm conviction that his task is, ultimately, to promote preaching, the scope of his work is hopelessly narrowed down. This is seen sufficiently in the desperate struggle of church-orientated exegetes (notably Stuhlmacher), kicking against the goads of historical criticism and trying to avoid presenting 'negative' (or merely negative) results.[18] If we stop artificially maintaining the bond between exegesis and preaching, there is no reason why there should be a problem in presenting 'negative' results.[19] In fact, the history of biblical study is full of examples from Galileo through Strauss to Albert Schweitzer which demonstrate that it is the 'negative' results which have most forcefully driven research forwards. Who today is seriously interested (except for historical reasons) in

Galileo's 'positive' attempt to show that the heliocentric world-view does not contradict the Bible?[20]

Obviously, we are on our way into 'a culturally (even if not statistically[21]) post-Christian period'.[22] Christianity today is only one 'system of orientation' among others in any Western society. The normative documents of Christians cannot then be binding for a society, as was thought to be the case some centuries ago. Exegesis cannot impose a normative interpretation of the Bible on a society (nor, for that matter, will attempts to impose such an orientation on a church be successful either). What exegesis can do instead is to provide sober information on the background, rise and early history of Christianity (Petzke, above, p. 85).

A consequence of this aim is the recognition that detailed exegesis of each biblical verse (criticized as 'micrology' by Wrede, above, p. 15) is not of much interest to society. What is relevant is the elucidation of the main lines. The present flood of commentaries is only comprehensible in a church context, as a survival from the good old days when exegesis could still be seen as normative.[23] It is revealing that there is a shortage of commentaries as soon as we leave the canonical writings and move into the realm of the Apostolic Fathers, and that there are hardly any commentaries at all on the host of pseudepigraphical writings.

One might venture to say that there is in fact far too much exposition of the Bible in present-day scholarship. True innovations apart, it is not very meaningful from the point of view of society for scholars to go through the same terrain over and over again. Nor is this state of matters necessarily meaningful from a church point of view either; for the churches notoriously accept and appropriate much less of the flood of exegesis than is available.[24]

Thus the discipline might profit from a redirection of its resources. Much more attention could be paid to *non-canonical* literature, the *history of the influence* of the Bible, and perhaps – moving from historical to theological issues – problems of *actualizing*.

Historical information about Christianity is by no means dead knowledge in a modern society. Knowledge rightly presented paves the way for understanding. It is a question of the roots of our religion, of how it all began, and at the same time largely of the roots of our whole culture. Such research as elucidates the early history of Christianity serves almost automatically to clarify the identity of a modern Westerner as well.[25] The Bible is 'a major element in our own imaginative tradition, whatever we may think or believe about it'.[26]

The global perspective, too, demands that the task be conceived in terms of critical information rather than proclamation. In our situation it would be irresponsible for experts on the study of religion to concentrate on propagating their respective traditions. A globally meaningful aim is to make a tradition (be it one's own, be it an alien one) comprehensible and to relate it to other traditions.[27] In this process, both one's own tradition and those of others have to be understood with *empathy*.[28] *Fair play*, or the application of the philosophical Golden Rule if you like, is a necessary requirement in the study of religions today. Even if a comparative approach in such a spirit may not overly impress representatives of alien traditions, as is probably the case today e.g. with regard to most Muslim communities, it can be of great heuristic value for a Westerner in search of understanding his or her own tradition.

The history of the discipline of New Testament theology tells us that most often a kerygmatic way of conceiving the task has been accompanied by a caricature of rival systems. Thus the Judaism of New Testament times has been blackened, so that the light of the gospel may shine forth all the more brightly. On a smaller scale this is surely true of the treatment of Stoicism and Gnosticism as well.[29] The recognition of this error of perspective alone demands a new way of framing the task. Any rival systems (Judaism, Stoicism, mystery religions, Gnosticism), as well as any Christian interpretations that compete with each other, must be understood on their own terms.[30] They are to be compared, and the comparison must be fair. If (relative) value judgments are made, the strengths and weaknesses of each tradition have to be assessed in a balanced way. In practice this may mean that one should pay particularly careful attention to the weaknesses of one's own tradition and to the strengths of those of others – not because one's own tradition is necessarily 'worse', but for the sake of balance: it has been done the other way round down the ages anyway.

It is surely of great significance for the present encounter of religions and traditions to study corresponding encounters in history. A special case for the historian of early Christianity is, of course, the contest connected with the emergence and separation of Christianity from Judaism. It is extremely important, both from the viewpoint of science and of global understanding, to study such conflicts as impartially as possible. Instead of putting oneself at the outset, say, on Paul's side, one has to weigh the case of those opposed to him just as seriously. The strengths and weaknesses of each position have to be considered in their own right rather than from the scholar's confessional point of view. Weak arguments or inconsistent reasoning in the ideological struggle are to be noted, on whichever side they may occur.[31]

In this regard a societally and globally orientated exegesis will be notably different from a church-orientated one. The latter may, and perhaps should, continue to regard it as its ultimate task to assist modern man to make a decision of faith similar to that made by people in the early church.[32] To what extent a fair treatment of rival systems is at all possible on this basis is still an open question.

(c) The New Testament or early Christianity?

Wrede made a clear distinction between a history of early Christian religion and New Testament theology. An important dividing line is the question of the canon. A scholar who confines his task essentially to the interpretation of the canonical New Testament writings (even if he uses extra-canonical documents for purposes of comparison and elucidation) bases his work on a decision of the church which has arisen in the course of history.[33] In the framework of an ecclesial interpretation of the Bible for kerygmatic and catechetical purposes such a limitation is quite meaningful. In historical work it is, by contrast, arbitrary.

Of those scholars who have reflected on the issue, most endorse Wrede's distinction.[34] Schlier's comments are of particular interest (above, p. 54). This convert to Catholicism admits that limiting oneself to the canon is arbitrary from a historical point of view. In nevertheless opting for New Testament theology rather than for a history of early Christian religion, he knowingly makes a faith decision which cannot, and need not, be argued historically.[35] Consistently, Schlier also utters the wish that a New Testament theology may lead to a *biblical* theology which covers *all* canonical literature. The canon divorces things that have belonged together historically, and it also joins together things that have had no historical connection.

Faced with the issue of canon, then, a scholar must decide whether he wants to produce, within canonical limits, a 'New Testament theology' (and, if he remains consistent, also a theology of the whole Bible) or else a history of early Christian religion independent of the canon. At the turn of the century it was not yet realized what far-reaching consequences this decision would have. Even Wrede thought that in practice it would affect only the treatment of the second Christian generation, which was in a secondary position anyway. Jesus, Paul and John would in any case preserve their position as the high-points of the presentation, and for the reconstruction of their thought, for all practical purposes only canonical sources were available (above, p. 14).

Since that time we have become aware in quite a new way of the diversity of the early church during and even before Paul's time. A canon-centred study of Paul can concentrate on clarifying and interpreting Paul's thought. A historical study must integrate Paul into a field to which belong also those Christians who were independent of him, as well as his opponents, and even the latter possess an equal right to the sympathetic attention of the scholar. In an ecclesial New Testament theology Paul may be taken as a norm. For the history of religion Paul is, instead, one figure among others. The scholar must try to understand him with empathy, out of his own intentions – but he must also try to understand Paul's opponents with empathy, out of *their* own intentions.[36]

The discovery of the Nag Hammadi texts has brought to light plenty of material which probably includes relatively early layers. What it means to take these texts seriously in a history of early Christian literature can be studied in Koester's work (above, p. 83). Their yield to an account of early Christian religion is probably no less. For the first time it is possible to study Gnosticism (both in Christian and non-Christian versions, it seems) with the aid of sources which are not tainted by polemics at the outset.

In an ecclesial New Testament theology the texts of Nag Hammadi probably have no intrinsic significance. In a history-of-religions work the same attention has to be paid to them as to any other contemporary sources. 'Orthodoxy' and 'heresy' are, from the point of view of early Christian history, misleading categories which are to be dismissed. They can have a historical significance only: they tell us what was regarded as orthodox or as heretical by some groups at some period of time.[37] Such concepts as 'revelation' or 'inspiration' also remain outside history-of-religions works[38] (except when one analyses what early Christians may have understood by 'revelation'[39] or how they conceived 'inspiration').

In practice, much history-of-religions work has also been carried out in church-orientated New Testament theologies. Bultmann, above all, moves beyond the boundaries of the canon in a sovereign way, and his work offers a good basis for an even more consistent history of religion. By contrast, attempts to sketch *historical* lines of development on the basis of *canonical* texts alone (such as Kümmel's) are methodologically hybrid. From canonical texts one can paint individual pictures of the theologies of various writers, and these pictures can be compared with one another. Yet the narrowness of the perspective renders truly historical work impossible at the outset.

One question that looms large in most New Testament theologies and is sometimes even considered the most important of all will be notably absent, or play a minor role, in a history-of-religions account of early Christianity: the question of unity behind diversity.[40] We will recall that Kümmel, for one, recognized that this question only arises for a Christian reader anxious to learn about the accountability of his faith (above, p. 69). To be sure, there is nothing inherently impossible in such a question to be asked from a historical perspective.[41] Yet to be meaningful, such a question presupposes a body of literature close enough in space and time and in any case clearly limited over against other writings. It might be a meaningful question to ask whether there is unity behind diversity between the Synoptic Gospels, or between the writings combined to constitute the Pauline corpus. But the totality of early Christian literature (including non-canonical literature) is obviously of such diversity that the question could be asked only on a very high level of abstraction.[42] The question of the unity or diversity in the New Testament belongs basically to actualizing theology, to the (possible) second stage of critical work, at which one ponders problems of present-day Christianity. In present-day Christianity the canon is, of course, a given fact and an influential factor.[43]

(d) The relevance of the 'history of influence'

Some scholars have defended their limitation to the canon with an argument from the history of the influence of the Bible. It is precisely the canonical writings that have had an influence on the history of Western culture; therefore, even humanistic research has a special reason for focusing on the study of them.[44]

The influence of the biblical canon on Western history is indeed an important, and so far much neglected, scholarly task. This influence should be carefully studied *in its own right*. A careful distinction should be made here between history of influence and history of interpretation.[45] Surely the latter must partly be seen as a history of suppression. It also testifies to the influence of other forces than the text in question. Moreover, the history of influence should by no means be limited to the function of the Bible in theology and religion. On the contrary, special attention should be paid to influences in the realms of politics and culture at large.

The influence of the canon has been whatever it has been, independently of how the writings that eventually became canonical came into being. Thus, the letter to the Romans has not exerted its historic influence primarily as Paul's statement on certain problems in certain places in the 50s CE. Instead, it has had an impact as part of what was conceived to be God's revelation (comprising the Old Testament and the New), interpreted in the light of a host of other writings (of which the most important, the Christian creeds and confessions, are later than the New Testament – in some cases a millennium and a half later). For the greater part of church history this letter was more influential in a Latin translation than in the original Greek version. It is quite possible that the greatest influence of all has been exerted by those sections of Romans which are regarded neither as very central nor as very characteristic of the author by modern exegetes.[46] It was the opinion of Leopold von Ranke, at any rate, that Romans 13.1–7 – the passage on the state authorities – is the most important text that Paul ever wrote.[47] It is a plausible view that 'most historical relationships are ironical in character' and that 'the course of history has little to do with the intrinsic logic of ideas that served as causal factors in it'.[48]

Moreover, it is not just 'the texts' that have had an impact on those who have used them. It may well be that some quite mundane affairs, notably the sack of Jerusalem which relegated the intrinsically Jewish understanding of the Christian message to insignificance, or the politics of Constantine the Great, have had a much greater influence on subsequent developments than any biblical text(s). Still, some texts *have* had a great deal of influence, sometimes beneficial, sometimes disastrous (anti-Jewish texts), but others have not;[49] surely there is a whole spectrum of degrees of importance in this regard. And one ought to make careful distinctions between, say, the texts as such and the texts as interpreted in some later framework. What has really been influential in Western history is the *total process* that led to the formation of the Christian church into the body it became. *This* process, of which the canonical texts are a part, no more and no less, cannot be outlined without recourse to a great number of non-canonical sources and non-textual factors. The history of influence is very important, but that fact should not be used as an argument for limiting an exegetical synthesis to the canonical writings.

If exegetical study takes the importance of the history of influence very seriously, a result will be a new allocation of space between the discussion of various writings, with some surprises from the viewpoint of conventional New Testament theology. Surely Acts and Pastorals would rise high up on the scale as writings that were really formative of subsequent developments.[50]

(e) Religion or religious thought?

The next decision, or prior choice, is more of an optional nature. 'Early Christian religion' is a vast area of study. Of the several components that make up a religion, the intellectual or theological one is only one among several. It is this side of the Christian religion – religious thought or the intellectual content of faith – that has been the focus of 'New Testament theology'. Wrede protested against this feature, too, in the traditional way of conceiving the task: the history of early Christian religion was to study the life of the believers rather than theology. Liberal and history-of-religions scholars were well aware that religious thought is only one, relatively small, part of a religion. They emphasized the religious experiences reflected in the texts; 'theology' was nothing but a set of conceptual interpretations of pre-theological experiences. Most often a rather negative attitude was taken toward such interpretations. The history-of-religions school broadened the perspective in a communal direction, underlining the significance of common cultic experiences as well.

I am in full agreement with these insights. Yet I am personally still inclined to maintain some continuity with traditional 'New Testament theology' in focusing on a discussion of religious *thought* in Early Christianity. This is not because thought is the most important aspect in a religion (or, specifically, in Christianity); that is disputable. It is rather a personal decision, partly made for pragmatic reasons: one must begin *somewhere*, and a comprehensive history of early Christian religion (cult, rite, myth, communality) would be too immense a task to be at all realistic except as teamwork. An account of early Christian thought is a task worth undertaking, no matter what its relative importance as compared with other tasks may be. For this reason, there can be no 'threat' to such an approach from the side of 'contextualisms' (see above, 87f.). The study of religious thought is one branch in the study of religion. Ideas and mental conceptions loom large enough among the influences on Western culture that have emanated from Christianity to keep some interest in them alive. The analysis of how these influential conceptions arose and developed within the total process can consequently aid a Westerner to come to terms with his or her history and identity.[51]

One all-important qualification is immediately needed. I will not study Christian thought alone, as if it were a world of its own, independently of historical, psychological and social realities – of the 'total process' (cf. already Wrede, above, p. 15).

I have, after all, criticized many 'New Testament theologies' for doing just that. A history of early Christian thought as I see it ought to make abundantly clear the connections of the thoughts and ideas with the experiences of individuals and groups. The development of thought is to be analysed precisely in the light of the interaction between experiences and interpretations.[52] Thus even those dimensions of religion which are not the primary object of the study would be part of the picture, some even having a crucial position.

The relation between thought and experience is of so vital importance for the whole enterprise that a special section must be devoted to a discussion of it (see below, 122ff.).

(f) Purely historical?

In distinguishing between history of religion and theology, Wrede wished to leave theology completely to the dogmaticians. Historical research had no aims beyond history itself. Yet it should be clear, after the discussions in hermeneutics and the philosophy of science this century that the person of the scholar cannot be wholly bracketed out in historical work. The scholar's perception is influenced by his or her own situation and interests. An actualizing concern always exists, consciously or unconsciously. But the concerns of the reader can be kept under control within certain limits. 'It is true that complete objectivity is not attainable, but a high degree of objectivity is attainable, and a high degree of it is very much better than a low degree.'[53]

The understanding of a text takes place between two foci, the pastness of the text and the presentness of the reader. In penetrating deeper into understanding, the reader learns to relate what he or she understands in an increasingly organized way between these foci (rather than simply letting the 'two horizons' fuse together). He or she learns to discern similarities and dissimilarities, points of contact and lack of them, possibilities and limits of interpretation.[54] It is probably misleading to speak of two chronologically successive separate stages in the process of research. The scholar presumably thinks both of the past and of the present all (or most of) the time. But it is still possible to keep the horizons distinct. And it would be helpful to keep them apart when presenting the results to readers.

The statement that historical study is about 'what the text meant' (Stendahl) is surely somewhat oversimplified. Nonetheless this slogan points in the right direction. It remains possible to inquire 'what kind of readings can do justice to the text in its historical context'. Despite the plurality of possible interpretations, historical study can – and should – still insist that the number of legitimate interpretations of a text are limited and 'seek to give the text its due by asserting its original meanings over and against later dogmatic usurpations'.[55]

The question of actualizing emphasis in an *ecclesial* New Testament theology may be left for those to consider who want to perceive their work in that way. Suffice it to say that it seems consistent that such a theology should have an actualizing and even normative character. Why should New Testament theology be practised in the church as a purely historical discipline in the first place, when the limitation to the canon already implies a theological decision? The real problem is, what sort of actualizing is carried out? Is the aim to keep as close to the confessional tradition as possible (e.g. Kümmel, Goppelt), or to assess the tradition more critically by content-critical criteria (Bultmann and his followers)?

Orientation towards *society* does not exclude the possibility of an actualizing perspective. I have insisted that, ultimately, exegesis has to serve society and even the global community by performing certain critical and hermeneutical tasks. But it would be utterly presumptuous to assume that a biblical scholar can without further ado (or even after some hermeneutical reflections) make a big leap to present-day issues and act as an arbiter in modern debates, though this is precisely the procedure adopted in so many 'New Testament theologies'. We have found that in many of them a normative function for seemingly historical study is simply taken for granted; in others, a normative layer is distinguished from the rest by way of content-criticism. In both cases a direct applicability of the findings is assumed.

But meaningful applications of the tradition to modern problems can only be made if all pertinent disciplines co-operate. There seem to be good reasons for an exegete to write a history of early Christian thought in which he clings as consistently as possible to the historical task – setting forth 'what has been' rather than 'what ought to be'. The more neutral the synthesis, the greater the profit it can bring to phenomenology or philosophy of religion, church history, history of dogma, systematic theology, or to anyone wishing to back up an assessment of the modern situation with historical knowledge.[56] Only when the biblical scholar gives up theological pretensions will sufficient space be left for considerations arising from other perspectives.

What I have just written is not at all to be understood in the sense of nineteenth-century historicism. The person of the biblical scholar, his problems and those of the modern world are always part of the picture. Nevertheless, the ability to distinguish between the past and the present is essential. But history can be presented in such a way that the manner of presentation also facilitates the use of the material in conjunction with modern problems (see below, pp. 117f.). I would argue for a historical interpretation which is so constructed that those who want to can also attempt a theological interpretation on its basis. This (Gablerian!) concern will affect the *structure* of the synthesis in that it favours the choice of a thematic presentation.

It is customary to speak of the problem of (historical) 'reconstruction' and (theological) 'interpretation' as the key question in New Testament theology.[57] This pair of terms is somewhat misleading. After all, there can be no reconstruction without interpretation.[58] Therefore it is more appropriate to talk of the relation between two sorts of interpretation: historical and actualizing. A historical interpretation is not independent of the situation of the interpreter. Modern problems affect the choice of perspective and the way various phenomena are emphasized.

For example, in view of the present global situation, *tolerance* and ability to engage in a *dialogue* appear as virtues that cannot be forgotten in biblical interpretation. If the New Testament is read on its own terms alone, tolerance will hardly emerge as a central value. By putting some weight on it – one may recall here the indictment of fanatical features in the New Testament by liberal scholars – the interpreter introduces (relative) value-judgments coloured by knowledge and evaluation of post-New Testament developments and his or her own situation. The historical interpretation thus receives a colouring which it would otherwise lack. As a special case of the issue of tolerance and intolerance, our awareness of the subsequent effects of the anti-Judaism present in parts of the New Testament will necessarily affect the *questions* put to the ancient authors. But it is very important that the modern situation is not allowed to dictate the results, as often happens when scholars sensitive to the issue of anti-Judaism attempt to interpret Paul and other New Testament writers artificially in such a way that all anti-Jewish tendencies are eliminated. That elimination must take place in the application by way of overt criticism of the problematical features, and not in exegesis.

As another example of how modern considerations may affect the choice of topic and approach (but not, in principle, the results) I take the liberty of referring to my own work on *Paul and the Law*. My starting-point was the history of Paul's influence, i.e. his actual position in much modern theology and the tendency of modern theology to use his statements normatively as models to be followed in inter-religious debates.[59] My discussion of first-century issues is undoubtedly coloured by the effort to determine whether Paul's theology is usable for such a purpose; yet it seeks to move in a framework which does not distort Paul's historical situation. In the end some brief (far too brief) theological intimations are added to suggest the direction in which subsequent actualizing thought might move.[60]

I think, then, that a historian of the religion of the early church can and should deal with his material so that it can be effectively utilized even by a reader who is mostly concerned with the modern situation. But such shaping is only possible as regards the questions asked and the manner and order of presentation. The results, of course, must remain independent of the interests of any group of readers.

All this moves on the level of historical interpretation (Gabler's 'true' biblical theology). It depends on the scholar himself whether he wants to move, following Gabler's lead, *at a second stage of the work*, to theological questions proper, i.e. to reflections on what his historical findings can mean for men and women of today. This move will be discussed below, in section 3.

(g) The attitude of the scholar

Church orientated New Testament theology demands faith of the scholar, although this faith cannot be controlled or even defined. For some, for all practical purposes the faith of the scholar amounts to his confidence that behind diversity a theological unity is found in the New Testament.[61] For others, faith implies that one has to distill from the New Testament with the help of content-criticism such emphases as are meaningful for the modern reader. It is part of the picture that one person's faith is heresy or sheer unbelief in the eyes of another.[62]

Such faith cannot and must not be demanded of a scholar of the history of early Christian religion. The only attitude that can be presupposed is the will to take the material seriously. (In practice, no other attitude can be required from a theological interpreter either.[63]) Empathy is all-important, but 'empathy stops short of belief'.[64] This is often denied by theologians with a hermeneutical orientation, but a moment of reflection on the study of religions other than one's own should make clear that empathetic understanding is fully possible without ultimate commitment to the tradition studied.[65] As Barr (1980, 26) puts it,

> Empathy and personal involvement are not to be identified with the acceptance of the theological or ideological position of the matter studied. If this were strictly so, it would lead to an impossibly solipsistic position . . . It would mean that no one could express a valid opinion about a theology or a philosophy unless they were themselves adherents of that opinion. Theologians themselves of course do not at all conform to this ideal: they feel free to express judgments about (shall we say) gnosticism, without being in the slightest convinced of the validity of that intellectual system.

Personal (Christian, Jewish or any other) faith is not prohibited, but neither is unbelief.[66] Each different existential attitude to Christian (or Jewish) systems of orientation includes peculiar assets as well as peculiar dangers which have been well characterized by Stendahl (1984, 22): 'The believer has the advantage of automatic empathy with the believers in the text – but his faith constantly threatens to have him modernize the material . . .[67] The agnostic has the advantage of feeling no

such temptations, but his power of empathy must be considerable if he is to identify himself sufficiently with the believer of
the first century.'

A further differentiation is called for. A scholar's own faith
only helps him to understand certain types of expressions of
religious life – those congenial to himself. What is worse, an
unwary interpreter will tend to discover his own image at
possible and impossible points in the sources. This is evident in
the shortcomings of the liberal exegetes whose historical
accounts were distorted precisely because of their faith. They
believed in a certain kind of Jesus, and so they only cared to take
seriously that kind of Jesus, dismissing such features in the
sources as conflicted with their ideal.[68] The faith of Richardson
made him construct an Anglican Jesus (above, p. 53), and so on.
A scholar who identifies himself with Paul (often enough, with
a Paul interpreted through Reformation lenses) does not necessarily (to put it mildly) understand the Christian faith-world of
the apostle's 'Judaizing' opponents. If genuine understanding is
to take place, the ability of the scholar to distance himself from
his own dearest values is also a quite necessary requirement.[69]

Bultmann's sophisticated demand for believing preunder-
standing breaks down totally in face of this necessary widening
of perspective.[70] The fact is certainly worth pondering that the
very scholar who wrote so eruditely about the conditions of
understanding was totally incapable of doing justice to the
Jewish religion, of which he drew a gloomy caricature.[71] By
contrast, scholars who have written little on the theory of
understanding have succeeded far better than the master of
hermeneutics in understanding the rival tradition. Bultmann
accepted Barth's starting-point: one can only understand a text
if one has an inner relationship to its real message. This
statement may be accepted, if 'inner relationship' is understood in quite general terms (so that 'critical sympathy' or
'genuine interest' will qualify); for Bultmann, however, 'faith'
as a religious and existential commitment was at stake. But
the claim that a Christian can never 'understand' a Muslim
text, or vice versa is simply obscurantist.[72]

With astonishing naiveté, 'faith' always seems to mean
Christian faith in these hermeneutical discussions. Not even
the existence of Jewish faith has been taken seriously (not even

in Old Testament theology, until quite recently).[73] But Jewish faith will produce a very different picture of the New Testament from that drawn by Christian faith, and so will Muslim faith or a Hindu conviction. The inevitable widening of perspective makes as objective an approach as possible imperative on the level of historical interpretation. That such an approach is possible is sufficiently demonstrated by the work of J. Weiss and A. Schweitzer: they dared to paint a Jesus who held a faith different from their own.

Whatever one's personal prejudice, it has to be held under control. For 'the relativity of human objectivity does not give us an excuse to excel in bias, not even when we state our bias in an introductory chapter'.[74] An important practical criterion with which the attitude of a scholar can be tested is that of *fair play*: can he do equal justice to all parties of the process he is studying?

One last point ought to be self-evident, but is almost never made in hermeneutical discussions.[75] It is not only the significance of faith for exegesis that ought to be discussed, but also the significance of critical *exegesis for faith*. Experience shows that 'in the biography of every other theological student' the encounter with exegesis brings about a crisis for the faith of the person.[76] This crisis should be assessed positively: it opens up the possibility that a person finds her or his way to an independent stance or to personal freedom in relation to a tradition with massive claims on him or her.[77] The faith of the scholar should not be spoken of as a static 'given' (or not 'given'). It should, rather, be seen as something dynamic and changing. What is really important is the scholar's willingness to struggle with the texts whole-heartedly.

(h) The prehistory of early Christian thought

The distinction between historical and dogmatic study of the Bible (Gabler) soon also led to a dichotomy within the historical task itself. Old Testament theology and New Testament theology parted ways. For pragmatic reasons at least both realms of biblical exegesis must indeed retain their independence, for no individual can any longer master the material of both. But considering a synthesis of early Christian religious thought one must also ask questions about its relationship to earlier thought and about the bearing of that relationship on the synthesis.

Of those working within a Christian theological framework, an increasing number of scholars now longs for a comprehensive 'theology of the whole Bible' that would transcend the barrier between the Testaments. Schlier suggested relatively early that a church-theological view of the New Testament actually implies a vision of the unity of the Old and the New Testament. Recently, many have undertaken to move toward a theology of the whole Bible (e.g. Stuhlmacher, see above, pp. 8of.). But if the New Testament canon is detached from contemporary non-canonical literature and made an objective of study on its own, this is a Christian theological (rather than a historical) decision. Then one can ask: Would not consistency require that all canonical material be treated together? In other words: a 'theology of the New Testament' alone is a methodological compromise that can be defended only on pragmatic grounds. In for a penny, in for a pound: let the advocates of a canonical approach try to write theologies of the whole Bible.[78]

The history of early Christian religion finds itself in a different position. In it, the New Testament writings cannot be detached from other writings either synchronically or diachronically. Synchronically, they must be interpreted in conjunction with other materials from the Hellenistic period, as Koester has stressed. Diachronically, they are to be interpreted as part of a process which is rooted in the cultural and religious history of Israel (and of the whole of the Near East) and which continues in the history of the church and of Western culture down to the present day. An appropriate interpretation presupposes that at least that part of the process that lies behind be taken into account.

The symbolic universe that determined the way in which early Christians interpreted their experiences had been formed during the history of Israel. Therefore the student of early Christianity must, to some extent, illuminate the path that had led to the situation with which he is ultimately concerned. Then the Old Testament material is relevant in conjunction with any other available contemporary material, e.g. archaeological material. Even more important is the subsequent development. Early Judaism as the seed-bed of the early church is a focal point of interest.[79] The limits of the canon are of no importance. The development of the tradition from the Exile on is important to the scholar of early Christianity (although in practice the presentation must be restricted to a minimum).

It is important to realize that the Deuteronomic view of God's dealings with man which prevails in the Old Testament is originally only the view of one 'party' on the religious history of Israel[80] and has its rivals even within the Old Testament itself, notably the Wisdom tradition. In an 'Old Testament theology' the Deuteronomic view may become the centre of the whole enterprise. In a balanced history of Israelite religion, by contrast, it will be presented as the view of one group among many. A history of Israelite religion will be quite different from an Old Testament theology, if the latter is to stick relatively close to the visions found in the Old Testament itself.[81]

Where should a history of early Christian thought end? One could well suggest the time of Constantine the Great as an appropriate boundary line. In practice it would be difficult to go as far as this.[82] Bousset stretched his description of the christological development down to Irenaeus (above, p. 21), and as a milestone of incipient Catholicism this theologian who unites so many lines of development in himself undoubtedly constitutes an appropriate limit. It would also be possible to regard the apologists of the second century as the limit (Wrede). All such limitations are, however, pragmatic decisions arising from the limits of the scholar's capacity. Nor have they too great a significance, if exegesis and church history or history of dogma co-operate closely, one taking up the work where the other has left off, with the same method and within a similar way of setting the task. As for the actualizing perspective, it might be ideal if the exegetical presentation already included some hints of the development of the themes in question in subsequent church history and the history of ideas.[83] But at this point, at the very latest, the tension between the ideal and what is possible may well become too great.

(i) Finished products and earlier stages

Authors of New Testament theologies have disagreed whether

or not the proclamation of Jesus as reconstructed with historical methods belongs to their province. Bultmann excluded Jesus as belonging only to the *presuppositions* of New Testament theology (above, pp. 39f.). This was indeed an inevitable consequence of Bultmann's definition of 'theology'. If there is Christian theology only after Easter, Jesus' pre-Easter proclamation is, *by definition*, something else (unless the earthly Jesus already proclaimed the post-Easter Christian message).

Even if one deems there to be much more continuity between Jesus and the church than did Bultmann, limiting oneself to the canonical texts (which Bultmann did not do) should mean that a historically reconstructed Jesus is not a theme of New Testament theology.[84] One scholar to perceive this early on was Theodor Zahn, not exactly a radical theologian (above, p. 44).[85] If a synthesis intentionally deals with the thoughts expressed in the *canonical* writings, then it is consistent to focus on the final products and on their canonical point of view, as Schlier insists. Traditio-historical reconstructions (the source Q, the teachings of the Hellenists) may help here to clarify the viewpoint and theology of a canonical author (e.g. Luke, Paul), but should not be given an independent significance. Such reconstructions as are ultimately dispensable from the canonical point of view also include the message of the historical Jesus. The New Testament authors were not interested in a reconstructed Jesus, but in Jesus as he was remembered – or in Jesus as people wanted to remember him.

For the sake of consistency, church-theological New Testament theology should concentrate on Jesus as remembered, on the 'faith image' of Jesus.[86] By contrast, historical and traditio-historical reconstructions are suited to provide material for non-church study of early Christian religion.[87] Such a presentation self-evidently includes the historical figures of John the Baptist and Jesus (in so far as they can be reconstructed); likewise the Hellenists around Stephen or the bearers of Q. The Q document is important in helping to delineate the thoughts of Matthew or Luke, but it is equally important in its own right in providing glimpses into the thought-world of a particular segment of early Christianity.[88]

A consistent concentration on the finished products would also exclude any special interest in such putative reconstructions as early creeds (Conzelmann) and in general in any oral traditions that may have preceded the production of the New Testament writings.[89] The logical outcome would be to start with the earliest New Testament writings, i.e. with Paul. This solution is indeed suggested by Strecker (although in part for dubious reasons)[90] and, independently of him, is put in practice by Morris.

(j) Historical or thematic structure?

Most New Testament theologies have been organized in chronological or traditio-historical terms according to persons or groups (of persons or of writings): Jesus – the early community – Paul – John, etc. Subdivisions (e.g. the teaching of Jesus or of Paul) have then been treated thematically. An overall thematic structure was put forward by Stauffer, Albertz and Richardson (with poor results, above pp 45,50,53) and, somewhat more successfully, by Schelkle (p. 55).[91] Bultmann treats parts of his material (the Hellenistic church, post-Pauline developments) thematically, not without success.[92]

In a presentation of early Christian thought both types of organization of the material are possible in principle. Each has its advantages and disadvantages. A chronological account helps to discern historical lines of development that are broken in a thematic presentation. The latter, again, can more clearly delineate the ideological and theological problems, and models for their solution. Something has to be sacrificed in any case. Some authors have indeed given at least some hints as to what their discussion would look like if organized differently. At the end of a chronological account a systematic survey of some basic questions is added; a thematic account is prefaced with a short outline of the historical development. Such a combination indeed seems wise.

The ideal would be for a reader to have both chronological and thematic syntheses in hand. Both viewpoints cannot receive equal attention in a single work. I personally am inclined to favour slightly a thematic structure.[93] The thematic treatment must, however, be prefixed with a short diachronic survey of the various groups in the early church and of the main lines of their thought.[94] The following reasons would seem to support a thematic decision.

(a) The available material is very fragmentary.[95] No continu-

ous lines of development can be drawn. The geographical location of many writings and groups is quite uncertain, too.[96]
Moreover, the documents available for the earliest period are all
occasional writings.[97] The body of texts that has survived
inevitably gives a distorted picture. Important though his contribution was, Paul is bound to receive a much more decisive
position than is historically plausible, simply because he wrote
letters that survived while others did not. If one wishes to write a
'New Testament theology' from a church perspective, the preponderance of Paul may be all right. If, however, one chooses a
historical perspective, one should keep in mind that Paul was a
very controversial person in his time and only became accepted
in larger Christian circles when he had been 'domesticated' by
Acts and the Pastorals. In a presentation of early Christian
religion, therefore, he should be one among many 'heroes' – no
more and no less.

(b) Due to the paucity of the material, traditio-historical
reconstructions need to remain extremely conjectural.[98] For
instance, the picture of the 'Hellenists' in Jerusalem can be drawn
in quite different ways.[99] Yet it is probable that this very group
had a great significance in the formation and early expansion of
what became Christianity. The reconstruction of the message of
Jesus is notoriously disputed. Any account of the thought of the
earliest church, if given in the form of chronological development, would be quite hypothetical on crucial points. The reader
would have to grope in darkness for a long time; not until
reaching Paul could he see more clearly. Hypothetical constructions are more tolerable in a thematic account in which various
models in addressing a problem are considered together. Even if a
given reconstructed model never existed as such, it could still
throw light on the nature of the problem![100]

(c) Reasons related to the history of influence also favour a
thematic structure. I have argued that one aim of a synthesis is to
help the reader assess subsequent developments, and ultimately
his own situation as a product and a receiver of the Christian
tradition. It may be more important to the reader to
learn what sort of ideas existed, say, about sin, salvation or the
last things in the early church than to know exactly what the
total theology of a Paul or a Matthew was like. Also, it is likely
that what has really been influential is not so much particular

texts as the Christian religion as a whole. Of course both questions are intermingled. In view of subsequent developments it will be relevant to know what options there were, and also what sort of contexts they once belonged to.

(d) In recent study the difference between New Testament introduction and New Testament theology has been diminished, as 'introductions' pay increasing attention to the religion and theology manifested in the various writings.[101] To avoid duplication, it might be wise to choose a different perspective when one is focusing on theology.

(e) A thematic structure is often associated with a harmonizing approach which does away with the internal divergences in the New Testament.[102] However, this does not follow from a thematic structure as such. By contrast, a thematic viewpoint provides the possibility to delineate sharply the differences between the various ideas, as is shown by the work of Braun (above, pp. 62f.) and Dunn (above, p. 82). Within a thematic overall structure the ideas of different groups and persons have to be clearly distinguished,[103] i.e., the thematic structure must be subdivided in longitudinal terms.

In summary, it may be more suitable to characterize the project described as a *phenomenology* of early Christian religious thought than as its history.

(k) Where to start?

For a thematic account it is important to find a proper starting-point which is really central in the sources. Obviously, it would not be wise to start an account of early Christian thought with an exposition of the Trinity.[104] It also seems that the decision, favoured by existentialist theology, to choose anthropology as a starting point, leads to undue modernizing.

The two serious alternatives would seem to be christology and eschatology. In a sense, the whole proclamation of the early church is an interpretation of the significance of the Christ. Therefore christology would be a possible starting-point.[105] However, christology can be seen as part of a larger whole, eschatology. In Jesus' own mission the eschatological reign of God seems to have been a more fundamental theme than his own person. Eschatological expectation connects early Christianity inextricably both with the religion of Israel as documented in the

Old Testament (diachronically) and with contemporary Judaism (synchronically). It therefore seems meaningful to start from eschatology or, considering the roots of Old Testament eschatology, from the idea of history.[106] In fact it almost seems possible to present the rise and development of early Christian thought as a whole within a eschatological framework (which would of course include the issue of the decline of eschatology as well).[107]

The chapter on eschatology would have to start with a brief consideration on the notion of Yahweh as acting in historical events (battles) and on the significance of the discrepancy between great memories and actual political and social conditions for the religion of Israel. Eschatology is to be seen as the memories of the ancient victories achieved by Yahweh projected on to the screen of the future. Without this development the rise of Christianity cannot be understood.

How could a thematically structured presentation go on? I can imagine something like following outline (in catchwords): eschatology would be followed by chapters on the nature and attainment of salvation (soteriology); the life in the Spirit (ecclesiology, pneumatology, means of revelation, spiritual gifts, baptism and the Lord's supper; the cult; mission and ministry); the relation of the new community to Israel (mutual antagonism; appropriation of the sacred symbols of Israel – Scripture, Torah, circumcision; the opening toward Gentiles); christology;[108] the human condition (anthropology; sin);[109] the new morality.

(l) Some relevant emphases in recent research

The centrality of eschatology leads to a brief discussion of other major emphases that would have to figure in a new synthesis. It is a sad fact that there is a growing gap between monographs and syntheses in the field of New Testament and related studies. The syntheses bearing the title 'New Testament theology' show little signs of many insights gained in the discussion of recent decades. This is even true of eschatology, although its centrality was discovered as early as the last century. Bultmann does start his presentation of Jesus with eschatology, but it soon turns out that this belongs to the unimportant husk, not to the existential core of the message. To start here, and to take eschatology seriously, amounts to an attempt to diminish the gap mentioned above. A related issue is the new interest in and evaluation of apocalyptic, which can no longer be seen merely as fanciful and absurd day-dreaming.[110]

A major point in a new synthesis will be the changed view of the Jewish religion. For Bultmann, the old view of Judaism as an anthropocentric legalistic religion (in the pejorative sense of the word) was fundamental to his whole construction. Recent work has taught us to take a less partisan look at Judaism, trying to see it from an insider's point of view. This is an area in which the vision of an empathetic historical interpretation, which is not committed in advance to the position of any one side in the ongoing struggle, becomes all-important. It makes all the difference whether the author of the synthesis takes, say, Paul's view of the law as a normative prescription, or whether he perceives it as a problem to be analysed, so that a person engaged in theology proper on the next stage of work can either accept, reject or modify Paul's view.[111]

These are only samples of approaches which have been present for some time in specialized studies but have not yet made their presence sufficiently felt in syntheses. Other points would include the redaction-critical assessment of the contributions of the Synoptists,[112] the neglect of which in the theological syntheses is undoubtedly due to the fear of losing sight of the unity of the New Testament message, and an evaluation of the Q document in its own right.

The development of new approaches, in themselves alternatives to doing 'New Testament theology', has to be taken into account in the study of the early Christian thought-world. Thus the social and sociological analysis which has seen a considerable progress in the last two decades has an obvious bearing on an attempt to portray the interplay between (social) experience and interpretation. The introduction of social anthropology serves as still another control, designed to hold cultural anachronism in check.[113] The contribution of linguistics and structuralism seems less obvious, except that it, too, may serve as a control: various textual features are not to be exploited theologically, if their function in the context is really different.

(m) Conclusion

I have opted for Wrede's vision in a modified form. According to it, biblical studies are to serve society and mankind within their own limited resources, but not the church in particular.

The task is not proclamatory, but informative and understanding. The material has to be treated impartially, with no distinction between 'orthodox' and 'heterodox' views.

The canon cannot be the starting point in exegesis orientated on society. Therefore the objective of the synthesis should not literally be 'New Testament theology' but early Christian thought. By contrast, scholars of the church can, in a church context, concentrate on the canon and outline theologies of the New Testament or, more consistently, of the whole Bible, in the light of their respective confessions.

An account of early Christian thought should not prescribe what the reader should think of Christianity or how Christianity ought to be interpreted today. Nevertheless, the actualizing point of view is not to be forgotten. The material should be organized and treated in such a way that even a reader asking actualizing questions may profit from it as much as possible. A phenomenology of early Christian thought does not answer questions about the present significance of that thought, but it must provide materials and clues to assist the reader who asks such questions.

The personal pre-understanding of the scholar is always present. It is not, however, a static factor, but can develop in the process of research. Neither 'faith' nor 'unbelief' can be required of the scholar. Yet he ought to be conscious of the advantages and disadvantages of his particular religious (or non-religious) attitude.

An account of early Christian thought will start from the development of tradition in Israel, especially from the Exile on, in order to move next to early Judaism. The rise and development of Christianity will be elucidated as part of a process that can, in principle, be followed both backwards and onwards endlessly. Thought must not, however, be isolated as a world of its own. The connections of religious thought with the concrete historical and social experiences of individuals and groups are to be taken very seriously. The rise and development of early Christian thought has to be described as an interplay between tradition, experience and interpretation.

In the present state of research a thematic organization of the material seems preferable. Eschatology provides the most appropriate starting point.

2

Historical Interpretation: A Model

(a) The dialectic between tradition, experience and interpretation

I have suggested that an account of early Christian thought should describe this thought in terms of an interplay between tradition, experience and interpretation. In what follows, a model for such description is worked out.

It was Friedrich Schleiermacher who, in his *Speeches on Religion*, brought piety and emotion to the centre of the study of religion. He distinguished between faith and beliefs, or between piety and theology. Religion, including Christianity, is a matter of intuition and feeling, above all of the feeling of absolute dependence and of union with the infinite. Christian doctrines are to be interpreted as expressions of this feeling, which has an aesthetic flavour.[1]

Schleiermacher's starting-point was fruitful. Theoretical theology can be seen as a set of conceptual interpretations of something that is itself not of a theoretical or intellectual nature. However, this 'something' was understood by Schleiermacher far too narrowly as *feeling*, no doubt partly due to his own Moravian piety. How incapable he was of understanding different forms of piety is evident from his statements on Judaism in his fifth speech. 'Judaism is long since dead', he said and went on: 'Those who yet wear its livery are only sitting lamenting beside the imperishable mummy, bewailing its departure and its sad legacy.'[2] As has been described above, it has been a characteristic flaw of subsequent research also that it did not understand or do justice to other ways of religious experience than those sympathetic to the scholar himself. The history of the treatment of Judaism in Christian exegesis is a case in point.

Liberal theology followed the route pointed by Schleiermacher (though a direct connection is difficult to establish) in distinguishing between experience and interpretation. The history-of-religions school shared this concern and even widened the scope in paying attention to communal cultic experience as well as the mystical feelings of individuals. Dialectical theology, however, put an end to the interest of theologians in experience.[3] An all-devouring concern for the *text* and its message left any interest in its author or in the process that had produced the text on one side.

Banned from theology, the concern for experience and emotion as the core of religion found a place in comparative religion, which was about to establish its position as an independent discipline. It was Rudolf Otto, himself a theologian influenced by Kantian philosophy of religion, who transmitted the heritage of Schleiermacher into the new discipline. He became the mentor of an influential branch of phenomenology of religion (represented e.g. by G. van der Leeuw and Mircea Eliade) which tries to penetrate through the varying manifestations of religion to its inmost 'essence'. The place accorded in Schleiermacher's theology to the feeling of dependence and union is taken in Otto's construction by the experience of the *numinous*, or the *holy*. It is the experience of a 'wholly other', frightening and fascinating mystery that constitutes the essence of religion.[4]

Whereas religious feeling as depicted by Schleiermacher resembled inner music, the encounter with the holy as characterized by Otto amounts to an experience of a tremendous volcanic power which includes terrifying features. Religion develops, however; the numinous takes on ethical and rational traits. In an ideal case, represented (of course!) by the faith of Jesus, the irrational and the rational are in a harmonious balance.

Otto's analysis is substantially based on biblical and Jewish–Christian (but also on Indian) materials, his classic paradigm being Isaiah's call vision (Isa. 6). A weakness in his approach is his one-sided concentration on the inner experiences of individuals, and on experiences of a quite specific type at that. In this regard the views of both Schleiermacher and

subsequent Protestant theology and of Otto need to be complemented with Baur's insight into the significance of conflicts
and with the cultic emphasis of the history-of-religions school;
i.e. social realities have to be taken into account.

Recently there have been some signs in biblical study of a
return to an emphasis on experience. In Peter Stuhlmacher's
case, experiences are interpreted in a normative doctrinal
framework, and a reference to my earlier brief discussion of his
article (above, p. 81) must suffice here.[5] A programmatic
attempt which draws largely on Otto and Eliade, but also on
Peter Berger's sociology of knowledge, is made by Luke T. Johnson. A parallel experiment (focusing on Paul) in the framework
of Greimas' structural semantics comes from Daniel Patte.
Berger himself, consciously leaving his role as an empirical
sociologist, has pursued the dialectic of experience and interpretation further on a wider, global front in a series of illuminating
publications.[6] Following Schleiermacher, Otto and Eliade, he is
concerned to find a contemporary possibility of religious
affirmation for globally orientated modern man. The following
analysis will reveal that that 'religious experience' on which
Johnson and Berger focus is defined by both in rather narrow
terms. Along with Otto's merits they have preserved the
weaknesses of his conception. Patte's construction is beset with
other difficulties.

(b) Global mystical experience: P. Berger and M. Eliade

Berger underlines the fundamental difference between religious propositions and religious experience. If one keeps to the
level of propositions and beliefs, not much is left of religion for
modern men and women. This follows already from the global
perspective which is inevitable today. Every assertion or belief
is countered by other quite different ones.[7] Today, no one can (or
should!) separate his own tradition from the totality of human
traditions. Anyone who wants to take religion seriously must
penetrate into the *whole* scale of human religious experience.
Knowledge about others is available as it never was before.

Yet theoretical assertions are no more than reflection caused
by fundamental experiences. 'At the heart of the religious
phenomenon is prereflective, pretheoretical experience' (1980,
34). Berger sees it as imperative that the 'final objective of any

inquiry into the religious phenomenon' be the *core experience* in its various forms (50, cf. 59). This amounts to concentrating on the 'religious virtuosi', as Max Weber called them. The rest of humanity will have had, 'at best, fugitive and intimational experiences in this area' (31).[8] The average person's knowledge of the core experience is dependent on a socially mediated tradition, by which experience is institutionalized and 'frozen'. For Berger, the positive significance of tradition from the viewpoint of the religious search seems to be not much more than that it provides the possibility to have the 'frozen' memories 'unfrozen' every now and then (114).

In true religious ('supernatural') experience[9] a man or woman is overwhelmed by an awareness of a 'radically other' reality invading or impinging upon the reality of ordinary life (39, 108). Such an experience involves 'the sense of startling and totally certain insights', the feeling of 'a sudden passage from darkness to light'. The 'categories of ordinary experience are transformed', especially those of space and time. It is such highly distinctive experiences that are 'at the core of the phenomenon of religion' (43) or indeed constitute its 'essence' (125). This more or less mystical core experience recurs, according to Berger, in an astonishingly similar shape within different traditions.[10]

Berger thus reduces what really counts in religion to a timeless, individual experience of union with the infinite. In this he is partly following Schleiermacher and, even more clearly, Eliade. Eliade too posits 'the fundamental unity of religious phenomena'[11] and invites modern man to escape from the profanity of everyday life and from the 'terror of history' into the timeless eternity of myths, rites, and symbols.[12]

I find Berger's distinction between experience and its theoretical interpretation crucial. But I wish to understand 'experience' in a much broader sense. Unlike Berger and Eliade, I wish to outline a conception in which precisely the 'profane' everyday reality,[13] bound in time and history, is taken with utmost seriousness. It is this reality that has evoked most of those experiences which appear in the Bible.[14]

(c) Core experiences and the Bible

If biblical study followed Berger's suggestion and concentrated merely on experiences of radical 'otherness', its material would be drastically reduced. The biblical material would supply a few additional cases to William James' classical display of the varieties of religious experience.[15] The New Testament has rather little to say about core experiences in themselves. Their existence is presupposed, and there are some references to them; most texts, however, are concerned with the everyday life that follows upon the transition from darkness to light. We learn a lot about *interpretations* of the initiation rite of baptism; what sort of experiences those baptized may have had is a matter of educated guessing.

As far as I can see, there is not a single first-hand description of a core experience in the New Testament, unless Paul's casual reference to his journey to heaven (II Cor. 12) is counted as such.[16] Luke, of course, presents his version of Paul's Damascus experience, and he even makes the apostle do so in his own words. But what we have in Acts is a stylized account by a later generation. On the basis of Paul's first-hand references it is hardly possible to reconstruct the experience. Instead, we can draw conclusions as to what that experience *meant* for Paul's life and thought. Paul's values were radically changed (Phil. 3); he received a new task for his life: the mission to Gentiles (Gal. 1, 15f.). And yet it is hard to tell the *immediate* consequences of the experience for Paul's life and thought from what dawned on him *later on*, under the influence of quite different later experiences (such as social conflict). Thus there is some disagreement in Pauline research whether Paul came to the conviction that a man is justified by faith, without works of the law right away, simply on the basis of his call or conversion experience, or whether this was the consequence of later conflicts with 'Judaizing' opponents.

As regards the rise and development of Christianity, core experiences do not suffice to explain why the new movement emerged as a new religion, distinct from Judaism. In view of this development, so crucial to the history of our culture, it is essential to find out why *Paul* drew conclusions from his ecstatic vision that were different from those that e.g. James and other Jerusalemites drew from their visions. As far as the history of influence is concerned, the role of social conflict seems much more important than core experiences.

(d) The biblical experience of the sacred: L. T. Johnson

Johnson begins by painting on a broad canvas, discussing Jewish and Hellenistic experiences in the Roman world and showing the great importance of the fact of the *imperium* itself: its existence alone forced man to redefine his place in the world (23–82). Thus a most 'profane' experience, literally connected with the 'terror' of history, came to have the utmost significance for the development of religion in the ancient world. A striking modern example of a this-worldly experience (not without a religious dimension, to be sure), with a tremendous impact on many symbolic worlds, referred to by Johnson himself (16–17), is the experience of the Holocaust.

When turning to the New Testament, however, Johnson narrows down his scope considerably. He reduces the experiences of the early Christians to a numinous experience of *power* (87–111). The experience of power is accompanied by a sense of a 'transcendent and commanding presence' (103). The numinous experiences include visions of the risen Jesus, but also experiences of his power, the Holy Spirit, even years later.

The experience of power no doubt plays a major role in the sources. It is, however, only one aspect in a larger picture. The Easter experiences of Jesus' followers were a necessary presupposition of the emergence of Christianity. It is another matter whether they were a *sufficient* presupposition of it. Johnson does not distinguish clearly enough between an experience and its interpretation. Thus he misleadingly speaks of resurrection *experiences*. Yet talk of Jesus' 'resurrection' already implies a particular *interpretation* of the event in question.[17] It would be correct to say that the disciples experienced *something* which they *interpreted* with the help of *categories of resurrection belief* (which are already known). Had they lacked the conceptual framework supplied by apocalyptic Jewish eschatology, they would have been bound to search for a different explanation of what they had seen. An average Greek might have claimed to have seen the immortal soul of Jesus freed from the bonds of matter.[18] The experience of the disciples was probably 'numinous', but this does not yet account for their talk precisely of Jesus' being *resurrected*.

Another point to be made is that in Johnson's work the bond

between the Easter experiences and the historical Jesus is cut. Yet it is important to see that in interpreting their experience the disciples understood that they had encountered that very Nazarene who had preached a particular message and invited them to a particular way of life. In this sense, too, the Easter experiences point to a wider framework, to previous experiences (already interpreted). They are not a single experience that could be isolated from everything else. On the contrary, they gain their meaning only as a link in a chain of experiences. They are less important as once-and-for-all *Erlebnisse* than as part of ongoing *Erfahrung*.[19] Without a pre-existing interpretative frame of reference the Easter experiences would have remained mute, or ambiguous, as are apparitions and other experiences of the 'paranormal' for most people who have had such experiences in our day. The frame that provided the Easter apparitions with meaning consisted of both traditional elements (the eschatological thought world) and recent ones (the experience with the earthly Jesus).

Thus examination of the Easter experiences, 'supernatural' as they may have been, by no means leads us away from the 'terror of history' (Eliade) to a timeless eternity. On the contrary, we are dealing with experiences and interpretations which are inextricably connected with a particular historical situation. It seems artificial to reduce them to a single universal type of 'core experience'. Symptomatically, Peter Berger does not regard the difference between 'spatial' and 'temporal' dualism as significant at all. It does not matter whether the supernatural reality is located 'up above' as opposed to 'here below', or in 'the age to come' as opposed to the present age, for 'either form of symbolic expression points to the same underlying experience – one in which the categories of ordinary reality are radically contested, exploded, *aufgehoben*' (1980, 39–40). But how helpful is a method that makes Plato and John the Baptist interpreters of the same religious experience?

It may be a basic error of much modern thought on religion (including Berger's) to postulate a fundamental unity of religious experience.[20] At the very least, one has to move to a very high level of abstraction to make such a generalization. It might be worth pondering at a second, philosophical stage, but in a historical account of empirical religions it is surely misplaced.[21]

Therefore, instead of searching just for a certain type of inner core experience, it seems worthwhile to examine the whole spectrum of experiences, including quite mundane ones, as reflected in the material. It does not seem appropriate to limit oneself to explicitly 'religious' experience, even if religious experience is understood in broader terms than just as a mystical or numinous experience.[22] In fact it is not clear that 'religious' experiences can be singled out as a distinct type of human experience at all. It is arguable that 'religious' experiences are psychologically similar to certain 'non-religious' reality-transforming experiences such as the experience of creativity.[23]

Perhaps it is simply the case that a certain type of experience is *interpreted* by some persons or groups in religious terms, and by others in different terms. Of course even the concept of 'religion' itself is the objective of an endless debate, and the argument that it is ultimately an abstraction and that we would do better to operate with such concepts as 'cumulative tradition' and (personal) 'faith' has much to be said for it.[24]

(e) The symbolic universe and experience

'Man is an empirical animal . . . his own direct experience is always the most convincing evidence of the reality of anything.'[25] This does not mean, however, that man is a *tabula rasa*, covered little by little with new 'knowledge' through new experiences. On the contrary, all experience and all perception is deeply coloured by existing 'theory'.

A human being is born into a community, and a community has its own tradition. The attempts of previous generations to 'make sense out of experience, to give it form and order'[26] have been construed into an authoritative total vision of what the world is ultimately like: what is important in it, how it works, what is the place of an individual in it. Peter Berger and Thomas Luckmann introduced the concept of 'symbolic universe' in their helpful and influential analysis of this vision.[27] A symbolic universe is a social construction. A person perceives the world in the way he is taught to perceive it by the community (not necessarily the 'society'; the more pluralistic a society is, the more partly competing 'symbolic universes', each maintained by a sub-group of the wider society, it can comprise). The concept of symbolic universe comes close to that of 'world-view', but the formation of the picture in a social process (ensocialization) is in focus. A symbolic universe can be defined as 'a system of shared meaning that enables us to live together as group', involving 'in particular the fundamental perceptions that ground the community's existence and that therefore do not need debate or justification'.[28] To the last point one might add the qualification that such fundamental perceptions often do not tolerate debate either. If, for some reason or another, a debate arises, the issue of justification or legitimation becomes vital.

A community, then, provides its members with a framework into which the experience of the individual is integrated from the start. The process of learning the language of the group in particular is a process which prepares the individual to perceive the world in a certain way. His experiences are not 'bare' ones, but laden with *interpretations*. 'We tend to experience what we have symbols for; the remainder is filtered out of perception.'[29] An experience also always has to be related and accommodated to the inherited values and beliefs of the community; this process mostly takes place unconsciously. Thus the symbolic universe deeply affects one's experience, or makes experience possible in the first place.[30]

It is not, however, a one-way traffic. A symbolic universe is exposed to changes. 'All socially constructed worlds are inherently precarious.'[31] A person can pause to reflect on this or that experience which does not quite seem to fit with the tradition.[32] To be sure, most experiences support, or can be claimed to support, the inherited symbolic universe; this universe is, after all, the accumulated result of earlier interpretations of earlier experiences within the community. But there is always also a chance that experiences may render part of the tradition questionable. In that case a tension between tradition and experience arises, which has to be released in one way or another.

Either the experience has to be given, in retrospect, an interpretation which makes it seem acceptable within the inherited symbolic universe, or there is the possibility that reflection on a particular experience leads to a *change* within the symbolic universe.[33] If the change is accepted by (leading members of) the community (which often involves acts of *legitimation* that actually camouflage the change and suggest that none has occurred or at least stress continuity with the past), the symbolic universe will be modified. If a new turn is not thus accepted, this may lead to a break with the community on the part of some of its members who are then forced to construct a new symbolic universe. In this process they will legitimate their stance by drawing heavily on elements of the old one and often stressing their continuity with the past. Often they will be anxious to maintain that it is *their* interpretation, rather than that of the early community, which upholds true continuity with the great values of the past.[34]

Thus the dialectical interaction between tradition (symbolic universe), experience and interpretation governs the way in which the world is perceived and interpreted by groups and individuals.

Also, a reflective person may theorize about his or her symbolic universe without any obvious experiential impetus. Many features of Gnostic or apocalyptic speculations about heavenly secrets[35] may belong to this category, as may many patristic reflections on the person of Christ or the Trinity. Even in these cases, however, there is probably mostly an external (social) stimulus which encourages one to get to 'know' more, say, by drawing conclusions from premises suggested by the symbolic universe (e.g. in order to refute some opponents). It should also be recalled that tradition can be deliberately exploited – whether by asserting parts of it, or by way of reinterpretation – on behalf of ideological interests (take the case of Constantine).

(f) Some biblical examples

This is not the place to engage in elaborating biblical examples of the interaction between tradition, experience and interpretation at any length; that is what the whole enterprise of a historical interpretation of early Christian thought, as I see it, would be all about. Let me just add a few random examples to those already discussed in the previous sections (the experiences of a resurrection appearance).

The account of Peter's dealings with Cornelius (Acts 10.1–11.18) describes *positive experiences* (a vision, the experience of ecstasy on the part of some Gentiles) which lead to a new practice (rejection of circumcision as a rite of initiation) and a new interpretation of God's plans for Jews and Gentiles.[36] This amounts to a change in the old symbolic universe at a very strategic point – a change that was not accepted by the earliest community and accordingly led to a host of attempts at legitimation[37] and, eventually, to the formation of a wholly new system of orientation ('Christianity').

Along with such *specific* positive experiences we may also think of *enduring* ones. Thus Grant suggests (1950, 244) that 'it was the realization of the new life in Christ which led Paul and many others to take high, and even higher, views of the nature of the one in whom and through whom this "newness of life" had been made possible and was now effected'. Or, as Dennis Nineham puts it: early Christians asked, 'Who must Jesus have been and what must he have done in order to have made possible the quality of life and relationship to God we now enjoy?'[38]

Again, Grant (1950, 252) explains the 'logic' of the atonement in experiential rather than rational terms:

> Our sins really *are* forgiven; we are certain of this, with an assurance which no animal sacrifice, no acts of penitence, no practice of piety has ever sufficed to give us; the explanation can only be that Christ's death has really effected what all our previous practice of religion . . . has only dimly reached out toward.

A negative experience, too, or an experience *of crisis* can act as a mighty catalyst. In Israelite tradition, the 'law' of cause and effect, of sowing and reaping, had a central place. Attempts abound to accommodate seemingly contrary experiences to this feature of the symbolic universe. Even the national catastrophe of the sack of Jerusalem was legitimated within the symbolic universe: the Deuteronomic and Chronistic history works paint in dark colours the sins of Israel which *must* have been the cause of the event.[39] But later on, the persecution of the pious by Antiochus Epiphanes was just too much to be accommodated into the old scheme. When the pious are systematically destroyed and the renegades are saved, the symbolic universe seems to be upside down.[40] A change is needed for it to survive at all; so the idea of an other-worldly retribution in the form of a resurrection (at first, partial) makes its appearance and in the course of time is accepted by (most of) the community. It is hardly coincidental that the new idea needed to overcome the problem of theodicy stems from an alien (Iranian) tradition. Often the encounter of traditions brings about something novel in crisis situations.

Another crisis with profound effects on subsequent Christian thought was the experience of the rejection of the gospel by most Jews. Paul's grappling with this issue finds a moving expression in Romans 9–11 where the apostle, struggling with this problem, tries as it were three different solutions (divine hardening; human obstinacy; partial divine hardening as part of a plan for saving all and sundry).[41]

A different sort of crisis is treated in II Peter 3. The experience to be interpreted is the non-occurrence of the parousia – *the experience that nothing has happened*. This has caused some to question the Christian symbolic universe at a central point. In his reply to these people, the author tries to interpret the situation in such a way that the symbolic universe is kept intact. His effort to *legitimate* the tradition which has become endangered leads him to *rationalize* the situation: God is only showing his forbearance in leaving people time for repentance (v. 9) – but why, then, should Christians forfeit this respite by hastening on the coming of the great day by means of a holy life (vv. 11–12)? Here we are faced with the well-known socio-psychological problem of *cognitive dissonance*.

This is an intrinsic problem for Christian legitimation. But even in a wider perspective early Christian writings represent a battle over *legitimation*: who is the authentic interpreter of the great tradition? It often seems that decisions once made on other grounds (e.g. the partial abandonment of the precepts of the Torah) are later rationalized in theological terms; here, too, one may also speak of attempts to overcome cognitive dissonance. In this connection, theology often means exegesis: the new position has to be justified in the light of the Bible. A synthesis of early Christian thought should not conceal the problematical features (forced exegesis, *ad hoc* arguments, sweeping assertions, etc.) in this ideological battle, no matter on which side they may occur.

Another enduring crisis that is extremely significant in this connection is what might be called a *cultural crisis* – the enduring confrontation with another culture. Israel in Canaan, the exiled Jews in Babylon, the Jews in the Hellenistic Diaspora – all such accumulating experiences have meant a very great deal for gradual changes in their respective symbolic universes.

These examples confirm that 'experience' is to be understood in very broad terms. Here the word does not denote only a momentary change of consciousness (it can refer to that too, but not very often), but also an ongoing positive or negative experience, such as the experience of communion with Jesus of Nazareth or the experience of hopes unfulfilled. It often refers to participation in events that need not be either spectacular (although they sometimes are: the destruction of a city) or 'inward'. Among these events social conflict looms large.

The process under examination can, it seems, be interpreted as the gradual abandonment of an existing (Jewish) symbolic universe[42] and the construction of a new one, first by Jewish believers engaged in what came to be Christianity and then by Gentile Christians attempting to assimilate the Jewish legacy to their present spiritual possession.

(g) On D. Patte's semantic universe

The primacy of experience is also emphasized by Daniel Patte in his structural reading of Paul's letters (1983). Drawing on Greimas' semiotic work, he makes a fundamental distinction between 'convictions' and 'ideas'. Conviction is closely associated with faith, idea with thinking. Faith is characterized by a system of convictions, a 'semantic universe' (a concept virtually identical with Berger's symbolic universe, cf. 268).

While this distinction has merit, the way Patte locates Pauline statements now in convictions, now in ideas, seems arbitrary.[43] Thus the centrality of Christ is relegated to the realm of theological ideas; 'Christ' is not counted among Paul's central convictions. No wonder Patte is unable to make sense of Paul's 'in Christ' statements.

I think that we should draw the crucial line of demarcation not between 'convictions' and 'ideas' (which cannot be neatly separated), but between experiences and their interpretations. Even the most basic (new) convictions result from interpretations of some experiences. The resulting interpretations include a whole spectrum of notions from very basic convictions to *ad hoc* ideas which never reappear in the writings of the person in question (in this case, Paul).[44] Instead of dividing Paul's thoughts into two different groups, one might wish to establish a hierarchy ranging from the all-important and constant to the casual. For example, the conviction that Jesus was sent by God to save all human beings is more basic to Paul than is the idea that God has hardened Israel for a period of time.[45]

(h) On the problem of 'reductionism'

At some point in the course of a research project like the present one the question of 'reductionism' is likely to arise. Is it not 'reductionist' (and, so the argument runs, wrong) to speak of what is referred to as revelation and as acts of God in the sources as human experiences and interpretations?

The scholar does not, however, claim *a priori* that what the Bible – or any other scripture for that matter – presents is 'only' the result of psychological experiences. It is beyond the reach of scholarship to answer the question what it was that *ultimately* gave rise to the experiences described or presupposed in the Bible, or in the Qur'an, or in the Bhagavadgita, or what exactly led to the particular interpretations that came into existence. It is not for historical scholarship to say whether there is a 'metaempirical' factor behind this process or not. What it can do is prepare the ground for theological or philosophical reflection on such matters.

Commenting on what such preparation might imply amounts to a transition from historical interpretation to an assessment of its philosophical or theological significance, which is the topic of my last chapter. It is possible, indeed normal, that the study of the empirical dimensions of a religion may reduce the terrain left for the potentially meta-empirical. This is what happens when a believer's view of the supernatural basis of his religion presupposes interpretations of *empirical* matters that must be questioned by serious scholarship.[46] The cumulative effect of such cases can *a posteriori* be at least a partly 'reductionist' view of the religion in question.

The actual pluralism of the religious traditions forces a scholar concerned with truth-questions to a certain kind of reductionism: he is bound to reduce the often absolute claims found in his sources to a more relative size, if for no other reason than that he has to relate them to claims found in *other* sources

(unless he is content with simply reproducing the rival claims).
Taking one's sources seriously cannot possibly mean that the
scholar must give everything the same significance as the
sources themselves do.[47] For instance, it is impossible to accept
simultaneously on an objective level both the claims made by
New Testament writers about Jesus and the claims made in the
Qur'an about the revelation received by Muhammad. A scholar
acknowledges that both sets of claims are based on genuine
experiences. But if he wants to penetrate into truth-questions he
has to reduce either set of claims, or both, to a more moderate
scale. Some sort of reductionism, or at least an analysis which
may lead to a reduced view, seems inescapable. In general it
seems fair to say that religious traditions attach exaggerated,
generalizing meanings to things important to them; in this,
Christian tradition is no different from others.[48]

In general, biblical scholars still take a rather particularist
attitude to the objective of their study. Surprisingly seldom is it
recognized – or spelt out – that the Bible is full of strongly
generalizing and therefore one-sided interpretations of various
experiences.[49] It is the duty of scholarship also to call attention
to such features; in this regard the liberal and history-of-
religions scholars at the turn of the century displayed more
candour. Often enough, putting two biblical interpretations of
the same event or matter side-by-side is sufficient to relativize
one or both. What was the ultimate truth in Antioch did not
necessarily have the same status in Jerusalem. But our accumulated experience from the subsequent centuries should also
evoke critical comments. The absolutizing interpretation given
by the early Christians to the 'Christ event' would seem to be
somewhat exaggerated – now, at the latest, from the perspective
of two millennia of frustrated hope for the Kingdom of God. It is
the duty of serious scholarship not to shy away from such
uneasy questions, although perhaps mostly at the second,
theological stage of work.[50]

3

Actualizing Interpretation

Throughout this study, a distinction has been made between the historical and the theological tasks that confront the exegete. I have argued that Gabler was basically right: these two tasks are to be kept apart. The previous chapters in this section have been concerned with historical interpretation. In this last chapter I will now take up the question of the theological interpretation of the historical findings.

If an exegete chooses to limit himself to the historical task, as Wrede did, this is a respectable decision that can be well defended. But if he prefers to work, at least occasionally, on a second stage as well, he should be encouraged to do that. For just as war is said to be too important to be left to the soldiers, it may be that theology is too important to be left to dogmaticians.[1]

An exegete can, and perhaps should, reflect on problems of actualizing, i.e. problems of the present-day significance of his historical findings. This would not result in a theology 'of' the early Christian sources, for these sources contain divergent theological standpoints, nor can any modern position be built exclusively on them. Rather, the actualizing efforts of the exegete can only result in theologizing *about* the sources.[2] This would include reflection on how to use those sources in constructive theology. In practice, though, the emphasis may fall on reflecting how *not* to use them. For while it is very hard to discover how one should go about using the Bible positively in theology, if one is not simply to fall back on pre-critical modes, it is surely possible to point out cases of overly strained application or downright misuse of the documents.[3] At the very least, exegesis can function as the 'historical conscience' of theology.[4]

This kind of reflection can, of course, take place independently of the historical work in another connection; in a different book or article. But perhaps it could also take place in a concluding section of the historical work, or in an appendix following the historical account. Indeed, why not in the same book, if the reflections are not intermingled with the historical-phenomenological account? After all, as I have argued, it is present-day concerns that keep alive the interest of most readers in the subject in the first place.[5]

In using the terms 'theology' and 'theological' I conceive of them in a very broad sense. Exegetes, let alone systematic theologians, often speak of theology in a narrow, authoritarian and traditionalist sense. But of course I am not recommending a move to a narrowly ecclesial framing of the task even at a 'higher' stage of work. Theology, too, can and should adopt a broad societal and global point of view. Despite some inevitable tensions, this is not impossible even for many theologians who work in a church context, or with an eye towards the church.

This contention is, it seems to me, basically in agreement with the visions of such systematic theologians as Wolfhart Pannenberg (1976)[6] and Gordon Kaufman (1981). Pannenberg sees it as the task of 'theology' to take seriously and check religious truth claims (by any religion) in terms of their consistency and their effects on the life of believers, and also to check them against present experience.[7] Theology has 'God' as its objective; not, however, as a given starting-point but as a *problem*.[8] This statement is crucial. It recognizes that sound scholarship requires that one does not apply to one's own tradition a method different from that applied to alien traditions. The philosophical Golden Rule must apply. Our own tradition is not *a priori* in possession of privileged knowledge, as Gerd Theissen rightly contends.[9]

For Pannenberg, theology is a two-stage project in that systematic theology has to confront the findings of historical theology with modern experience and knowledge. But historical theology (e.g. exegesis) must also have a 'systematic' viewpoint, a concern for truth questions, in order to be able to contribute to the theological task. In my view this concern comes to light partly at the first stage (in the structure of the work), but mostly at the (possible) second stage.[10]

Pannenberg rightly maintains, against most contemporary theologians, that while theology, whether historical or not, cannot be value-free or 'objective', it can refuse to start from an absolute point of departure. It can deal with 'God' or 'revelation', not as its ground, but as hypotheses to be critically checked.[11]

Similarly, an exegete is not bound to any predetermined absolutes either when reflecting on actualizing questions. On the contrary, any demand that the present significance of the texts must be found in a given direction rather than in another (so that e.g. the tradition of a church is inevitably the horizon of the actualizing interpretation) must be excluded.[12] Kaufman makes it very clear that theology 'can no longer take it for granted that there is a fixed body of belief which is simply to be interpreted and explained'. 'On the contrary, the central task of theology in the present situation is to ascertain just what beliefs or concepts inherited from the tradition are still viable, and to determine in what ways they should be reconstructed so that they will continue to serve human intellectual and religious needs.'[13]

An actualizing interpretation is then far more dependent than any historical interpretation on the theological or philosophical presuppositions and the religious or non-religious background and vision of the interpreter, and rightly so.[14]

However important biblical and historical materials are to the reflection of the theologian, they never can function as final authorities. In every generation it is the theologian herself or himself who makes the final decision about what contours the notion of God will have on the pages being written.[15]

Moreover, not only are very different religious interpretations of the material possible. It is also the case that both applications committed to a religious faith and applications opposed to such faith[16] can be based on the same exegetical material, and in many cases even on the very same historical interpretation of it. Also, both these basic possibilities comprise an incalculable variety of very different shades and variations.[17]

Gerd Petzke, too, very critical of the aprioristically (traditionalist) theological attitude generally adopted by exegetes, wishes to entrust them with a philosophical-critical task: exegetes are to criticize values and institutions that prevail in society by showing how they have come into existence. Herbert Braun's 'New

Testament theology', which attempts to answer the question what 'God' ultimately means in the New Testament in a modern (in a sense, atheistic) way, can be understood as an actualizing reinterpretation of the Christian tradition, based on historical work. A classic example of a philosophical critique or reinterpretation of the tradition carried through with the aid of exegetical ammunition is, of course, the work of David Friedrich Strauss. Its aims were initially quite positive: Christian faith was to be assisted in freeing itself from being tied to the biblical history, for a christology based on the historical Jesus stood on too weak a foundation. Rudolf Bultmann in part continued in the same vein, and Robert Morgan (though shrinking from Strauss's actual christology) was right in appealing to Strauss in order to encourage exegetes to theological work proper.

A critical second-stage reading of the material will certainly require what Elizabeth Fiorenza calls an 'ethics of accountability' that accepts responsibility 'for the ethical consequences of the biblical text and its meanings'. 'If scriptural texts have served not only noble causes but also to legitimate war, to nurture anti-Judaism and misogynism, to justify the exploitation of slavery, and to promote colonial dehumanization', then scholars must expose such effects.[18]

Clearly a biblical scholar is qualified to make statements on modern religious questions in so far as the Bible is appealed to in support of modern decisions.[19] But that is where his competence normally reaches its limits. The point of view I am outlining implies, however, that the development of the tradition as a whole is viewed as a process in which the Bible cannot be isolated from everything else. Thus it would not be very meaningful for a biblical scholar, whose province is the first pre-Christian and Christian centuries, to make strong value judgments on the total process.[20] Truly founded statements can only be reached, if the different disciplines co-operate. Thus the main contribution of a biblical scholar at a theological level would be a critical reflection on the role of the Bible within the post-biblical development, and a rational assessment of the biblical ideas and values from some modern point of view.[21]

This is a far cry from establishing a modern theological position. The leap from history to theology is a big one. Such a move requires much more than exegetical knowledge and insight. It is simply not possible to construct a viable present-day theology from biblical building-bricks alone, and it never was. Biblical scholars have been surprisingly reluctant to admit this, as the history of 'New Testament theology' amply testifies.[22] Gabler was far ahead of his time in separating the historical task from the theological, although he could not anticipate how tenuous and precarious the yield of 'true (i.e., historical) biblical theology' would prove to be as the years passed by.[23]

A partial apology for the premature attempts of the exegetes at normative, theologically binding presentations is the fact that systematic theology has seldom taken the findings of exegetes very seriously, and therefore exegetes have felt a pressure to act as theologians too.

Fortunately, in recent times some systematic theologians have fully responded to the challenge from biblical studies. They have even taken the critical enterprise further, combining the exegetical challenge from within with the even more radical challenge from without: the problem of the claim to 'Christian uniqueness' in the face of the global encounter between different religious and philosophical traditions.[24]

Biblical scholars will soon find themselves at a crossroads. Will they remain guardians of cherished confessional traditions, anxious to provide modern man with whatever normative guidance they still manage to squeeze out of the sacred texts? Or will they follow those pioneering theologians and others con-genial to them on their novel paths, fearlessly reflecting on the biblical material from a truly ecumenical, global point of view?

BIBLIOGRAPHY

Albertz, M., *Die Botschaft des Neuen Testamentes* I-II, Zürich *1947–1957*

Almond, P. C., *Rudolf Otto*, Chapel Hill *1984*

Baird, R. D., *Category Formation and the History of Religions*, RaR 1, The Hague-Paris *1971*

Baltzer, K., 'Exegese, Wozu? Anmerkungen zu G. Petzke: Exegese und Praxis', ThPr 10, *1975*, 20–5

Barbosa da Silva, A., *The Phenomenology of Religion as a Philosophical Problem*, Uppsala *1982*

Barker, M., *The Older Testament*, London *1987*

Barr, J., *Explorations in Theology* 7, London *1980* = *The Scope and Authority of the Bible*, Philadelphia *1980*

—, *Holy Scripture. Canon, Authority, Criticism*, Oxford *1983*

Barth, K., *The Epistle to the Romans*, translated from the sixth edition by E. C. Hoskyns, London 1968 (*1933*)

—, 'Ein Briefwechsel zwischen K. Barth und A. von Harnack', in J. Moltmann, (ed.), *Anfänge* (*1962*), 325–9, 333–45

—, *Der Römerbrief (Erste Fassung) 1919*, Karl Barth – Gesamtausgabe 16 (ed. H. Schmidt), Zürich *1985*

Batson, C. D. – Ventis, W. L., *The Religious Experience. A Social-Psychological Perspective*, New York – Oxford *1982*

Bauer, W., 'Heinrich Julius Holtzmann', in: *Aufsätze und kleine Schriften*, ed. G. Strecker, Tübingen *1967*, 285–341

Baumgärtel, F., 'Gerhard von Rad's Theologie des Alten Testaments', ThLZ 86, *1961*, 802–15, 895–908

Baur, F. C., *Vorlesungen über neutestamentliche Theologie*, Darmstadt 1973 (= Leipzig *1864*)

Berger, K., *Exegese des Neuen Testaments*, UTB 658, Heidelberg *1977*

—, *Exegese und Philosophie*, SBS 123/124, Stuttgart *1986*

—, *Einführung in die Formgeschichte*, UTB 1444, Tübingen *1987*

—, *Hermeneutik des Neuen Testaments*, Gütersloh *1988a*

—, 'Neutestamentliche Theologien', ThR 53, *1988b*, 354–70

Berger, P., *The Social Reality of Religion*, London *1969*

—, *A Rumour of Angels. Modern Society and the Rediscovery of the Supernatural*, London and Garden City *1970*

—, *The Heretical Imperative. Contemporary Possibilities of Religious Affirmation*, New York and London *1980*

—, and Luckmann, T., *The Social Construction of Reality*, Garden City *1967*

Best, E., Review of J. D. G. Dunn, *Unity and Diversity in the New Testament*, *SJTh* 32, *1979*, 287f.

Best, T. F., Review of J. D. G. Dunn, *Unity and Diversity in the New Testament*, *Encounter* 40, *1979*, 81f.

Beutler, J., Review of E. Lohse, *Grundriss der neutestamentlichen Theologie*, *ThPh* 57, *1976*, 586–7

Beyschlag, W., *Neutestamentliche Theologie oder Geschichtliche Darstellung der Lehren Jesu und des Urchristenthums nach den neutestamentlichen Quellen*, 1–2, Halle *1891–1892*

Block, P., Review of R. Kieffer, *Nytestamentlig teologi*, STKv 56, *1980*, 35–8

Boers, H., *What is New Testament Theology? The Rise of Criticism and the Problem of a Theology of the New Testament*, Philadelphia *1979*

Bonsirven, J., *Théologie du Nouveau Testament*, Théologie 22, Paris *1951*

Bousset, W., 'Zur Methodologie der Wissenschaft vom Neuen Testament', *ThR* 2, *1899*, 1–15

—, 'Die Religionsgeschichte und das Neue Testament', *ThR* 7, *1904*, 265–77, 311–18, 353–65

—, 'William Wrede. Zur zweiten Auflage von Wredes *Paulus*', in: Wrede, *Paulus* (*1907*), 3–10

—, *Kyrios Christos. Geschichte des Christusglaubens von den Anfängen des Christentums bis Irenaeus*, FRLANT NF 4, Göttingen ²*1921*

Bouttier, M., 'Théologie et Philosophie du NT', *ETR* 45, *1970*, 188–94

Bowden, J., *Jesus: the Unanswered Questions*, London and Nashville *1988*

Braun, D., 'Heil als Geschichte. Zu Oscar Cullmanns neuem Buch', *EvTh* 27, *1967*, 57–76

Braun, H., *Gesammelte Studien zum Neuen Testament und zu seiner Umwelt*, Tübingen *1962*

—, 'Die Problematik einer Theologie des Neuen Testaments', in: Strecker (ed.), *Problem* (*1975*), 405–24

Brown, R. E., Review of J. D. G. Dunn, *Unity and Diversity in the New Testament*, *CBQ* 40, *1978*, 629–31

Brückner, M., 'Die neuen Darstellungen der neutestamentlichen Theologie', *ThR* 16, *1913*, 363–86, 415–36

Büchsel, F., *Theologie des Neuen Testaments. Geschichte des*

Wortes Gottes im Neuen Testament, Gütersloh *1937*

Bultmann, R., 'Vier neue Darstellungen der Theologie des Neuen Testaments', *MPTh* 8, *1911/12*, 432–43

—, *Theology of the New Testament* I–II, New York and London *1951, 1955*

—, *Essays Philosophical and Theological*, London *1955*b

—, 'Karl Barths "Römerbrief" in zweiter Auflage', in Moltmann (ed.), *Anfänge* (*1962*), 119–42

—, 'Das Problem einer theologischen Exegese des Neuen Testaments' (1925), in Moltmann (ed.), *Anfänge* 2 (*1963*), 47–72

—, *Theologische Enzyklopädie*, ed. E. Jüngel & K. W. Müller, Tübingen *1984*

Catchpole, D., Review of G. E. Ladd, *A Theology of the New Testament*, *Theol* 79, *1976*, 126–7

Childs, B., *The New Testament as Canon: An Introduction*, London and Philadelphia *1984*

Clavier, H., *Les Variétés de la pensée biblique et le problème de son unité. Esquisse d'une Théologie de la bible sur les textes originaux et dans leur contexte historique*, S.NovTest 43, Leiden *1976*

Conzelmann, H., *The Theology of St Luke*, London 1960 reissued London *1982*

—, *An Outline of the Theology of the New Testament*, London *1969*

—, *Grundriss der Theologie des Neuen Testaments*, UTB 1446, fourth edition edited by Andreas Lindemann, Tübingen *1987*

Cullmann, O., *Christ and Time. The Primitive Christian Conception of History*, Philadelphia and London ³*1962*

—, *Salvation in History*, London and New York *1967*

Dahl, N. A., 'Rudolf Bultmann's *Theology of the New Testament*', in *The Crucified Messiah and Other Essays*, Minneapolis *1974*, 90–128

Deissmann, A., 'Zur Methode der biblischen Theologie des Neuen Testaments' (*1893*), in Strecker (ed.), *Problem*, 67–80

Dentan, R. C., *Preface to Old Testament Theology*, New York *1963*

Dewailly, L-M., Review of R. Kieffer, *Nytestamentlig teologi*, SEA 43, *1978*, 136–8

Dodds, E. R., *The Greeks and the Irrational*, Berkeley *1951*

Dreyfus, F., 'Exégèse en Sorbonne, exégèse en Église', *RB* 82, *1975*, 321–59

Dunn, J. D. G., *Unity and Diversity in the New Testament*, London *1977*a

—, 'Demythologizing – The Problem of Myth in the New Testament', in: *New Testament Interpretation* (ed. I. H. Marshall), Exeter *1977*b, 285–307

—, *Christology in the Making. An Inquiry into the Origins of the Doctrine of Incarnation*, London *1980*

—, 'The Task of New Testament Theology', in: J. D. G. Dunn –

J. P. Mackey, *New Testament Theology in Dialogue*, Biblical Foundations in Theology, London *1987*, 1–26

Ebeling, G., 'The Meaning of "Biblical Theology"', in *Word and Faith*, London and Philadelphia *1963*

Eichrodt, W., 'Hat die alttestamentliche Theologie noch selbständige Bedeutung innerhalb der alttestamentlichen Wissenschaft?' *ZAW* 47, *1929*, 83–91

Eissfeldt, O., 'Israelitisch-jüdische Religionsgeschichte und alttestamentliche Theologie', *ZAW* 44, *1926*, 1–12

Eliade, M., *The Myth of the Eternal Return*, London *1954*

—, *A History of Religious Ideas*, 1–2, Chicago *1979–1982*

Esler, P. F., *Community and Gospel in Luke–Acts. The Social and Political Motivations of Lucan Theology*, SNTS. MS 57, Cambridge *1987*

Evang, M., *Rudolf Bultmann in seiner Frühzeit*, BHT 74, Tübingen *1988*

Fascher, E., 'Eine Neuordnung der neutestamentlichen Fachdisziplin? Bemerkungen zum Werk von M. Albertz: Die Botschaft des Neuen Testamentes', *ThLZ* 83, *1958*, 609–18

Feine, P., *Theologie des Neuen Testaments*, Leipzig [7]*1936*

Fiorenza, E. S., 'The Ethics of Biblical Interpretation: Decentering Biblical Scholarship', *JBL* 107, *1988*, 3–17

Fredriksen, P., 'Paul and Augustine: Conversion Narratives, Orthodox Traditions and the Retrospective Self', *JTS* 37, *1986*, 3–34

Frei, H., 'David Friedrich Strauss', in N. Smart et al. (ed.), *Nineteenth Century Religious Thought in the West* I, Cambridge *1985*, 215–60

Frye, N., *The Great Code. The Bible and Literature*, London *1982*

Fuller, R. H., Review of G. E. Ladd, *A Theology of the New Testament*, *AThR* 58, *1976*, 381–4

Gabler, J. P., 'On the Proper Distinction Between Biblical and Dogmatic Theology and the Specific Objectives of Each', in Sandys-Wunsch and Eldredge (*1980*), 134–44

Geertz, C., *The Interpretation of Cultures. Selected Essays*, London *1975*

Georgi, D., 'Bultmann's *Theology of the New Testament* Revisited', in Hobbs (*1985*), 75–87

Gerrish, B. A., *A Prince of the Church. Schleiermacher and the Beginnings of Modern Theology*, Philadelphia and London, *1984*

Gese, H., *Essays on Biblical Theology*, Minneapolis *1981*

Gilkey, L., 'Cosmology, Ontology, and the Travail of Biblical Language', *JR* 41, *1961*, 194–205

Goppelt, L., *Theology of the New Testament* I–II, Grand Rapids and London *1981–2*

Grant, F. C., *An Introduction to New Testament Thought*, New York and Nashville *1950*

Grässer, E., 'Offene Fragen im Umkreis einer Biblischen Theologie', *ZThK* 77, *1980*, 200–21

—, 'Albert Schweitzer und Rudolf Bultmann. Ein Beitrag zur historischen Jesusfrage', in Jaspert (ed.) *Rudolf Bultmanns Werk und Wirkung* (*1984*), 153–69

Gulin, E. G., *Die Freude im Neuen Testament* 1–2. Helsinki *1932–6*

—, 'Die Theologie des Neuen Testaments', *TAik* 45, *1940*a, 409–17

—, *Uuden testamentin teologia*, Helsinki *1940*b

Gunkel, H., *Die Wirkungen des heiligen Geistes nach den populären Anschauungen der apostolischen Zeit und nach der Lehre des Apostels Paulus*, Göttingen *1888*

Guthrie, D., *New Testament Theology*, Leicester *1981*

Güttgemanns, E., 'Literatur zur neutestamentlichen Theologie', *VuF* 12/2, *1967*, 38–87

—, 'Linguistisch-literaturwissenschaftliche Grundlegung einer Neutestamentlichen Theologie', *LingBibl* 13/14, *1972*, 2–18

Halse, P., Review of R. Kieffer, *Nytestamentlig teologi*, *TTK* 54, *1983*, 206–8

Hammond, P. E., 'Religion in the Modern World', in Hunter-Ainlay (*1986*), 143–58

Hargrove, B. (ed.), *Religion and the Sociology of Knowledge. Modernization and Pluralism in Christian Thought and Structure*, Studies in Religion and Society 8, New York – Toronto *1984*

Harnack, A. von, 'Ein Briefwechsel zwischen K. Barth und A. von Harnack', in Moltmann (ed.), *Anfänge* 1 (*1962*), 323–5, 329–33, 346–7

Harrington, W., *The Path of Biblical Theology*, Dublin *1973*

Harris, H., *David Friedrich Strauss and his Theology*, Cambridge *1973*

Hasel, G. F., Review of L. Goppelt, *Theologie des Neuen Testaments*, *AUSS* 15, *1977*, 231–4

—, *New Testament Theology: Basic Issues in the Current Debate*, Grand Rapids *1982* (= 1978)

Haufe, G., Review of K. H. Schelkle, *Theologie des Neuen Testaments*, *ThLZ* 94, *1969*, 909–10; 104, *1979*, 506–10

—, Review of W. G. Kümmel, *Theologie des Neuen Testaments*, *ThLZ* 96, *1971*, 108–11

Hay, D., 'Asking Questions About Religious Experience', *Religion* 18, *1988*, 217–29

Hayes, J. H. – Prussner, F. C., *Old Testament Theology. Its History and Development*, Atlanta and London *1985*

Hellholm, D. (ed.), *Apocalypticism in the Mediterranean World and the Near East*, Proceedings of the International Colloquium on Apocalypticism Uppsala, 12–17 August 1979, Tübingen ²*1989*

Hiers, R. H. – Holland, D. L., 'Introduction', in Weiss *1971*, 1–54

Hick, J. – Knitter, P. (ed.), *The Myth of Christian Uniqueness*, Maryknoll and London *1988*

Hobbs, E. C. (ed.), *Bultmann Retrospect and Prospect. The Centenary Symposium at Wellesley*, HThS 35, Philadelphia *1985*

Hodgson, P. C., *The Formation of Historical Theology. A Study of Ferdinand Christian Baur*, New York *1966*

Holtz, T., Review of L. Goppelt, *Theologie des Neuen Testaments*, ThLZ 101, *1976*, 424–30

Holtzmann, H. J., *Lehrbuch der neutestamentlichen Theologie* 1–2, Freiburg i.B.– Leipzig ²*1911*

Hübner, H., 'Das Gesetz als elementares Thema einer Biblischen Theologie?', KuD 22, *1976*, 250–76

—, 'Biblische Theologie und Theologie des Neuen Testaments. Eine programmatische Skizze', KuD 27, *1981*, 2–19

—, '*Vetus Testamentum und Vetus Testamentum in Novo receptum*. Die Frage nach dem Kanon des Alten Testaments aus neutestamentlicher Sicht', in *Zum Problem des biblischen Kanons*, JBTH 3, *1988*, 147–62

Hunter, J. D. – Ainlay, S. C. (ed), *Making Sense of Modern Times. Peter L. Berger and the Vision of Interpretive Sociology*, London *1986*

Hurtado, L., Review of J. D. G. Dunn, *Unity and Diversity in the New Testament*, JBL 98, *1979*, 135–7

James, W., *The Varieties of Religious Experience*, New York and London ⁵*1970*

Jaspert, B. (ed.), *Rudolf Bultmanns Werk und Wirkung*, Darmstadt *1984*

Jeffner, A., *Vägar till teologi*, Berlings, Arlöv *1981*

Jeremias, J., *New Testament Theology*, I, *The Proclamation of Jesus*, London and Philadelphia *1971*

Johnson, L. T., *The Writings of the New Testament. An Interpretation*, Philadelphia *1986*

Jülicher, A., 'Ein moderner Paulusausleger', in: Moltmann (ed.), *Anfänge* 1 (*1962*), 87–98

Kaftan, J., *Neutestamentliche Theologie*, Berlin *1927*

Kalusche, M., 'Das Gesetz als Thema einer biblischen Theologie?' ZNW 77, *1986*, 194–205

Käsemann, E., 'The Problem of a New Testament Theology', NTS 19, *1972/73*, 235–45

Kaufman, G. D., *The Theological Imagination. Constructing the Concept of God*, Philadelphia *1981*

—, 'Religious Diversity, Historical Consciousness, and Christian Theology', in Hick–Knitter, *The Myth of Christian Uniqueness* (*1988*), 3–15

Keck, L. E., 'Problems of New Testament Theology. A Critique of

Alan Richardson's *An Introduction to New Testament Theology', NovT* 7, *1964–65*, 217–41

Kieffer, R., *Nytestamentlig teologi*, Lund *1977*

—, *Die Bibel deuten – das Leben deuten. Einführung in die Theologie des Neuen Testaments*, Regensburg *1987*

Kiehn, A., et al., *Bibliodrama*, Stuttgart *1987*

Klein, G., 'Bibel und Heilsgeschichte. Die Fragwürdigkeit einer Idee', *ZNW* 62, *1971*, 1–47

Knitter, P. F., *No Other Name? A Critical Survey of Christian Attitudes Toward World Religions*, Maryknoll and London *1985*

Knoch, O., Review of K. H. Schelkle, *Theologie des Neuen Testaments*, *ThRev* 70, *1974*, 364–8; 73, *1977*, 23–6

Koester, H., 'The Intention and Scope of Trajectories', in Robinson – Koester, *Trajectories* (*1971*), 269–79

—, 'New Testament Introduction: A Critique of a Discipline', in: J. Neusner (ed.), *Christianity, Judaism and Other Greco–Roman Cults I (Studies for Morton Smith at Sixty)*, Leiden *1975*, 1–20

—, *Introduction to the New Testament 2. History and Literature of Early Christianity*, Philadelphia *1982*

—, 'Early Christianity from the Perspective of the History of Religions: Rudolf Bultmann's Contribution', in Hobbs (*1985*), 59–74

Kraus, H-J., *Die Biblische Theologie. Ihre Geschichte und Problematik*, Neukirchen–Vluyn *1970*

Krüger, G., *Das Dogma vom Neuen Testament*, Giessen *1896*

Kubo, S., Review of J. D. G. Dunn, *Unity and Diversity in the New Testament*, *AUSS* 18, *1980*, 111–13

Kümmel, W. G., Review of A. Richardson, *An Introduction to the Theology of the New Testament*, *ThLZ* 85, *1960*, 921–5

—, *Das Neue Testament im 20. Jahrhundert. Ein Forschungsbericht*, SBS 50. Stuttgart *1970*

—, *The New Testament. The History of the Investigation of Its Problems*, Nashville and London *1973*

—, *Theology of the New Testament According to Its Major Witnesses. Jesus – Paul – John*, Nashville and London *1974*

—, 'Ein Jahrzehnt Jesusforschung (1965–1975)', *ThR* 41, *1976*, 295–363

Küng, H., *Christianity and the World Religions. Paths of Dialogue with Islam, Hinduism, and Buddhism*, New York and London *1987*

Ladd, G. E., *A Theology of the New Testament*, Guildford – London *1975*

Laeuchli, S., *Das Spiel vor dem dunklen Gott. 'Mimesis' – ein Beitrag zur Entwicklung des Bibliodramas*, Neukirchen *1987*

Lange, D., *Erfahrung und die Glaubwürdigkeit des Glaubens*, Tübingen *1984*

Lemche, N. P., *Ancient Israel. A New History of Israelite Society*,

Sheffield *1988*

Lemcio, E. E., 'The Unifying Kerygma of the New Testament', *JSNT* 33, *1988*, 3–17

Levenson, J. D., *Sinai and Zion. An Entry into the Jewish Bible*, Minneapolis *1985*

Lindbeck, G. A., *The Nature of Doctrine. Religion and Theology in a Postliberal Age*, London *1984*

Lindemann, A., 'Jesus in der Theologie des Neuen Testaments', in *Jesus Christus in Historie und Theologie*, FS H. Conzelmann, Tübingen *1975*, 27–57

Lohse, E., *Grundriss der neutestamentlichen Theologie*, Stuttgart *1974*

Lüdemann, G., Review of H. Koester, *Introduction to the New Testament, RSR* 10, *1984*, 116–20

—, 'Die religionsgeschichtliche Schule', in B. Moeller (ed.), *Theologie in Göttingen. Eine Vorlesungsreihe*, Göttingen *1987*, 325–61

Luz, U., 'Wirkungsgeschichtliche Exegese', *Berliner Theologische Zeitschrift* 2, *1985*, 19–32

Malherbe, A., Review of H. Koester, *Introduction to the New Testament, RSR* 10, *1984*, 112–16

Malina, B. J., *The New Testament World. Insights from Cultural Anthropology*, Atlanta and London *1983*

Marxsen, W., 'The Resurrection of Jesus as a Historical and Theological Problem', in C. F. D. Moule (ed.), *The Significance of the Resurrection for Faith in Jesus Christ*, London *1968*, 15–50

McCann, D. P., Review of P. Berger, *The Heretical Imperative, JR* 61, *1981*, 214–17

Meeks, W., Review of W. G. Kümmel, *Theologie des Neuen Testaments, Int.* 29, *1975*, 297–300

—, Review of J. D. G. Dunn, *Unity and Diversity in the New Testament, ThTo* 36, *1979–80*, 118–21

—, Review of H. Koester, *Einführung in das Neue Testament, JBL* 101, *1982*, 445–8

Meinertz, M., *Theologie des Neuen Testaments* I–II, Bonn *1950*

Merk, O., *Biblische Theologie des Neuen Testaments in ihrer Anfangszeit. Ihre methodischen Probleme bei Johann Philipp Gabler und Georg Lorenz Bauer und deren Nachwirkungen*, MarbThSt 9, Marburg *1972*

—, 'Biblische Theologie II. Neues Testament', *TRE* 6, *1980*, 455–77

—, 'Gesamtbiblische Theologie. Zum Fortgang der Diskussion in den 8oer Jahren', *VuF* 33, *1988*, 19–40

Moltmann, J. (ed.), *Anfänge der dialektischen Theologie* 1–2, TB 17, *1962–1963* (³1974)

Morgan, R., *The Nature of New Testament Theology. The Contri-*

bution of William Wrede and Adolf Schlatter, SBT Second Series 25, London *1973*
—, Review of W. G. Kümmel, *Theology of the New Testament*, *Theol* 77, *1974*, 649–52
—, 'A Straussian Question to "New Testament Theology"', *NTS* 23, 1976–*1977*, 243–65
—, 'Gabler's Bicentenary', *ExpT* 98, 1986–*1987*a, 164–8
—, 'The Historical Jesus and the Theology of the New Testament', in L. D. Hurst and N. T. Wright (eds.), *Studies in Christology in Memory of G. B. Caird*, Oxford *1987*b, 187–206
—, *Biblical Interpretation* (with J. Barton), The Oxford Bible Series, Oxford *1988*a
—, Review of B. Jaspert (ed.), *Rudolf Bultmanns Werk und Wirkung*, *JTS* 39, *1988*b, 333–4
Morris, L., *New Testament Theology*, Grand Rapids *1986*
Müller, K., 'Die religionsgeschichtliche Methode. Erwägungen zu ihrem Verständnis und zur Praxis ihrer Vollzüge an neutestamentlichen Texten', *BZ* 29, *1985*, 161–92
Müller, M., *Einleitung in die vergleichende Religionswissenschaft*, Strassburg *1876*
Neill, S., *Jesus through Many Eyes. Introduction to the Theology of the New Testament*, London and Philadelphia *1976*
Neusner, J., *Judaism in the Beginning of Christianity*, Philadelphia *1984*
Nikolainen, A. T., *Der Auferstehungsglauben in der Bibel und ihrer Umwelt* I–II, AASF B 49, 3; 59, 3, Helsinki *1944–1946*
—, *Uuden testamentin tulkinta ja tutkimus. Uuden testamentin teologian kokonaisesitys*, Porvoo *1971*
—, 'Om planläggningens problem i en totalframställning av Nya testamentets teologi', *SEA* 38, *1972–73*, 310–19
Nineham, D. E., *The Use and Abuse of the Bible*, London *1976*
Oeming, M., *Gesamtbiblische Theologien der Gegenwart. Das Verhältnis von AT und NT in der hermeneutischen Diskussion seit Gerhard von Rad*, Stuttgart *1985*
Otto, R., *The Idea of the Holy*, London *1959* (1917)
Painter, J., *Theology as Hermeneutics. Rudolf Bultmann's Interpretation of the History of Jesus*, Sheffield *1987*
Pannenberg, W., *Theology and the Philosophy of Science*, Philadelphia and London *1976*
Patte, D., *Paul's Faith and the Power of the Gospel. A Structural Introduction to the Pauline Letters*, Philadelphia *1983*
Perrin, N., 'Jesus and the Theology of the New Testament', *JR* 64, *1984*, 413–31
Petzke, G., 'Exegese und Praxis. Die Funktion der neutestamentlichen Exegese in einer christlichen oder nachchristlichen Gesellschaft', *ThPr* 10, *1975*, 2–19

Piper, O. A., Review of E. Stauffer, *New Testament Theology*, *ThTo* 14, *1957*, 134–5

von Rad, G., *Old Testament Theology* I and II, Edinburgh *1962*, *1965* reissued London 1975

Räisänen, H., Review of D. Guthrie, *New Testament Theology*, *ThLZ* 110, *1985*, 889f.

—, *The Torah and Christ*, Publications of the Finnish Exegetical Society 46, Helsinki *1986*

—, *Paul and the Law*, WUNT 29, Tübingen ²*1987a*

—, 'Römer 9–11: Analyse eines geistigen Ringens', *ANRW* II 25.4, *1987*b, 2891–939

—, 'Paul, God, and Israel: Romans 9–11 in Recent Research', in J. Neusner et al. (ed.), *The Social World of Formative Judaism and Christianity, Essays in tribute to H. C. Kee*, Philadelphia *1988*, 178–206

—, *The 'Messianic Secret' in Mark's Gospel*, Edinburgh *1989*

Regner, F., 'Johannes Weiss: "Die Predigt Jesu vom Reiche Gottes". Gegen eine theologiegeschichtliche *fable convenue*', *ZKG* 8, *1973*, 82–92

Reicke, B., 'Einheitlichkeit oder verschiedene "Lehrbegriffe" in der neutestamentlichen Theologie?' *ThZ* 9, *1953*, 401–15

von Reventlow, H. Graf, *Problems of Biblical Theology in the Twentieth Century*, London and Philadelphia *1986*

Rhoads, D. – Michie, D., *Mark as Story. An Introduction to the Narrative of a Gospel*, Philadelphia *1982*

Richardson, A., *An Introduction to the Theology of the New Testament*, London *1958*

Riesenfeld, H., 'Biblische Theologie und biblische Religionsgeschichte. II. NT.', *RGG* 1, *1957*, 1259–62

—, 'Nytestamentlig teologi', in B. Gerhardsson (ed.), *En bok om Nya testamentet*, Lund *1969*, 359–459

Robinson, J. M. and Koester H., *Trajectories through Early Christianity*, Philadelphia *1971*

Robinson, J. M., 'Introduction: The Dismantling and Reassembling of the Categories of New Testament Scholarship', in Robinson and Koester (*1971*), 1–19

—, 'Die Zukunft der neutestamentlichen Theologie', in *Neues Testament und christliche Existenz*, FS H. Braun, Tübingen *1973*, 387–400

Robinson, R., *An Atheist's Values*, Oxford *1964*

Rollmann, H., '*Paulus alienus*: William Wrede on Comparing Jesus and Paul', in P. Richardson – J. C. Hurd (eds), *From Jesus to Paul. In Honour of F. W. Beare*, Waterloo *1984*, 23–45

Rowland, C., *The Open Heaven. A Study of Apocalyptic in Judaism and Early Christianity*, London *1985* (1982)

—, *Christian Origins. An Account of the Setting and Character of the Most Important Messianic Sect of Judaism*, London ²*1987*

Rudolph, K., 'Die Problematik der Religionswissenschaft als akademisches Lehrfach', *Kairos* 9, *1967*, 22–42

—, 'Der Beitrag der Religionswissenschaft zum Problem der sogenannten Entmythologisierung. Ein Versuch', *Kairos* 12, *1970*, 183–207

Saebo, M., 'Johann Philipp Gablers Bedeutung für die Biblische Theologie', *ZAW* 99, *1987*, 1–16

Saliba, J., *'Homo Religiosus' in Mircea Eliade. An Anthropological Evaluation*, Leiden *1976*

Sandberger, J. F., *David Friedrich Strauss als theologischer Hegelianer*, STG 5, Göttingen *1972*

Sanders, E. P., *Paul and Palestinian Judaism. A Comparison of Patterns of Religion*, London *1977*

—, *Jesus and Judaism*, London *1985*

Sanders, J. T., *Ethics in the New Testament. Change and Development*, London and Philadelphia *1975*

Sandys-Wunsch, J. – Eldredge, L., 'J. P. Gabler and the Distinction Between Biblical and Dogmatic Theology: Translation, Commentary, and Discussion of His Originality', *SJT* 33, *1980*, 133–58

Schelkle, K. H., *Theologie des Neuen Testaments* 1–4, Düsseldorf *1968–1976*

Schillebeeckx, E., *Christ. The Christian Experience in the Modern World*, New York and London *1980*

Schlatter, A., *Der Glaube im Neuen Testament*, Leiden *1885*

—, *Die Theologie des Neuen Testaments. I: Das Wort Jesu, II: Die Lehre der Apostel*, Calw & Stuttgart *1909–1910*

—, 'Karl Barths "Römerbrief"', in Moltmann (ed.), *Anfänge* 1 (*1962*), 142–7

—, 'The Theology of the New Testament and Dogmatics' (1909), in Morgan *1973*, 117–66

Schlaudraff, K-H., *'Heil als Geschichte'? Die Frage nach dem heilsgeschichtlichen Denken, dargestellt anhand der Konzeption Oscar Cullmanns*, BGBE 29, Tübingen *1988*

Schleiermacher, F. D. E., *On Religion. Speeches to its Cultured Despisers*, reissued New York *1958*

Schlier, H., 'Biblische und dogmatische Theologie', in Strecker (ed.) *1975*, 425–37

—, 'Über Sinn und Aufgabe einer Theologie des Neuen Testaments', in Strecker (ed.) *1975*, 323–44

Schmithals, W., *Die Theologie Rudolf Bultmanns. Eine Einführung*, Tübingen *1966*

Schnackenburg, R., *Neutestamentliche Theologie. Der Stand der Forschung*, Munich *1963*

Schnelle, U., *Gerechtigkeit und Christusgegenwart. Vorpaulin-*

ische und paulinische Tauftheologie, GTA 24, Göttingen ²*1986*

Scholder, K., 'Ferdinand Christian Baur als Historiker', *EvTh* 21, *1961*, 435–58

—, *Ursprünge und Probleme der Bibelkritik im 17. Jahrhundert. Ein Beitrag zur Entstehung der historisch-kritischen Theologie*, Munich *1966*

Schottroff, L., 'How my Mind has changed oder: Neutestamentliche Wissenschaft im Dienste von Befreiung', *EvTh* 48, *1988*, 247–61

Schweitzer, A., *Paul and His Interpreters. A Critical History*, London *1912*

—, *The Quest of the Historical Jesus*, London ³*1954* reissued London 1981

Schäffer, W., *Erneuerter Glaube – verwirklichtes Menschsein*, Zürich *1983*

Scott, E. F., *The Varieties of New Testament Religion*, New York *1946*

Scroggs, R., 'Can New Testament Theology Be Saved? The Threat of Contextualisms', *USQR* 42, *1988*, 17–31

Shipps, J., *Mormonism. The Story of a New Religious Tradition*, Chicago *1985*

Smend, R., 'Johan Philipp Gablers Begründung der biblischen Theologie', *EvTh* 22, *1962*, 345–57

Smith, M., 'The Present State of Old Testament Studies', *JBL* 88, *1969*, 19–35

—, *Palestinian Parties and Politics that Shaped the Old Testament*, New York *1971*, reissued London 1987

Smith, W. C., *The Meaning and End of Religion*, New York and London, *1964*

Stauffer, E., *New Testament Theology*, London *1955*

—, *Die Botschaft Jesu damals und heute*, Dalp-Taschenbücher 333, Bern *1959*

Stendahl, K., *Meanings. The Bible as Document and as Guide*, Philadelphia *1984*

Strauss, D. F., *The Life of Jesus Critically Examined*, Philadelphia and London *1973* (1835)

Strecker, G. (ed.), *Das Problem der Theologie des Neuen Testaments*, Wege der Forschung 367, Darmstadt *1975*

—, 'Das Problem der Theologie des Neuen Testaments', in Strecker (ed.), *Problem* (*1975*), 1–31

—, *Eschaton und Historie. Aufsätze*, Göttingen *1979*

—, '"Biblische Theologie"? Kritische Bemerkungen zu den Entwürfen von Hartmut Gese und Peter Stuhlmacher', in D. Lührmann and G. Strecker (eds), *Kirche, Festschrift G. Bornkamm*, Tübingen *1980*, 425–45

—, 'Neues Testament', in G. Strecker (ed.), *Theologie im 20. Jahrhundert, Stand und Aufgaben*, UTB 1238, Tübingen *1983*,

61–145

Strecker, G. – Schnelle, U., *Einführung in die neutestamentliche Exegese*, UTB 1253, Göttingen ³*1988*

Stuhlmacher, P., *Vom Verstehen des Neuen Testaments. Eine Hermeneutik*, NTD Ergänzungsreihe 6, Göttingen *1979*

—, *Versöhnung, Gesetz und Gerechtigkeit. Aufsätze zur biblischen Theologie*, Göttingen *1981*

—, 'Exegese und Erfahrung', in *Verifikationen* (FS G. Ebeling), ed. E. Jüngel et al, Tübingen *1982*, 67–89

Syreeni, K., 'Matthew, Luke, and the Law. A Study in Hermeneutical Exegesis', in T. Veijola (ed.), *Das Gesetz in der Bibel und in ihrer Umwelt*, Schriften der Finnischen Exegetischen Gesellschaft, Helsinki *1989*

Theissen, G., *Biblical Faith. An Evolutionary Approach*, London and Philadelphia *1984*

—, *On Having a Critical Faith*, London and Philadelphia *1979*

Thüsing, W., *Die neutestamentlichen Theologien und Jesus Christus, I, Kriterien*, Düsseldorf *1981*

Tiele, C. P., *Einleitung in die Religionswissenschaft* 1, Gotha *1899*

Tracy, D., *The Analogical Imagination*, New York and London *1981*

Tuckett, C. M. (ed.), *The Messianic Secret*, IRT 1, London *1983*

Uro, R., *Sheep Among the Wolves. A Study on the Mission Instructions of Q*, AASF Diss. Hum. 47., Helsinki *1987*

Verheule, A. F., *Wilhelm Bousset, Leben und Werk. Ein theologiegeschichtlicher Versuch*, Amsterdam *1973*

Watson, F., *Paul, Judaism and the Gentiles. A Sociological Approach*, SNTS MS 56, Cambridge *1986*

Weinel, H., *Biblische Theologie des Neuen Testaments. Die Religion Jesu und des Urchristentums*, Tübingen ⁴*1928*

Weiss, B., *Lehrbuch der Biblischen Theologie des Neuen Testaments*, Berlin ⁴*1884*

—, 'Die biblische Theologie des Neuen Testaments', in Strecker (ed.), *1975*, 45–66

Weiss, J., 'Das Problem der Entstehung des Christentums', ARW 16, *1913*, 423–515

—, *Earliest Christianity. A History of the Period A.D. 30–50*, 1–2, Gloucester, Mass. *1970*

—, *Jesus' Proclamation of the Kingdom of God*, Philadelphia and London *1971* (1892/1900)

Wernle, P., *Der Christ und die Sünde bei Paulus*, Freiburg and Leipzig *1897*

—, *Die Anfänge unserer Religion*, Tübingen – Leipzig ²*1904*

Westerholm, S., *Israel's Law and the Church's Faith. Paul and His Recent Interpreters*, Grand Rapids *1988*

Westermann, C., *Elements of Old Testament Theology*, Atlanta *1982*

Wiles, M., 'Reflections on James Dunn's *Christology in the Making*', *Theology* 85, *1982*, 92–6

Wilson, S. G., 'Paul and Religion', in M. D. Hooker and S. G. Wilson (eds), *Paul and Paulinism, Festschrift C. K. Barrett*, London *1982*, 339–54

Windisch, H., 'Zwei neue Darstellungen der neutestamentlichen Theologie', *ZwTh* 52, *1910*, 193–231

—, 'Die neuesten Bearbeitungen der neutestamentlichen Theologie und die zwei Leitmotive des Urchristentums', *ZwTh* 54, *1912*, 289–329

Wrede, W., *Paulus*, RVB, Tübingen ²*1907*

—, *The Messianic Secret*, Cambridge *1971* (1901)

—, 'The Tasks and Methods of "New Testament Theology"' (1897), in Morgan *1973*, 68–116

Wuthnow, R. et al. (ed.), *Cultural Analysis. The Work of Peter L. Berger, Mary Douglas, Michel Foucault and Jürgen Habermas*, London *1984*

Wuthnow, R., 'Religion as Sacred Canopy', in Hunter–Ainlay (*1986*), 121–42

Zahn, T., *Grundriss der Neutestamentlichen Theologie*, Leipzig *1928*

NOTES

Introduction

1. The mass of material has not deterred scholars from producing valuable syntheses of 'New Testament Introduction'.

2. Nonetheless, hidden theological valuations quite often tend to affect seemingly historical study. The 'quest of the historical Jesus', not only before Schweitzer but also after him, is a case in point; see E. P. Sanders 1985, 330, and passim.

3. Or, for that matter, when general statements are made on the purpose of New Testament study.

4. It is castigated by Morton Smith 1969. He regards the 'painstaking studies of tradition' by scholars like Gerhard von Rad as 'great achievements' (35), but finds modern Old Testament theology 'unspeakable' (32).

5. From now on I will use the masculine pronoun in an inclusive sense in the hope that this conventional usage may not hurt (justified) feminist sensitivities too much. My mother tongue happens not to know grammatical genders – there is only one common word for 'he' and 'she' – which makes me prone to skip this particular problem.

6. Methodologically, the most acute presentation of the history of New Testament theology is that of Boers 1979. Morgan 1973, 1–67 is rewarding; Kümmel 1970, 123–46, is informative. See also Goppelt 1981, 251–281; Hasel 1982, 13–139, is more a list of problems and positions than a grappling with the issues. Merk 1972 thoroughly discusses Gabler and G. L. Bauer and then presents a survey of more recent developments (207– 72). There is a shorter version: Merk 1980. K. Berger 1988b is more critical; he offers incisive, if mostly tantalizingly brief, comments on several modern works.

7. Many issues which are in themselves very important (for instance, the extent of pagan Hellenistic influences on early Christianity) are not discussed at all.

8. These include B. Weiss and W. Beyschlag.

Part One: From Gabler to Wrede

1. *The Dual Programme of Biblical Theology*

1. Kümmel 1973, 51ff.

2. E.g. Kümmel 1970, 115; Smend 1962, 345; Boers 1979, 23; Morgan 1973,

2–3. On Gabler's programme cf. Smend 1962; Merk 1972, 29–140; Sandys-Wunsch and Eldredge 1980; Saebo 1987; Morgan 1987a.

3. The page references are to the translation by Sandys-Wunsch and Eldredge 1980.

4. Cf. Kraus 1970, 56–7. Boers 1979, 24, 27, etc., praises Gabler for aiming at a biblically grounded dogmatics and for being concerned with the theological task in its totality; cf. also Morgan 1987a.

5. Cf. Boers 1979, 30–1, 38; Sandys-Wunsch 1980, 147; Morgan 1987a, 166. Although Gabler emphatically distinguishes between religion and theology, he regards even religion as divine doctrine, but a doctrine simpler and easier than the subtle philosophizing of the theologians.

6. On p. 142 the decision seems to belong to the first stage, on p. 143 to the second.

7. Smend 1962, 348.

8. Smend 1962, 353f., 345.

9. 'Pure' means purified from being time-conditioned. Boers 1979 uses Gabler's evocative pair of terms. I was tempted to follow his lead (and actually did so both in the Finnish articles on which this book is based and in its penultimate draft). However, I am grateful to Robert Morgan for pointing out that the preservation of Gabler's terminology does not make for clarity in the present situation.

One could speak of a distinction between (historical) reconstruction and (actualizing) interpretation; cf. Bultmann 1955, 251; Boers 1979, 35, and Merk 1972, passim. The problem with this vocabulary is that there is, of course, no reconstruction without interpretation. Therefore, it might be better to speak of historical and actualizing (or theological) interpretation respectively.

2. *Towards a Historical New Testament Theology*

1. On the importance of Strauss in the history of theology see Harris 1973, ix-x, 274–84, and above all Frei 1985. Harris is justified in correcting Karl Barth, who claimed that Strauss was no 'thinker' at all (!). According to Frei, 224, Strauss was 'not a profound thinker, either in originality or constructive synthesis', but 'nonetheless a brilliant critic and intellectual narrator'. Morgan 1977 deals with the significance of Strauss's study for 'New Testament theology', which has seldom if ever been seen with such clarity.

2. Cf. Dunn 1977b, 289–90 (of all places, in a programmatic collection of articles by authors professing to be 'conservative evangelicals', edited by I. H. Marshall): 'His painstaking scrutiny of individual narratives, his careful analysis of what the miracle intended by the evangelist would have involved, and his ruthless exposure of the shifts and artifices to which rationalist explanations of Gospel miracles resorted, is without equal in NT scholarship . . . Perhaps above all, Strauss showed the importance of starting with the text as it stood, and of respecting the purpose of its author . . .' This squares with the comments of Schweitzer ³1954, 95f. Stuhlmacher (1979, 139, 140) differs; he tries to brand Strauss's criticism of the Gospels as 'speculative' and methodologically confused.

3. Cf. Harris's list of events interpreted by Strauss as 'mythical' (1973, 48–51): virginal conception, birth in Bethlehem, the star of Bethlehem, the

temptations of Jesus, his transfiguration, the miraculous cures, the resuscitations of dead people, the feeding of the five thousand, the turning of water into wine, the passion predictions, the details of the passion story (the triumphal entry, the scene in Gethsemane, the words from the cross, the spear thrust into Jesus's side, the burial in a tomb owned by Joseph of Arimathia, the setting of guards over the tomb), the ascension; the appearances of the risen Christ are mystical visions without a base in reality. (Harris includes, with some reservations, the predictions of the parousia, but these are not considered inauthentic by Strauss.) Today one could glean a very similar list from almost any non-fundamentalist book on Jesus (with the exception perhaps of the triumphal entry and the burial; and of course the interpretation of the Easter visions is a most controversial issue). The mention of the cures in this connection needs qualification; they are dealt with by Strauss in a more differentiated way than Harris suggests (he by no means denies the historicity of all cures).

4. Cf. Schweitzer ³1954, 92 ('sometimes one almost seems to be reading Johannes Weiss').

5. See Sandberger 1972, 86.

6. This would have been perfectly possible; cf. Schweitzer ³1954, 91; Frei 1985, 234, 236–8. Not until 1864 did Strauss construct a portrait of Jesus; then, however, he came to disown many of his own insights.

7. The *Glaubenslehre* from 1840–41 signals a radicalized phase in Strauss's theology. He now no longer strives at a theological synthesis, but at a mere antithesis. See Sandberger 1972, 161.

8. See Sandberger 1972, 87–91, 156.

9. See Sandberger 1972, 87.

10. Cf. e.g. Dunn 1977b, 290–1. It is naive, however, to trace all (!) of Strauss's historical decisions back to the premise that miracles do not happen since there is no transcendent personal God (thus Harris 1973, 43, 89, 283–4).

11. Cf. Morgan 1977, 243: 'Despite possible reservations about Strauss's mechanistic world-view the essential points of his critical position have become commonplace.'

12. See Sandberger 1972, 143, cf. 111–12; cf. Frei 1985, 239.

13. Baur (1864, 9ff.) criticized his precursor G. L. Bauer, who mixed a dogmatic interest in his work by looking for truths of the reason, applying the principle of accommodation and regarding his task as establishing whether Christianity is a rational and divine religion. These criticisms would probably apply to Gabler as well. G. L. Bauer and his significance is dealt with at length by Merk 1972, 141–203.

14. For Baur as historian see Scholder 1961.

15. G. L. Hahn, who had taken as his lead the treatment of the self-consciousness of the apostolic church, is criticized by Baur (1864, 31f.) for being vague and apologetic. Such a procedure serves to by-pass doctrinal differences and to emphasize incorrectly only unitive factors.

16. K. Berger 1986, 29ff., also traces the influence of Schelling and Kant on Baur.

17. The influence of Hegel on Baur should not be exaggerated. Morgan 1988a, 71f., points out that Baur did not force his history into a Hegelian pattern, but reached his view on the basis of an exegetical study of Paul's letters, even though 'his theological evaluation of historical development

as the self-expression of the divine Spirit (learned from Hegel) no doubt encouraged him'.

18. Hodgson 1966, 146, 266; cf. Morgan 1977, 255f., 257f. on the combination of history and theology in Baur's conception.

19. Cf. Boers 1979, 40.

20. Bultmann 1955, 245. For an enthusiastic review by a contemporary see Brückner 1913, 425–36; cf. also Bultmann's review (1911/12), where the work is called a 'masterpiece' (432) and a 'permanent milestone of research' (435).

21. Now and then Holtzmann inserts a critical comment on modern 'school theology' which tries to make dated New Testament notions palatable to modern taste; cf. e.g. 1,369 n. 2; 2, 110, 116–17.

22. Bultmann 1955, 245; Kraus 1970, 158.

23. Brückner 1913, 428–9, observes that Holtzmann's first volume comes close to Wrede's subsequent programme. In the first volume the history-of-religions method predominates; in the second volume the method of 'doctrinal concepts'. The first volume presents an overall picture of the development which is illustrated in the second volume through individual cases. In the second edition, Holtzmann's openness towards the history of religions is even more pronounced. See his fundamental statement in Holtzmann 1, 21–2; cf. Brückner 1913, 426–7; Bauer 1967, 333–4. A history-of-religions foundation for the presentation of New Testament theology had been demanded in 1893 by Deissmann (69ff.).

24. Holtzmann is quite vague as to the positive content of this 'fire'. Despite the occasional affirmation that the kernel of Christianity must consist in some basic views of Jesus that are capable of being transmitted by teaching (1,178), he never makes clear what this kernel is. We only hear of universalism, love, *Gesinnungsethik*, filial relationship to God, etc., on a very general level; cf. Bultmann 1911/12, 435. Moreover, Holtzmann (1,418) even states that in the mouth of any other teacher the teachings of Jesus would not have been of lasting significance; his teaching is inseparably bound to his person. So what happens to the kernel capable of being taught?

25. Jesus only knew and offered the undissected fruit as a whole (1,412, cf. 244). But as reformers always show their superiority at those points on which they are innovators, Holtzmann feels justified in separating Jesus' permanent accomplishment from his talk of the eschatological kingdom (416). Holtzmann is inclined to trace a development in Jesus' thought, so that toward the end of his career the national limitations of his message diminished more and more.

26. According to Holtzmann, the conversion experience meant that Paul broke down under the burden of the law (2,216).

27. Time and again Holtzmann finds contradictions which result mostly from the fact that Jewish and Hellenistic–Greek lines of thought cross each other in his mind; see e.g. 2, 36–8, 160 (the law); 48f., 56, 81 (sin); 167 (indicative and imperative); 223 (eschatology).

28. Holtzmann also finds such generalization in Paul's theology of baptism: Paul 'died to sin' in connection with the conversion experience on which his baptism followed; therefore he constructs a 'dogmatic theory which transcends all demonstrable experience', according to which this happens to all those who are baptized (2,127, 196f., cf. 164).

29. Holtzmann points out, however, that the remedies against such excesses can just as well be found in Paul's writings (2,254).

30. It is often regarded as a shortcoming of the work that Holtzmann does not sufficiently elucidate the historical process that has led from one 'doctrinal concept' to the other. He is said to be content with juxtaposing the different 'doctrinal concepts' and comparing them to each other. See Bultmann 1911/12, 435; Kümmel 1973, 191f.; Merk 1972, 242. Kümmel even speaks of an 'atomizing presentation of the New Testament world of thought'; cf. Hasel, 1982, 44.

I do not think that this line of criticism does justice to Holtzmann. Holtzmann does ask questions about the historical process, and he also suggests answers to them (whether or not the answers will hold is, of course, another matter). This is especially true of the chapter on the 'theological problems of early Christianity' (1,420–580), as even Wrede, critical as he was of the project (see above, pp. 13f.), acknowledged (Wrede 1973, 189 n. 40); but see also 1,27–159 (the chapter on Judaism on point after point stretches over into early Christianity). See the positive comments by Brückner 1913, 432f. Unlike Kümmel, I think that Holtzmann does sketch a quite 'intelligible development from Jesus to Paul and on into the early Catholic Church'. Paul constructs his theology in the attempt to interpret his conversion experience; his interpretative instruments are supplied by: 1. his pre-Christian Jewish theology; 2. memories of the historical Jesus provided by the earliest church; and 3. Greek thought. In the subsequent historical process, 3. comes increasingly to dominate over 1. and 2.

Hasel 1982 reveals on p. 45 that he is not acquainted with the book he is criticizing. He copies Schweitzer's (1912) summary of Holtzmann's section on Paul as if it applied to the whole work.

Schweitzer, for his part, criticizes Holtzmann's arrangement of the Pauline materials for leaving out of account 'the connexions inherent in the system' (1912, 102). I find this criticism (praised as 'brilliant' by Kümmel 1973, 434 n. 248) unfair. To be sure, one is entitled to think that the connections established by Holtzmann are often not the right ones, and Schweitzer is certainly correct in pointing out that eschatology is given far too little attention. But it is not true that Holtzmann finds no connections between Paul's views on different topics. One can just as well dispute many of the connections established by Schweitzer himself, who goes to the other extreme, over-emphasizing the role of eschatology. In the final analysis, Schweitzer is criticizing Holtzmann just for not establishing such connections in Paul's thought as he himself finds there to be.

31. He also makes it very clear that there is no unified 'New Testament' doctrine; rather, there is a variegated mixture of doctrines, 'a chaos' from which there could have been many other developments than actually happened in the historical circumstances (1,573; cf. 2,239).

3. *The History-of-Religions Programme*

1. On the history-of-religions school see Lüdemann 1987; a methodological evaluation is given by K. Müller 1985. Wrede himself did not carry out comparative work in the history of religions in his own research keeping rather strictly to the realm of the early church, but he followed it and was stimulated by it; see Bousset 1907, 3–10 esp. 6. Bousset 1899

subscribes to Wrede's programme, as does Windisch 1912, 289, 300. Brückner 1913, 363, tells how scales fell from his eyes, as it were, when he was listening to Wrede's lecture.

2. Even B. Weiss (1975, 46 = 1884, 2) regarded New Testament theology as practised by him as a 'purely historical discipline', although New Testament theology presupposes the normative character of the New Testament writings as the fundamental witness to God's revelation (1975, 45, 47–8 = 1884, 1–3).

3. For a mediating position see Windisch 1910, 201–2. He subscribes to Wrede's view of the task of New Testament theology. But he insists that providing materials for historians of the dogma is also an important part of the task. New Testament theology is not only a 'presupposition' of the history of dogma but its first, fundamental chapter. Undoubtedly Wrede would have agreed. What is important to him is that a systematic concern must not affect the exegetical results. Wrede's disagreement with Holtzmann hardly included the latter's frequent comments on, e.g., Paul's influence on the history of dogma (often regarded by Holtzmann as more apparent than real); see Holtzmann 1911, 2,237 and the section 'Paulinism in History' (2,242–50).

4. At this point he follows Krüger (1896).

5. The demand that New Testament theology must also deal with non-canonical writings amounts to a criticism of Holtzmann, who in his great work confined himself to the New Testament. In principle, however, Holtzmann agreed with Wrede: a more complete presentation would have to go beyond the boundaries of the canon. He had restricted himself to the New Testament partly for pragmatic reasons. In the second edition, however, Holtzmann also emphasizes the 'incomparable significance' which the New Testament canon has had for the Christian church and for our religious inheritance as a whole (1911, 1,ix). Thus the nub of the matter proves to be, after all, the relation of New Testament theology to the church, as Wrede realized.

6. See, however, 102–3, where Wrede shows that the limit is not to be conceived in a mechanical way.

7. Thus emphatically Bousset 1899, 7,15; cf. Deissmann 1893, 67f.; Windisch 1910, 198–9, 218.

8. Cf. Deissmann 1893, 74–5; Bousset 1899, 8–9; and already Gunkel 1888, 62. See also K. Müller 1985, 165.

9. The praise given to Holtzmann by Wrede (83–4) should emphatically be noted. Holtzmann's work was the best that New Testament theology had thus far produced. Even the method of 'doctrinal concepts' is praised for its effort at making differentiations between the 'doctrines' of the New Testament (74).

10. The term tradition history is not yet used by Wrede; on the subject-matter see Strecker 1975, 10–11; 1979, 340; Morgan 1973, 10–11. In this regard even Stuhlmacher (cf. above, p. 81) can be seen as a perpetuator of Wrede's line of thought.

11. See Morgan 1973, 12–13; Strecker 1979, 338–9.

12. ET: 'minute hair-splitting'.

13. Cf. Bousset 1899, 8.

14. Wrede does not use the word 'experience' here; what he does say is that Paul's doctrine of justification by faith 'had a practical origin'; Paul

would never have formed it 'had he not taken in hand the task of converting Gentiles'. In his book on Paul, Wrede is more specific: the doctrine 'provides the theoretical support for the emancipation from the Jewish precepts. The practice was here the mother of the theory, not vice versa . . .' (1907, 84). In this book I am using the word 'experience' in a much wider sense than just inward religious emotions, and from that point of view it is correct to say that the doctrine of justification by faith is linked to experience. More precisely, the theory has a legitimating function: it has been devised to justify a practical step which was taken first.

15. Wrede 1973, 190 n. 59, points out that Holtzmann has not put the question how the formula of justification by faith arose sufficiently sharply. By contrast, at this point Wrede can follow Wernle, who treats the doctrine of justification as part of a 'mission theology' (Wernle 1897, 79). Even today, the question of the rise of the 'doctrine' of justification is a kind of watershed in the study of Paul.

16. Cf. Strecker 1979, 355; Morgan 1973, 21.

17. See e.g. the most recent collection of articles on the subject: Tuckett 1983 (with a good introduction by the editor, 1–7); also Räisänen 1989.

18. See also Wrede's criticisms of Holtzmann's interpretation of 'Kingdom of God' (97; cf. 190 n. 52). But although the eschatological dimension of Jesus' proclamation was not foreign to Wrede (cf. also Rollmann 1984, 35f.), he sketches a portrait of Jesus in his book on Paul which is still very much in the liberal tradition (Wrede 1907, 89–97). He contrasts the simplicity of Jesus' ethical religion with the complex theological reflections of Paul. But this contrast does not necessarily result from Wrede's alleged preference for the simple religion of Jesus over the dogmatics of Paul. Rollmann 1984, 29, points out that it does not as such imply valuation. 'Wrede always remains enough of an historian . . . to separate his own religious preferences from what he considers to be necessary religio-historical developments' (30). Consequently he does not understand the movement from 'religion' (Jesus) to 'theology' (Paul) simply as damage but as a historical necessity (Wrede 1907, 102f.).

19. See recently Schnelle 1986; Räisänen 1987a; and the witty remarks of Westerholm 1988, 15.

20. Strecker 1979, 356. In a similar vein J. M. Robinson, another outstanding Bultmannian, states that Wrede's main arguments, set out brilliantly in his programmatic essay, are still convincing today. 'New Testament theology' ought indeed to be replaced with history of early Christian religion (1973, 388).

21. The presentation would start with a description of Judaism and go on with a statement of the preaching of Jesus. From Jesus one should move to the faith of the early community (due to the paucity of sources 'the chapter will unfortunately be short') and to Paul. A consideration of Paul's influence would bring one to the large and difficult section on 'faith and theology on Gentile Christian soil'. The presentation would be concluded by the theology of John, in connection with which the treatment of Ignatius would find its natural place. Within the main chapters a thematic subdivision would be adopted.

22. Cf. Boers 1979, 46–7.

23. Strecker 1975, 12.

24. On B. Weiss see above, n. 2. Beyschlag attempts in his New

Testament theology to combine a historical approach with a 'Christian and evangelical viewpoint' (1891, 5), his starting-point being the conviction of the revelatory nature of biblical religion.

25. Morgan 1973, 23, points out that Wrede 'brought into the open the tension between the historical approach to Christianity and traditional views of revelation' which had been concealed by Baur's quasi-theological theory about history as revelation. The concept of 'inspiration' is sharply rejected by Wrede. 'For logical thinking there can be no middle position between inspired writings and historical documents, although in fact there is no lack of partial doctrines of inspiration about the place (*obwohl es ja an mancherlei halben, Einviertel-und Dreiviertel-Inspirationslehren nicht fehlt*)' (69; German original in Strecker 1975, 83).

26. See Strecker 1979, 355.

27. Cf. Stuhlmacher 1979, 153: the systematic and historical theology of the time tended to raise historical-critical thinking to the dominant theological mode of thought; cf. especially Troeltsch.

28. It is cricitized by Boers 1979, 59–60; cf. Morgan 1973, 24–6.

29. Morgan 1973, 59–60.

30. Lüdemann 1987, 356.

31. Cf. Kümmel 1973, 288: 'a book written with traces of inspiration'; Bultmann 1955, 245: 'sprightly and impressive'; Kraus 1970, 166: 'vivacious and original'; Windisch 1910, 200 n. 1.

32. See Wrede 1973, 101. Wernle does *not* offer his work as a 'New Testament theology', though. Contrary to Wrede, he regards it as a presupposition for a 'New Testament theology' that the author has formed a clear opinion on each individual place in the New Testament which is only possible for a much more experienced scholar (Wernle refers to Holtzmann).

33. It is very important to Wernle that piety be based on genuine experience (cf. 256). He criticizes Paul's theological thoughts on the cross of Jesus for being only minimally rooted in experience; they have arisen from theoretical reflection.

34. This applies to Paul's account of Christian life as 'walking in the Spirit'. In sweepingly general terms Paul depicts the Christian ideal as if it were a fact. Sometimes reality did correspond to this ideal, but in countless cases it did not (189, cf. 195).

35. Among the things strongly criticized by Wernle is what he regards as narrow fanaticism, see e.g. 333 (on John), 428–9 (on the Pastorals). See also his comment on John's christology (what else is the Johannine Christ but a ghost? 353).

Having moved from New Testament study more and more to the study of the Reformation, Wernle was later alienated from the radicalism of his youth. He then rejects the programme of the history-of-religions school, taking the view that it reflected a failure to comprehend the peculiarity of the gospel. See Verheule 1973, 335–8.

36. For a nuanced appraisal see Windisch 1912, 303–15. This review combines praise (305: Weinel has 'at last with skill and understanding raised New Testament theology to a higher level'; 306: 'especially masterful' is the depiction of religious life in the early church) with a critique of the philosophical assumptions of the work (308–15). Cf. Bultmann 1911/12, 437–9; he regards the work basically as a success, but

criticizes the insufficient use of non-Christian materials and the section on Paul.

37. In judging this obvious tendency one should keep in mind that a more objective comparative approach was at that time almost foreign even in the discipline of comparative religion, then about to take its first stumbling steps. Its pioneers Müller and Tiele thought, for example, that by way of comparative study they could show that Christianity was the highest of religions. See e.g. M. Müller 1876, 34; Tiele 1899, 48; cf. 28, 182. Cf. Rudolph 1967, 22f.

38. For a critique see Brückner 1913, e.g. 416–18. For Weinel's picture of Jesus see especially Windisch 1912, 308–13; Kaftan 1927, 11–13.

39. Weinel here succumbs to modernization to a much greater degree than did Holtzmann, who recognized the Jewish nature of much of Jesus' message. Cf. Schweitzer ³1954, 398.

40. Cf. Brückner 1913, 423.

41. Bousset 1899, 1ff.

42. Bousset 1904.

43. Cf. Verheule 1973, 182.

44. On Bousset's philosophical background (Carlyle, Fries) see K. Berger 1986, 87ff.

45. See Sanders 1977, 39f.; 213–17.

46. The work was published posthumously in 1917; the references are to the ET of 1970.

47. See Verheule 1973, 324–7, on the differences between Weiss and Bousset. Weiss emphasizes above all the significance of the personality of Jesus for the early church as well as for Paul; see in particular Weiss 1913, 478–515. He stresses the alleged continuity from Jesus via the early church to Paul, but underestimates the importance of the Hellenist wing.

48. Over 500 pages are devoted to Paul. This amounts to about 60% of the whole! John, by way of comparison, gets a little less than 20 pages, i.e. 2.5%.

49. Weiss 1892, ET 1971; second edition 1900.

50. On Weiss's interpretation of Jesus see Regner 1973.

51. See the discussion in Hiers – Holland 1971, 16–24, in particular the quotation from J. Weiss, *Die Idee des Reiches Gottes in der Theologie* (1901), 113, on 17–18.

52. See Regner 1973, 85–7.

53. According to Weiss, this timeless kernel of Paul's religion also reveals the most profound essence of all religion: God reveals himself only to the one who surrenders himself to him, not to one who tries to reach him through his works (193f.). The same insight is found at the heart of the message of Jesus, but in a simpler and easier form than in Paul.

54. Windisch 1912, 315–29, had likewise sketched the programme for a New Testament theology conceived as early Christian history of religion which would have New Testament eschatology as its starting point. As the other *Leitmotif* (even in historical regard) the 'internalized piety' would have to be dealt with. This is a relatively independent undercurrent which is increasingly detached from eschatology (325).

55. He reflects e.g. on the problems that arise for those who have grown up in a Christian environment when one tries to establish Paul's conversion experience and his theology of stark contrasts, based on the former, as a norm for them (442–5).

56. See Weiss 1913, 433–4.

57. Weiss here agrees with a point emphasized by Wrede and, later on, by Bultmann. But Weiss goes on to note that the narrow connection between faith and thought which is part of Paul's historic contribution to Christianity has not necessarily been a blessing for the latter. The trend of the time towards Christianity without dogmas is endorsed by Weiss (423).

58. Weiss 1913, 450f.; see also 479: early Christianity let 'a stream of the noblest Jewish piety and ethics flow into a world religion', albeit in a strongly concentrated and intensified form.

59. Weiss (803) stresses that the evangelist was able to combine his high-flown mysticism with the church and its Lord as well as with the sacraments. In the light of subsequent literary-critical research, at least the connection with the sacraments is, of course, open to doubt. Had Weiss analysed the Gospel of John with anything like the thoroughness with which he analysed the Pauline letters, he should have discovered more problems in the former.

60. See above, n. 35.

61. Stuhlmacher 1979, 157–61; 1981, 271–301; Hasel 1982, 43; cf. even Dunn 1987, 12.

62. Bultmann 1955, 248–50; Käsemann 1972/73, 239 calls him Bultmann's only peer. Kraus (1970, 170–8), Boers (1979, 67–75) and Morgan (1973, 27–33) also deal with Schlatter at length, and Morgan offers a translation of his lengthy article on New Testament theology and dogmatics. The page numbers in what follows refer to this translation.

63. See Brückner's review (1913, 366–76). Merk 1972, 250, thinks that Schlatter has 'given up reconstruction for the sake of interpretation'. Cf. also Boers 1979, 75; Morgan 1973, 33.

64. Pace Bultmann himself! On the contrary see Merk 1972, 250; cf. also Morgan 1973, 28; Georgi 1985, 84. See also the critical review of the young Bultmann, 1911/12, 440–3, which ends up with the regretful question: 'How is such a lack of comprehension of serious historical work possible in a mind which is so open to the purely religious and untroubled by prejudices?'

65. Contra Käsemann. Schlatter would have bluntly rejected Bultmann's specific exegetical findings as well as those of Käsemann.

66. Morgan 1973, 172 n. 55, notes that one could almost read Schlatter's article as polemic against crude forms of Barthianism.

67. On the other hand, the historian setting up a New Testament theology should not content himself with 'a statistical account of the ideas in the New Testament', but should move on from statistics to 'aetiology' to ask how the convictions found in the New Testament arose. In this he does not yet 'trespass upon the dogmatician's territory'. Schlatter thinks of Bernhard Weiss as such a 'statistician' (136). It is not clear, however, why Schlatter can criticize others for departing from direct textual observations on the one hand and yet himself move beyond the texts to conjectures about the emergence of their ideas and combinations of the ideas found in different texts on the other.

68. See already Schlatter 1885, 9f., approvingly cited by Stuhlmacher 1979, 160.

69. Schlatter explicitly admits that the church's capacity for making valid observations about the Bible has been 'seriously damaged by a confusion of the two tasks', the historical and the dogmatic (128). Boers is

mistaken in repeatedly stating that Schlatter considered Calvin's *Institutes* to be historically more true to the New Testament than most historical works of his time (Boers 1979, 69, 72, 74). Schlatter refers to Calvin as part of his report on 'the objection to a historical theology of the New Testament' put forward by people more conservative than himself.

70. For criticisms see also Morgan 1973, 29, who points out that Schlatter's argument for separating the New Testament from later church writings could 'only be maintained on the assumption of the traditional views about its authorship'.

71. Brückner 1913, 366ff., gives many examples, including the following: 'Because of the end (= the resurrection of Jesus), we know (!) how he thought (!) of the beginning of his Sonship. It begins with God's giving him the body, as it is completed through God's returning the body to him' (Schlatter 1909, 474f.). Cf. also Kümmel 1970, 125.

72. Windisch 1910 has an excellent discussion of both the weaknesses and strengths of Schlatter's New Testament theology. Unlike Feine, Schlatter does not put forward objective observations (even though they are precisely what he emphasizes on the theoretical level). '. . . here is no critical-exegetical division of the subject-matter and its problems, but the reflection of the tradition on the mind and nature of a theologian who thinks deeply and has personally grown into the whole of the tradition, and therefore communicates the colouring of his own thoughts to the whole material. To the degree that one can perceive this change of perspective, one will really be able to evaluate . . . the work . . . Now one can see how a sensitive mind masters and changes the thoughts and traditions of the Gospels until they gain the miraculous unity and coherence which makes such an effect in the book' (224–5). The best contribution of the book is that the reader is allowed to penetrate into the thought-world of one profound theologian (225)! Schlatter brings scattered embryonic thoughts of the New Testament into a distinctive subjective whole (229).

73. Bultmann 1955, 249, with reference to Schlatter 1909, 10.

74. Bultmann 1955, 249, notes that Schlatter's statements might in themselves also be understood as a defence of historical relativism. Morgan 1973, 29, finds it striking how far Schlatter seems to be in agreement with Wrede on the level of theory.

75. For a discussion of Feine's work see Windisch 1910, 194–219, esp. 214–17; 1912, 289–97; Brückner 1913, 376–86; Bultmann 1911/12, 439f. Windisch 1912 demonstrates a development in an even more clearly church-dogmatic direction in the second edition, in which Feine follows von Hofmann's Erlangen salvation-historical theology.

76. Gulin 1940b, 15.

77. Bultmann 1955, 246.

78. Although the book did not appear until 1927, the manuscript was ready several years earlier (5).

79. Cf. e.g. Kaftan's comment that Jesus could not possibly understand his death along the lines of later dogmatics as an indispensable prerequisite of divine forgiveness, because he did forgive sins during his earthly mission.

80. From the perspective of future influence the question also has to be asked why should it be important for humanistic scholarship to acquaint itself in particular with the figure of Jesus as reconstructed with critical methods. After all, it is not this Jesus who has exerted influence throughout

the history of the church. Similarly, it is doubtful whether Paul as documented in his genuine letters has been as influential as the stylized figure portrayed in the Pastorals and in Acts.

81. Inconsistently, however, at the end of his book he introduced the notion of revelation (205).

82. See e.g. his comments on the church's doctrine of Jesus' sacrificial death (52, 117–22), on the place of the resurrection in the wider context (77f.) or on christology (105f., 202).

83. See e.g. 147f. In Rom. 9–11 Paul teaches absolute double predestination and the *apokatastasis panton* side by side. Apart from this acute observation it is typical (of the whole era) that Kaftan fails to see how important the issue of *Israel* is for Paul in the section in question.

84. Bultmann does mention Kaftan in a single sentence of his (admittedly brief) account (1955, 246), but Merk 1972 relegates him to a short footnote in his extensive treatment of the discipline (251 n. 137). Kaftan's contribution is discussed at some length by Kraus 1970, 178–81.

Part Two: From Wrede to the Present

1. *New Testament Theology and the Breakthrough of Neo-Orthodoxy*

1. A second, completely rewritten, edition appeared in 1922. The following page references are to the ET (1933), which was made from the sixth edition but includes the prefaces to the previous ones, of which those to the first and second edition will be of interest to us.

2. Barth 1962, 326. To be sure, Barth claims that his hermeneutical method is only an application of general hermeneutics: he would use a similar method in the exposition of Laotse or Goethe, if that were his job (1933, 12). But would Barth use the same method in interpreting both Paul on one hand and the opponents of the apostle on the other? If not, a special type of hermeneutics seems to be reserved for Paul. – As ideal scientific theologians Barth recommends Luther and – Paul (1962, 335).

3. Harnack 1962, 329–30, 346.

4. See the extracts given by Kümmel 1973, 365f., 369–71, and Moltmann (1962, 87–98, 119–147). See also e.g. Weinel 1928, 9: the movement initiated by Barth 'exposes with full force and one-sidedness the basic fault of biblicism: the will to artificial reinterpretation (*Umdeutung*), without which biblicism cannot hold fast to the absolute authority of the Bible, deteriorates here to a violation of the texts'. Weinel's comment is directed at Bultmann, too.

5. Jülicher 1962, 88–90.

6. In *ThLZ* 1922 (a review of the second edition), cited by Kümmel 1973, 369.

7. Jülicher 1962, 97. Cf. Stendahl 1984, 17: '. . . what is intended as a commentary turns out to be a theological tractate, expanding in contemporary terms what Paul should have said about the subject matter as understood by the commentator'.

8. Schlatter 1962, 145, cf. 144. Indeed, Barth shows no interest whatsoever in the question of the original purpose of the letter which is so central in its recent exegesis. Paul's problem with Israel in Romans 9–11 becomes

without further ado the problem of how 'the Church (!) confronts the Gospel' (1933, 332)!

9. Bultmann 1962, 140.

10. Bultmann 1962, 140–2.

11. As a prominent Swiss exegete Wernle was one of the central goals of Barth's attack. See Barth's letter to Wernle and the comments of the editor: Barth 1985, 638–46.

12. Barth 1962, 150. Cf. P. Berger's instructive analysis of Barth as a representative of 'reconversion'. Berger 1980, 77–9, points out that if key passages of Barths *Church Dogmatics* were translated into Muslim terms – and among other religions Islam is particularly instructive because of its proclamatory ('kerygmatic') understanding of revelation – 'very little in Barth's basic methodological assumptions would have to be changed' (78).

13. Jülicher 1962, 94.

14. P. Berger 1980 is unable to see the deeply religious character of Bultmann's work. On Bultmann as a theologian see e.g. Schmithals 1966; cf. also Painter 1987. On Bultmann's move from liberal to dialectical theology see Jaspert, in Jaspert (ed.) 1984.

15. This is admitted even by Stuhlmacher 1979, 172. Morgan, too, though quite appreciative of Barth, comments that his book more resembles a sermon than a scholarly study (1973, 36).

16. Down to the early 1920s, however, Bultmann himself had shared the liberal and history-of-religions point of view, including an emphasis on the historical Jesus and a distinction between theology and religion. On the theology of the young Bultmann see the careful study of Evang 1988, e.g. 188f. Bultmann's review of four New Testament theologies in 1911/12, in which he fully adopts Wrede's point of view (433–7), is characteristic.

17. Bultmann 1963, 50–4.

18. Bultmann states that 'a person who makes Paul's religious life or his life-sentiment the theme of his interpretation of Paul is clearly interpreting something in which Paul was not in the least interested' (1963, 52f.). But it is equally doubtful whether Paul would have taken any more interest in existential interpretation or demythologization.

19. In his rejection of the message of the historical Jesus as the core of New Testament theology Bultmann drew the consequences of the miscarriage of the quest as demonstrated by Schweitzer and by the incipient form-critical study of the Gospels in which Bultmann himself played a major part. Both Schweitzer and Bultmann saw the problem in quite similar terms, although their solutions differed markedly; cf. Grässer 1984.

20. Contrast Bultmann's own early view in 1911/12, 433–7, in which he emphasizes the centrality of experience. Later, in his New Testament theology Bultmann assessed this central aspect in the work of the history-of-religions school more positively: these scholars recognized religion 'as an independent force' and as 'an existential attitude' (1955, 247).

21. Bultmann manages to avoid the word 'experience' even when speaking of Paul's conversion. He describes even that event only in terms of 'self-understanding' language: Paul 'surrendered his previous understanding of himself' (1951, 188).

22. Bultmann 1963, 55–8. Having criticized some allegedly objective samples of exegesis (Holtzmann is blamed for idealism, 59f.), Bultmann refuses to give a sample of correct interpretation. His reason: such an

exegesis only exists in the living practice of interpretation, so that no criteria exist!

23. See Bultmann 1955b, 43f.; 1951, 11f.

24. Bultmann always sought to be a theologian of the church. For his early period see Evang's chapter on Bultmann's 'church orientation': 1988, 101ff. In recent times Bultmann has been increasingly recognized by church leaders also as a teacher of the church. Morgan, reviewing a recent collection of articles dedicated to Bultmann's work, notes that 'the general Church orientation of the . . . volume, signalled by an episcopal introduction, is indicative of the now generally recognized status and stature of Bultmann as a teacher of the Church. So we build the tombs for the prophets our fathers persecuted', Morgan 1988b, 334.

25. On the other hand Bultmann does assert that New Testament interpretation does not in principle differ in any way from the interpretation of other historical texts. There is at least a strong tension between his various statements.

26. Bultmann 1963, 66–8. On Bultmann's view of the task of theology see now Bultmann 1984, esp. 159–70.

27. Bultmann 1963, 70; cf. 1955, 251.

28. 1955, 251.

29. One of the most instructive assessments of Bultmann's New Testament theology is Dahl 1974, a sympathetic and critical review at the same time.

30. Did the earliest church really understand itself as an 'absolutely eschatological entity', as Paul did (1951, 54)? The kerygma of the 'Hellenistic' community is, by contrast, set out in more descriptive terms.

31. See e.g. Bultmann's criticism of the diluted eschatology of I Clement and my critique of this aspect of Bultmann's work: Räisänen 1986, 307–33. Perrin 1984, 417, points out that 'the comparative denigration of the literature of emergent Catholicism' is 'an indication of the fatal flaw in Bultmann's whole enterprise'.

32. For a critique of the notion of a *Sache* supposed to underlie the texts see K. Berger 1977, 242f., 249ff.

33. Merk 1972, 254, 257, and 1980, 464, puts Bultmann's decision on a par with Baur's procedure; similarly Hasel 1982, 32, 87. Yet Bultmann's reasons for separating Jesus from New Testament theology are opposite to those of Baur. For Bultmann, the message of Jesus is not yet Christian theology; for Baur, it alone is such theology in a pure form.

34. This being so, one might ask, does not contemporary Judaism belong to such presuppositions of New Testament theology as ought to be presented first? In Bultmann's representation the relation to Judaism tends to be antithetical, the Jewish religion merely making up a contrasting background to the kerygma. Is this not a step backwards in comparison with Holtzmann and Wernle?

35. See 1951, 190f.; cf. Boers 1979, 77f.

36. The procedure is openly stated when Bultmann is interpreting Paul's idea of 'original sin': 'Paul, it is true, never expounds this train of thought, but our right to develop it for the understanding of his statements is suggested by his conception of "world"' (1951, 253). Cf. 1951, 232, on 'flesh'.

37. The problems connected with this are well analysed by Boers 1979,

76–80. On Bultmann's relation to Heidegger cf. K. Berger 1986, 130ff.

38. For Bultmann it is enough to say that on a literal reading of Rom. 9.6–29 an insoluble contradiction would result in view of the character of faith as decision which is so central to Paul (1951, 330). The 'mystery' of the salvation of Israel which plays such a central role in recent study of Paul (Rom. 11.25) is not even mentioned by Bultmann in his section on Paul, but only in his account of the development towards the ancient church (1955, 232), where it is ascribed to 'speculative fantasy'. The 'salvation historical' features of Paul's thought do not withstand Bultmann's content-criticism.

39. 'The spirit powers represent the reality into which man is placed as one full of conflicts and struggle, a reality which threatens and tempts' (ibid.). Later on in the same chapter (vv. 35ff.), 'Paul lets himself be misled into adopting his opponents' methods of argumentation', so these verses should not be used in interpreting Paul's notion of *soma* (1951, 192). Paul's real intention is distinct from the mythology put forward in the passage in question (1951, 198).

40. See Dahl 1974, 113–15, and elsewhere.

41. Morgan 1977, 258, deems that Bultmann pays more attention to the canon than he can justify rationally.

42. Bultmann even states that Paul's theological thinking, as set out in Romans, 'only lifts the knowledge inherent in faith itself into the clarity of conscious knowing' (1951, 190). The consequence would be that all those Christians who thought differently were not conscious of the true content of their faith.

43. Cf. Dahl 1974, 100–1; Perrin 1984, 417.

44. Cf. Georgi's critical comparison of Bultmann with his history-of-religions predecessors (1985, 80–5).

45. Cf. Morgan 1977, 248 n. 4: 'Bultmann provides a theoretical framework in which the interpreter's prior understanding may be corrected through encounter with the text. Whether this happens in his own practice remains a question.'

2. Biblical History as Normative

1. Even these works appeared in a situation already coloured by the hermeneutical reflections of Bultmann and other dialectical theologians. Therefore it seems justified to locate them, too, in the 'shadow' of Bultmann's work, broadly understood.

2. Merk 1972, 251 n. 137, therefore regards him as the last representative of the method of 'doctrinal concepts' in New Testament theology.

3. Even Goppelt 1981, 276, finds that Zahn's work, though valuable from a historical-philological point of view, 'was hopelessly entrenched in historical conservatism'.

4. The 'essential difference' consists in the fact that the Synoptic Jesus does not talk of his heavenly origin or of his eternity as does John's (87). But Büchsel later states that the silence of the Synoptics does not mean that the idea of pre-existence does not go back to Jesus' own teaching. For the Synoptics 'treat the divine Sonship of Jesus as a mystery which they will not and cannot fully elucidate' (164). In a footnote (213 n. 2) he adds that acceptance of the eternity of Jesus is demanded because of the divine love

which has appeared in him.

5. Cf. Stendahl 1984, 20.

6. 'Apocalyptic' refers to a mode of thought which has the notion of a universal salvation-historical drama as its presupposition (19). Stauffer denies Hellenistic influences altogether. In a peculiar way he brands the 'Hellenists' of the early community as an insignificant group which lacked ability to persuade, ideas and a vocation (35, the ET is inaccurate)!

7. See e.g. the account of predestination in Jesus (Mark 4.11f.), Paul and John (52–5). From the saying of Jesus Paul develops the teaching (sic) about hardening found in Romans 9. The result is that 'the New Testament teaches the supralapsarian *praedestinatio gemina*' (54).

8. For instance, the Lord's Prayer or Jesus' demand to love one's enemies are mentioned only in passing – in the chapter on prayer (176, 179). The message of Jesus hardly figures at all in the book (in contrast to his 'way', which is interpreted in apocalyptic terms, 25–29).

9. Cullmann 1962, 26 n. 9, considers this organization in terms of 'redemptive history' to be the lasting merit of the work.

10. Merk 1972, 253. For critical comments see also e.g. Goppelt 1981, 274; Hasel 1982, 65. Even Ladd, who writes from an 'evangelical' viewpoint, criticizes Stauffer for not doing justice to the variety of the interpretations of Christ in the New Testament: 1975, 16, 33.

11. Cf. Goppelt 1981, 274: the book first found wide acceptance especially in conservative circles, as it seemed to demonstrate the coherence of New Testament thought. Goppelt criticizes the work for eclecticism, mythologizing and objectivizing.

12. Cf. Stendahl 1984, 20: 'A close study of Stauffer's NT theology makes it quite clear, however, that its method remains strictly descriptive . . .' From another perspective, Piper 1957, 135, in fact complains that Stauffer has presented a purely historical view of the New Testament.

13. Stauffer now portrays a non-apocalyptic Jesus who was 'quite alone in his own time' (1959, 10); his message was 'rejudaized' or 'qumranized' by the early church (9). There are great differences between Jesus and Paul (e.g. 18, 47f., 133). Now Stauffer is not content with describing New Testament thought, but strives to present the message of Jesus as a challenge for the present day. It is the deepest task of the church to proclaim the message of Jesus always and everywhere, and Stauffer's book is written to serve this very purpose (7).

14. A brief summary is found in Gulin 1940a. Gulin's two-part monograph on joy in the New Testament (1932, 1936) already contains the main lines of his subsequent synthesis.

15. Jesus – the early church – Paul – John – Hebrews – the post-apostolic age.

16. Gulin deals with Paul's theology in terms of four 'lines': the dualistic-eschatological line, the line of justification, the line of dying with Christ, and that of resurrection and sacraments.

17. By contrast, Judaism is strongly castigated by Gulin. See the caricatures in Gulin 1932, 73, 78, 83, 88f., etc.

18. For instance, Weinel's work does not do justice to the New Testament, for its unitary view of salvation is 'falsely dismembered' (15).

19. See 11f., 21, 36, 52f. The relation between experience and theology is stressed in connection with both christology and eschatology. 'It was the

realization of the new life in Christ which led Paul and many others to take high, and even higher, views of the nature of the one in whom and through whom this "newness of life" had been made possible and was now effected' (244). 'Our sins really are forgiven; we are certain of this, with an assurance which no animal sacrifice, no acts of penitence, no practice of piety has ever sufficed to give us; the explanation can only be that Christ's death has really effected what all our previous practice of religion . . . has only dimly reached out toward.' Accordingly, the 'logic' of the Atonement is not merely rational or categorical, but 'psychological', experiential, deeper than reason and understanding (252).

20. In this he differs from the contemporary work of Scott 1946; see in particular Scott's comments on Paul (98–115).

21. See e.g. 112, 138. 'That the (!) Christian view as set forth in the NT must naturally (!) lead (as it historically did) to the doctrine of the Incarnation is quite obvious' (141).

22. For instance the discussion of the doctrine of salvation opens with an interesting chapter on 'the antecedents' which includes intriguing comments on the 'primitive eudaemonism' which culminated in Old Testament apocalyptic (248f.). In the sequel, however, this soteriological prehistory does not lead anywhere. The religio-historical connection is broken, as the New Testament part does not open with Jesus' preaching but with Paul's metaphors of salvation (250).

23. Inconsistently Grant (198) nevertheless regards the reconstruction of the teaching of Jesus as part of New Testament theology.

24. The same theme forms the thread of Scott's book. He emphasizes the variety as an essential part of the New Testament message itself, since 'Christianity is the religion of freedom' (1946, 17f.).

25. Cf. Merk's criticisms (1972, 265f.).

26. In this, Grant's position is reminiscent of Gulin's (see above, 47f.). Both are aware of significant inner differences within the New Testament; both claim that the differences are not important in view of the similarities – without actually weighing the differences or explaining in concrete terms how the problems caused by them might be solved.

27. Grant (24) even claims that Jesus can much more appropriately be described in the language of the later creeds than in language derived from Palestinian apocalyptic.

28. See e.g. II/1, 180: Rom. 10.4 (Christ the *telos* of the law) and John 19.30 (it is fulfilled) together prove that the Torah is not abolished but fulfilled.

29. To refute Bultmann's programme of demythologizing it is enough to point out that, according to the Pastoral letters, there are no myths in the church (I/1, 10f.)!

30. But see Fascher's review article (1958).

31. For a comprehensive summary see Schlaudraff 1988.

32. 1962, xxviii–xxix; 1967, 64–74.

33. Cullmann seems to accept even the statements about the defeated angelic powers as history, though admitting that they cannot be verified (144). The story of the Fall, though non-historical, is still a depiction of a 'primal event' in which man rebelled against his divine task (146). Stendahl may have been right in noting, in 1962, that 'it is not quite clear how Cullmann understands the relation between such a descriptive biblical

theology in its first- and second-century terms and its translation into our present age' (1984, 19); since the publication of the German original of *Salvation in History* in 1965 it appears that Cullmann feels no need for a translation at all. It is not clear that he represents a two-step hermeneutics (thus D. Braun 1967, 65, 69); at least he needs the second step very rarely indeed.

34. Cullmann even claims that Jesus' attitude to Gentiles as depicted in the Gospels shows that he followed a universal plan of salvation (161f.). Conzelmann 1982 tried to show that the view outlined by Cullmann is held by Luke, yet one must not generalize Luke's view into the view of the whole New Testament. For a justified criticism of Cullmann's interpretation of John and Paul see Güttgemanns 1967, 47–9.

35. E.g. by Goppelt 1981, 280; Schlaudraff 1988, passim.

36. Cullmann finds continuity and salvation history even in Galatians 3–4, Romans 4 and I Corinthians 3 (as the Old Testament is referred to!). For criticisms see Klein 1971, 29–34.

37. Cullmann (266) has to attribute to Paul the following idea: in principle, God's revelation in creation and in the law could have led mankind to salvation, if men had believed in it. As they did not, salvation in Christ became a necessity. This explanation degrades Christ to a divine expedient in a situation in which God's previous attempts to get hold of the situation miscarried! No doubt such a view logically results from some Pauline statements. Paul did not however, draw the conclusion. He mostly stresses the exclusive and crucial significance of the Christ event so strongly that Cullmann's explanation is out of the question.

38. Cullmann's appeal to von Rad is misleading in that his talk of salvation history in the Old Testament is rather different from the latter's view. For Cullmann, salvation history is not the action of Yahweh in Israel's actual history, nor the history of Israel's witness to this action. Thus the Exodus event, actual or remembered, has no place in his construction! From the point of view of the New Testament this is natural, for the New Testament does not follow the tradition of the great deeds of the 'God who acts', and God's covenant with Israel is spoken of in a rather ambiguous way (II Cor. 3!). For this reason it is very difficult indeed to try to establish 'salvation history' as the scarlet thread which should hold the whole Bible together.

39. This holds true especially of the relationship between actual and interpreted history; see e.g. Klein 1971, 4–15. See also Klein, 23–8, on von Rad's attempt to join the Old Testament to the New by letting the latter appear as the last appropriation of the old tradition. The Old Testament is appropriated by different New Testament writers in different ways that cannot be harmonized with one another, and the ongoing history of the church gives the lie to the assertion that the appropriations of the Old Testament in the New should be the *last* ones. Of course there were other contemporary appropriations as well, and it is beyond the possibility of research to decide whether the history of the influence of the New Testament appropriations has been better than that of others (Klein). For an extensive criticism of von Rad's enterprise see Oeming 1985, 58ff. (see esp. 67ff. on von Rad's oscillating use of the term 'salvation history').

40. According to Cullmann (245f.), the surrender of imminent expectation does not mean distancing oneself from the inmost essence of the New

Testament message – in contrast to the surrender of the 'salvation-historical tension'; cf. also 219. Against this see e.g. J. M. Robinson 1973, 391.

41. Cf. Stendahl 1984, 19f.

42. Rightly noted by Hasel 1982, 74, 77; cf. Keck 1964/65, 224.

43. Cf. Keck 1964/65, 221. Richardson's outline also has surprising gaps; creation, anthropology and even the problem of the law (!) are missing. See Kümmel 1960, 922.

44. Keck 1964/65, 236, gives a list of things traced back to the teaching of the historical Jesus by Richardson – including the church's task of Gentile mission and the fact that the leaders of the church have to be shepherds and bishops.

45. Keck 1964/65, 237.

46. Kümmel 1960, 925; Merk 1972, 266. Keck 1964/65 offers a thorough and annihilating critique of Richardson's 'confessional handbook' (219) in which 'the iron hand of Church dogma and traditionalism is revealed under the velvet glove of piety' (223).

47. Correctly Merk 1972, 267. Yet in 1973 Harrington (186) could still claim that Richardson's work is 'the greatest New Testament theology we have'!

48. Braun's conception is rejected by Schnackenburg on the simple ground that its starting-point is not 'the primacy of God and his glory'.

49. Only (!) a person who acknowledges that the various witnesses regarded the (postulated) common theology as binding will be able to 'discern a harmonious chorale in the polyphonic choir' (18). K. Berger 1988b, 355, is right in commenting that 'the tendency to harmony is omnipresent' in Schnackenburg's book.

50. In this, Schnackenburg's conception resembles that of Conzelmann (above, pp. 64f.).

51. The two-part work of Meinertz (1950) does differ from traditional dogmatic biblical theologies (e.g. Ceuppens) which served first of all to provide systematic theology with biblical ammunition. Yet his approach is still awkwardly conservative. There are differences in the New Testament but no contradictions (I, 2f.). When the greatness of Christ, which surpasses all human proportions, is acknowledged, the whole testimony to him in the New Testament is organized into 'one marvellous harmony' (II, 338). John's Gospel complements the Synoptics; the Synoptics are not considered in their own right but only as sources for the teaching of Jesus. Paul's unified doctrine is constructed on the basis of all thirteen letters. The same criticisms apply to the work of Bonsirven (1951).

52. For thorough and good reviews see Haufe 1969 and 1979.

53. In itself this definition of unity leaves everything open as regards the contents!

54. The latter statement is, of course, far from being obvious. How normative is Freud for 'Freudian psychoanalysis', or Marx for Marxism?

55. Thus Part I opens with a section on the world and the creation, and eschatology is not dealt with until Part IV.

56. Haufe 1969, 910, justly points out that other legacies than that of the Old Testament ought to have been taken into account.

57. So also Haufe 1969, 910, and Merk 1972, 269.

58. Schelkle does note e.g. the existence both of the christology 'from

below' and of the christology 'from above' in the New Testament as well as the difference between them (II, 155f.), but he draws no conclusions from this fact. Nor does he distinguish consistently between Jesus and the Synoptic Gospels, nor even between the different Synoptics themselves. See Haufe 1969, 910; cf. also Knoch 1974, 366; K. Berger 1988b, 362.

59. This applies e.g. to Schelkle's view of the miracles, the resurrection, and the pre-existence of Jesus. See Haufe 1979, 507–9; Knoch 1974, 366; 1977, 25. As for the relation between the christologies from below and from above, Schelkle comments rather vaguely (II, 161) that today dogmatic theology attempts to do justice to the christology from below. On the attempts to interpret the virgin birth in non-historical theological terms he remarks that then the traditional doctrine of the infallibility of the Bible, of the teaching office and of the believing consciousness would have to be reinterpreted (II, 182).

Cf. K. Berger 1988b, 362: Schelkle represents 'a moderate Catholic Modernism with all the contradictions that such a position can contain'.

60. Cf. Riesenfeld's comments on the appropriation of the virgin birth in faith (412).

61. Nikolainen 1944–1946.

62. At length in his subsequent Swedish article (1972/73).

63. At one point, however, the author vigorously denies both unity and normativeness. In prohibiting women from teaching, the author of the Pastoral letters offers (in I Tim. 2.15) 'a justification which is not known or acknowledged in the rest of the New Testament' and which 'amounts to Judaism rather than Christianity'. In a modern society 'the prohibitions of the Pastoral letters cannot be in force' (218). For endless years Nikolainen was in fact the most prominent champion of the ordination of women in the Lutheran church of Finland (which was finally introduced in 1988).

64. Nikolainen considers at length the question at which point the preaching of Jesus should be presented (he gives his reconstruction only after having dealt with the Gospel tradition and the theologies of the Synoptics), but neglects the prior question whether it should be presented at all.

65. 1972/73, 315.

66. The attempt is not quite successful, however, since the presentation has gaps.

67. For assessments in Scandinavian languages see Dewailly 1978, Block 1980 and Halse 1983.

68. Cf. Güttgemanns' (1972) programme for a linguistic and literary-critical grounding of New Testament theology. What the resulting product would look like is not yet clear.

69. Kieffer (20) thinks that conventional biblical theologies mix up historical and structural analysis in a methodologically unsound way. A hypothetical line of development is interpreted in terms of value-judgments; e.g. the teachings of Jesus or Paul's doctrine of justification are raised to the status of absolute criteria, in the light of which further development appears a process of degeneration. This critique is justified. It is another matter whether it suffices to render all diachronic study of the theology of the early church suspect.

70. See also e.g. 22. Block 1980, 37, correctly points out that even though the comments on the uncertainty of many hypotheses and the critique of

the exaggerated self-confidence of some scholars are apposite, Kieffer obscures the fact that many hypotheses are the consequence of real problems. Even though lines of development can only be outlined hypothetically, it is 'extremely likely' that 'changes in conceptions' took place during the first explosive period of mission.

71. Dewailly 1978, 137, comments that it is difficult to find out what Kieffer really means by 'main structure and function'; cf. also Halse 1983, 207.

72. In conclusion, in the original Swedish edition Kieffer also draws some 'lines of development in the theology of the New Testament texts' (1977, 209–39). Not until here is the historical Jesus briefly given some attention; thus far Kieffer has, with methodological consistency, only dealt with the images of Jesus in the New Testament. From Jesus he does not, however, move to the theology of the early church or of the Hellenistic churches; instead, he presents rather summary longitudinal sections of 'eschatology', 'christology', 'soteriology and ethics', 'pneumatology' and 'ecclesiology'. The absence of the theme of the law, and of the problem of Israel in general, leaps to the eye. The matter is surely connected with the fact that Kieffer's main interest is directed to themes that have become classical in Christian theology.

In the German version this part is omitted, since it would be of interest more to the professional theologian than to the layman (1987, 25).

73. Cf. Halse 1983, 206. Block compares Kieffer to Goppelt and observes that both have combined 'scientific aspirations with a relatively traditional Christianity' (1980, 38).

74. In fairness to the work it should be noted that it is aimed at being a survey for seminary students, not an original contribution (5). Fuller 1976, 381, is therefore mistaken in his claim that the book is 'expressly designed to provide a conservative evangelical alternative to Bultmann'.

75. For criticisms of this see Hasel 1982, 123f.; Catchpole 1976, 126; Fuller 1976, 384.

76. K. Berger 1988b, 363, speaks of 'modernized fundamentalism'.

77. The internal tension in Ladd's conception which the insertion of this adjective indicates is observed by Hasel 1982, 122. Yet Hasel himself (204–20) also requires biblical theology as a 'historical-theological' discipline.

78. Catchpole 1976, 127, registers disagreement. Ladd states e.g. that the Apocalypse of Baruch 'reflects Jewish hopes for a happy future', whereas the Revelation of John 'forms a conclusion to the entire biblical narrative in which the purposes of God, expressed in the prophets, manifested in the incarnation of Christ, and explained in the epistles, are brought to a consummation' (32). But what prevents one from describing Revelation as a reflection of Christian hopes for a happy future or Baruch as an intended conclusion to the biblical narrative as understood by its author?

79. See Räisänen 1985.

80. He does treat even the letter of Jude in a separate section and still sums up its teaching in his concluding chapter (330).

81. Morris appeals to the fact that 'the church has always given the canonical writings a special place' and that 'it is to these books and no others that Christians refer when they wish to establish authentic Christian teaching' (11). Morris suggests that the book of Revelation is an exception to Wrede's claim that no New Testament writing was written as

canonical (12 n. 11). Even if this were true, it should be a source of embarrassment rather than confirmation for Morris' position, for the canonical status of precisely this book was long disputed. If any writing was finally accepted as canonical on the authority of bishops and theologians, this was. But of course a claim to authority is not identical with canonicity. Still, Wrede's statement should perhaps be modified: accepting the canon without question may amount to placing oneself not so much under the authority of bishops and theologians as under that of developing 'orthodox' practice.

Morris' further claim that 'the church has always regarded the canonical books as "inspired"' (11) is to be rejected, if 'the church' is meant to refer to something that existed in the first century.

82. Part One deals with Paul (the whole corpus!), Part Two with the Synoptic Gospels and Acts (each evangelist receives a separate treatment), Part Three with the Johannine writings (including Revelation), Part Four the catholic epistles (of which each receives a chapter).

3. Singling out the Normative

1. A case could be made that Goppelt's work ought to have been discussed in the previous section of this book. Conversely, it might have been possible to include Kieffer's work (above, pp. 58f.) in the present group.

2. Incidentally, this shows that a thematic treatment of New Testament theology need not of itself lead to harmonization.

3. For Braun, anthropology is the one constant feature in New Testament theology – a view that can be challenged.

4. E.g. Käsemann 1972/73, 241; Lohse 1974, 14; Merk 1980, 465: Braun has given up New Testament theology, unlike Conzelmann, who is said to have elaborated Bultmann's position critically.

5. Goppelt 1981, 269, recognizes Braun's consistency; his assertion that Braun signals the end of an epoch in the history of scholarship (270) may, however, prove premature. In any case it is strange that Goppelt should accuse Braun of 'historicism'.

6. Braun 1962, 243–82; cf. Boers 1979, 80–2, 84. Boers, a pupil of Braun, in essence follows the aims of his teacher, who has carried out the task of a 'pure' biblical theology, although in a way which Gabler could not yet envisage. For an appreciative discussion of Braun's work in the context of New Testament ethics see J. T. Sanders 1975, 23–8.

7. The page numbers refer to the ET of 1969.

8. Conzelmann in particular attacks such historicizing and 'positivistic' tendencies as he detects in recent exegesis (xiii). A main representative of such tendencies is, of all people, another theologically orientated Bultmannian, Ernst Käsemann (compare e.g. the hint on pp. xiii–xiv and the explicit statement on p. 36)!

9. Güttgemanns 1970, 49, seems to have noted the lack of clarity; cf. Morgan 1977, 249 n. 5.

10. That Conzelmann nevertheless does reconstruct the preaching of the historical Jesus when dealing with the Synoptic kerygma (97ff.) – a step regarded as progress beyond Bultmann by Stuhlmacher 1981, 10! – is inconsistent with his programme; cf. Kümmel 1970, 143. In the fourth

edition (1987) Lindemann has tried to move the focal point in the direction of the treatment of the Jesus material in the Gospels.

In the earlier editions Conzelmann dealt with the 'Synoptic kerygma' separately, apart from the rest of the 'kerygma'. Thus he did justice to the fact that the actual teaching of the earthly Jesus is of importance only to part of the New Testament writers. But historically speaking it was odd to separate the 'Synoptic kerygma' from the 'kerygma' of the primitive and the Hellenistic communities. This peculiarity has been corrected in the fourth edition by Lindemann.

11. The title of the first main chapter in the first editions. In the fourth edition of 1987 the section has been entitled 'The Kerygma of the Earliest Community' by Lindemann. There is no change in the substance of the subject-matter.

12. At first (29–32) Conzelmann does make the distinction, but in the actual presentation of the theological views it often plays no part (e.g. as regards the interpretation of Jesus' resurrection and death, 64–71). – Käsemann 1972/73, 241, points out that an early Christian creed as assumed by Conzelmann 'is already excluded by the variety of the existing formulae'.

13. See e.g. 187, 189, 196. In the contrasts set out in I Cor. 15.39ff. 'Paul's real meaning breaks through laborious expedients: the hope of resurrection cannot be reached from an analysis of the nature of man . . .' (189). As regards Romans 5, 'Paul is clear about the boundaries within which myth is capable of a contribution' (196).

14. Fellow scholars are right in pointing out that Conzelmann has failed to draw sufficient conclusions from his own redaction-critical work! Cf. Bouttier 1970, 190.

15. A short survey of the 'theological aspects' of Q is inserted into the 1987 edition by Lindemann (152f.).

16. It is inconsistent with this principle, however, for Strecker to state that in dealing with the Synoptic Gospels, in particular one should take source-critical and traditio-historical questions into account, e.g. the problem of Q (30 with n. 68). Why, if one is to concentrate on the finished products?

17. Käsemann seems to think that Wrede's programme entails the depiction of a unitary, organic development. But as Käsemann himself notes, Wrede was well aware of the gaps in our information. Käsemann asserts that 'the liberal notion of an organic development is now as bankrupt as the idealist unfolding of the divine Spirit in dialectical movement' (238). But it is one thing to believe that there have been 'organic lines of development' (not necessarily just one!); it is another to claim that the lines can be traced on the basis of extant material. Wrede's programme does not require anything like a complete picture of the early Christian religion with no gaps (that would be quite impossible). The real question is, Are we willing to describe early Christianity as a *religion*?

18. In what sense can New Testament theology be a 'historical' discipline and at the same time aim at serving the church? Käsemann talks of a historical task while in the same breath rejecting other positions on purely theological grounds (detaching Jesus from New Testament theology would turn early Christian preaching into ideology; Braun's anthropological interpretation is theologically unacceptable).

19. K. Berger 1988b, 359, speaks of a 'German Lutheran translation of Bultmann'.

20. In spite of that, Lohse by and large shares Bultmann's view of Paul's anthropology, with its merits and its weaknesses (112, 138f.).

21. Lindemann 1975, 47, points out this inconsistency.

22. Beutler 1976, 586f., points out that this solution is grounded in a mere postulate. Little attention is paid to such christological conceptions of the New Testament as do not put great weight on Christ crucified (Q!). K. Berger 1988b, 359 comments: '"Theology of the New Testament" becomes a systematic discipline when it resorts to content-critical judgments to such a degree.'

23. Kümmel 1974, 24, claims that Bultmann excluded Jesus from his theology of the New Testament on theological grounds; yet this decision was also a logical conclusion from Bultmann's definition of 'theology'.

24. Morgan in his review (1974, 650) notes that Kümmel's point is no strong argument for the inclusion of Jesus in New Testament theology; it indicates instead 'how far people's theological interests determine their structures here'. Reicke 1953, 406ff., realizes that a New Testament theology which concentrates on the 'most important authorities' ought to deal with the Synoptics, John, and Paul.

25. But see Morgan 1977, 259 n. 2: 'But why should he draw a line at Paul? And does he find all pre-Pauline theologies equally acceptable?'

26. This is justly criticized by Haufe 1971, 108.

27. It is somewhat strange in this perspective, however, that the Synoptic Gospels are not considered at all in their own right, but only as sources for reconstructing the 'testimony' of Jesus. In practice redaction criticism is altogether missing from the work (Meeks 1975, 299).

28. Morgan 1974, 651, rightly regards Kümmel's 'theological confession' as unsatisfactory.

29. Cf. K. Berger 1988b, 358.

30. Somewhat akin to Kümmel's book is Neill's popular introduction to New Testament theology (1976) in which the author categorically asserts: 'Every theology of the New Testament must be a theology of Jesus – or it is nothing at all' (10). One looks in vain for any grounds for this claim. Neill treats the theology of the early church according to groups of writings. His presentation resembles as much a (popular) introductory work as a theology of the New Testament which would be 'a systematic and ordered presentation of its teaching' (1). Actually Neill's approach is not systematic in the least. In his final chapter he asks the question 'What lies behind it all?' and sketches, as an answer, a picture of the message of the historical Jesus. He does not even attempt to show concretely how the postulated continuity between Jesus and the various groups in the early church should be understood.

31. See e.g. Kümmel's vague section on the pre-existence of Jesus (169–72): this is mythical talk, but it has its roots in a central concern of faith. One must ask whether this concern can be expressed today in another form, but it must not be neglected 'if one tries to understand and maintain Paul's proclamation of Christ in its ultimate significance' (172). Does Kümmel want to have his cake and eat it?

32. The references in what follows are to the ET (1981–82).

33. Hasel 1977, 232, thinks that here Goppelt is breaking new ground.

Actually there is more (though not very much!) of such a dialogue in Schelkle's work.

34. Goppelt points out that salvation history in Cullmann's sense is unknown to the New Testament. For instance, the salvation-historical statements of Romans 4 and 5 cannot be united in one inclusive picture (I, 280).

35. Goppelt's position has justly been called a 'dynamic biblicism': Holtz 1976, 425.

36. It makes itself felt in the comments on the perspectives of I Peter and Revelation which complement each other in polarity: the former summons 'to socio-political responsibility in a pre-Christian world', whereas the latter obligates one to maintain one's confession 'in a post-Christian (!) world that falls under anti-Christian ideology' (II, 196).

37. The vagueness of the expression recalls a similar difficulty in Kümmel, see above n. 31.

38. Reference should be made here to Jeremias' 1971 monograph on Jesus, which he entitled *New Testament Theology, Volume One*. As the book contains no reflection on the place of the preaching of Jesus in a New Testament theology and a second part never appeared, there is no reason to comment on it here except to note that the book is valuable as a classical study on Jesus. Jeremias's results are throughout criticized by Goppelt, often unfairly.

39. Goppelt thinks that although the Jesus tradition was not itself the direct content of missionary or catechetical proclamation, it did constitute its foundation (I, 5f.; this claim is contradicted by the description of the collection and use of the Jesus traditions on II, 28). Lindemann 1975, 49, points out the problematic nature of Goppelt's starting-point. Goppelt presupposes that the community always sought to and was able to distinguish between the words of the earthly Jesus and those of the risen Lord; yet e.g. I Cor. 14.37 (to which Goppelt refers) proves the opposite. Goppelt also stresses that the Jesus tradition was from the first shaped from a retrospective perspective, but this contradicts his earlier claim.

Goppelt's conception is characterized by a tension between two approaches: he wants to start from the New Testament writings on one hand and from a qualified 'salvation-historical' theological overall view (promise and fulfilment, the New Testament seen as the fulfilment of the Old) on the other. The former approach would logically require that he limit himself to the Christ proclaimed (cf. Zahn's insight, above p. 44); the latter naturally also includes the historical Jesus (and John the Baptist), as does any 'historically' orientated conception.

40. The passage on Jesus is not much different from the passage in which Goppelt later (II, 224–27), on the basis of the same verses, describes the theology of Matthew.

41. Kümmel 1976, 313, justly calls attention to an internal discrepancy in Goppelt's view of the eschatology of Jesus.

42. Goppelt would fall under E. P. Sanders's verdict (1985, 278f., 330ff., etc.) of doing theology under a historical guise. Cf. Sanders' note (404 n. 42) on an earlier work of Goppelt's: 'an extreme case of a fairly widespread tendency' to disguise confessions of faith as historical descriptions.

43. Faith comes to light in that a person who turns to Jesus, asking for help in his illness, forgoes self-help. This is a consequence of his having

received the message of the Beatitudes (I, 152f.). But of course any person turning to any miraculous healer expects help from beyond his own resources, and Goppelt does not document the connection with the Beatitudes at all. In the section on Paul Goppelt then claims that the central place of 'faith' in the Hellenistic church was due (apart from the Gentile mission) to the key role that Jesus himself had ascribed to 'faith' (II, 125)!

44. Nevertheless, a critic as sympathetic as Hasel still misses 'an explication of the unity of the New Testament' in Goppelt's work (1977, 233).

45. See e.g. the account of the significance of John the Baptist (I, 33–41, esp. 40f.) – those baptized by John did not really repent, and John's real vocation was that of baptizing Jesus! – or the interpretation of Isa. 53 (I, 198).

46. Despite his critical comments, Kümmel 1976, 315, states that Goppelt's book is 'presently the best and most trustworthy scholarly account of Jesus' proclamation and mission'. Should this statement be true, it says more about the level of Jesus research in the 1970s than about the level of Goppelt's book. K. Berger 1988b, 361, exaggerates a little, but goes in the right direction in assorting Goppelt's work to 'fundamentalistic historical credulity (*Historiengläubigkeit*)'.

4. *The Unrealized Programme of Separate Tasks*

1. By contrast, the Old Testament theology of Gerhard von Rad (1962, 1965) may, albeit contrary to its own express intentions (1962, vi–vii), be conceived as a two-stage project: a tradition-historically constructed history of Israelitic religion, by and large descriptive and empirical (cf. Baumgärtel 1961, 812, 895), is followed by a speculative account of the relation of the two Testaments which resorts to daring typological interpretations.

2. On the Old Testament side note the sharp formulation of the issue by Otto Eissfeldt in 1926. He demanded a sharp distinction between a history of Israelite religion and a theology of the Old Testament. The former is strictly historical study which refrains from absolute value judgments, does not use such concepts as God's word or revelation, pays no attention to the New Testament and leaves open the question whether the New Testament is the fulfilment of the Old. This kind of study can be carried out by representatives of all denominations and even by non-Christians on a common basis. By contrast, 'Old Testament theology' presupposes the concept of revelation. It is a confessional-ecclesiastical testimony, influenced by Christian faith experience, to what the particular denomination of the scholar in question has experienced to be revelation in the Old Testament. Such a theology can only be structured systematically, for 'faith has to do not with the past but with the present and with the timeless' (10f.). – Eissfeldt's dichotomy has been much criticized, but not necessarily on the right score. His description of the historical task is sound (e.g. Eichrodt's critique that Eissfeldt attempts to do a history 'chemically pure of evaluations' [1929, 87f.] distorts the latter's position, for he does speak of the necessity of relative value judgments). It is a weak answer to accuse Eissfeldt of positivism because of his perfectly sound opinion that history

cannot answer questions about absolute value and truth (thus Kraus 1970, 311). In dividing the work of the exegete in two Eissfeldt continues the tradition of Gabler. What is problematic is his unnecessarily denomination-centred conception of the second stage. Even an actualizing biblical theology could be conceived in more open terms.

3. Morgan 1988a, 74f., may be right in stating that 'most (!) modern biblical scholars have separated' historical reconstruction and theological interpretation from each other. It is all the more striking that none of this is evident when one turns to 'New Testament theology'.

4. Bultmann is praised, but Conzelmann is criticized rather harshly for trying to counteract current historicist tendencies with the wrong means: by putting greater weight on historical reconstruction than did Bultmann (392ff.).

5. In particular, Robinson has attempted to free himself from a static perception of the history-of-religions 'backgrounds' of the New Testament (1971, 8ff.).

Goppelt 1981, 271, states that the enterprise of Robinson and Koester means 'in terms of the history of research, a return to the programme of the history-of-religion school'. This is true, but why should it be regarded as a negative development? It was about time to take seriously the unfinished work of the 'school'! Correctly Lüdemann 1984, 117.

6. On Koester's particular contribution see above, 83f.

7. To be precise, he did this in 1977. Whether he still thinks of Strauss as a methodological model in 1988 is less clear.

8. On the material level, Morgan pleads for a relatively traditional theology; theologians are expected to 'articulate and defend the truth of their religion' (1988a, 174). He can state that Bultmann's christology is (just about) acceptable, while Strauss's is not (114f.). Christologies 'from below' are not satisfactory either, as they 'cannot say what Christians have to say about Jesus' (123). And although scripture is not to be confused with revelation, 'the Bible is authoritative for Christians' (194).

9. Cf. the deductive statement 1988a, 280: 'Theologians may, when interpreting the Bible, choose the methods whose corresponding theory offers them the best opportunities for articulating their sense of God.' Yet Morgan also stresses that theological interpreters must allow their underlying theory 'to be scrutinized, and if necessary criticized' (282).

10. Is it simply a question of applying *Sachkritik* in the course of historical work (cf. 1988a, 112f.)? Morgan 1988a largely leaves the impression that he would assign purely historical and theological interpretation of the New Testament to different scholars, the former to 'secular', the latter to 'believing' exegetes. This would be tantamount to taking leave of the vision of (Gabler and) Strauss, which he proposed as a methodological model, in 1977, according to which one and the same person is encouraged to pursue both aims at different times. However, Morgan also suggests (1988a, 180) that even 'secular' scholars need not restrict themselves to historical work, but they can also 'reflect in a disciplined and truth-seeking way upon the whole range of possible contemporary meanings' of their texts. But if a 'secular' scholar proceeds in this way, and if some separation of the tasks is to be upheld, is he not bound to do different things at different stages?

11. Scholars who pursue exegesis and 'content criticism' at one and the

same stage of work are criticized for apologetics – either conservative or progressive apologetics, as the case may be (108f.).

12. This does not mean that interest in exegesis has an antiquarian character. The point is that historical exegesis aims at quite specific statements on the events and experiences of the first century CE, and this goes with an interest on the part of the interpreter in specific issues today (116f.).

13. Somewhat inconsistently he also speaks of different '*New Testament* theologies', which means the theological outlines of the biblical authors (e.g. 1987, 186, 190). Yet his table of contents (201f.) makes clear that the boundaries of the canon play no part, as the Gospel of Thomas (but no other Nag Hammadi texts), the Didache, Barnabas, Ignatius, I and II Clement and Hermas are included.

14. An example: the similarities between Paul and Matthew reflected in the wording of Gal. 1, 15f. and Matt. 16.17 respectively (187).

15. These include not only Jerusalem, Antioch, Corinth, Ephesus and Rome, but also Damascus (where the Johannine writings are located in an attempt to account for the common traditions between Paul and John) and Caesarea Philippi (the location of the Gospel of Mark!).

5. *Some Recent Trends*

1. For a survey of the latest contributions see Merk 1988. His conclusion: 'the project of a "Biblical Theology" is now as before completely open' (37).

2. Cf. Kraus 1970; Reventlow 1986; Oeming 1985. See also the learned but slightly idiosyncratic work of Clavier 1976, which combines a broad history-of-religions perspective with openly Christian apologetics. Clavier is also a true heir of the history-of-religions school in that he finds the centre of New Testament theology (and of the Bible) in the gospel of Jesus, from which other New Testament authors more or less deviate. Paul is singled out for a number of theological criticisms (301f.).

3. See esp. Gese 1981.

4. Stuhlmacher 1981, 136–65. Hübner 1976 also explores the theme of the law in the context of a planned biblical theology. His treatment lacks the apologetic features of Stuhlmacher's presentation; cf. his critical comments on the 'Zion Torah' theory of Gese and Stuhlmacher in Hübner 1981, 3–5. It is too early to assess Hübner's conception of 'biblical theology'. His starting-point is the theological use of the Old Testament made by the New Testament writers (1981, 8; cf. 1988).

5. On the topic of the law see the detailed critique in Räisänen 1986, 337–65; cf. also Kalusche 1986. The following comment by Keck (1964/65, 230), made on Richardson's theology of the New Testament, would apply to Stuhlmacher's approach as well: 'Every biblical student can organize ideas and passages found in the OT in such a way as to build a bridge to the NT. Such constructions reveal the mind of the modern student, but are without value to the historian of early Christian thought unless it can be shown that the NT writers understood these passages in precisely the same way' (230).

6. Cf. the remarks on the history of the influence of the texts above, pp. 103f.

7. In this Stuhlmacher is no different from others at present practising 'biblical theology'. Georgi 1985, 85, is not unjustified in speaking of 'the ahistorical and acritical ventures in that area today'. See also Strecker 1980; Grässer 1980. Oeming 1985 presents useful criticisms of the existing enterprises (on Stuhlmacher see 119ff.), even though he shares the ideal and (aprioristically Christian) starting-point.

8. Dunn 1977a. Cf. K. Berger 1988b, 366: 'Precisely because of its fascinating overall conception, this book seems to me to be one of the most important contributions to New Testament theology in recent decades.'

9. Meeks 1979–80, 118, comments that Dunn 'might have mapped out the logic of his move from descriptive to normative statements more fully', and Hurtado 1979, 137, finds 'a strong "sermonic" intent to the whole treatment', wondering if this intent (that conservatives should be kind to liberals and vice versa) 'has perhaps guided Dunn's discussion too much'.

10. In a later essay, however, Dunn reveals that this is not how he conceives the task of 'New Testament theology'. New Testament theology should be engaged in a dialogue between the first and the twentieth century. Thus it is 'clearly part of dogmatic theology' and 'must be allowed to play its normative role' in those cases where dogmatic theology relates to New Testament issues (1987, 25f.).

11. The difference is that Kümmel is content with finding what unites his principal witnesses (Jesus, Paul and John), whereas Dunn is anxious to find a formula that would cover all New Testament writings and strata.

12. In the year in which the book in question was published, an article from Dunn's pen (1977b) also appeared in a programmatic book by 'conservative evangelicals'.

13. See e.g. Brown 1978; E. Best 1979; T. Best 1979. A negative attitude is shown by the fundamentalist Guthrie (e.g. 1981, 36 n. 53), and by Childs 1984, 29f., who tries in vain to defend his 'canonical' method. Lemcio 1988 argues against Dunn that there is a more comprehensive kerygmatic core common to all major representatives, genres and traditions of the New Testament: a statement about '(1) God who (2) sent (Gospels) or raised (3) Jesus. (4) A response (receiving, repentance, faith) (5) towards God (6) brings benefits (variously described).' I fail to see that this list really covers more than Dunn's formula does. It does point to the theocentric nature of the kerygma, and it calls attention to the response expected of the hearer; Dunn would certainly not disagree with either point.

14. Cf. the analogous tension between 'unitarian' statements and the actual findings in the works of Gulin, Grant, Kümmel and Nikolainen (above, p. 47f., 49, 57f., 70f.).

15. In a later work (1980) Dunn in fact states that 'John abandons any idea of a divine sonship given or enhanced by resurrection and presents Jesus . . . as conscious of his divine pre-existence as Son of God in heaven . . .' (59); 'When John opens the floodgates of his christology of pre-existent sonship it sweeps all before it and leaves no room at all for the earlier stress on Jesus' sonship as an eschatological status and power that opens the way for others to share in' (62). Cf. the critique of Wiles 1982, 94–5: John's 'backward extension of the Son of God language' (Dunn) 'does not simply enhance the status of that language but radically alters it'; 'if personal pre-existence is anything more than a highly pictorial way of saying the same thing as the earlier "impersonal (even if personified)" Wisdom Christologies, then it

cannot coexist with the other christological formulations. It is bound in the long run to distort and to devour them.'

16. Cf. Kubo 1980, 112–13: the earliest Christian community in Jerusalem either met the criteria given by Dunn for the limits of acceptable diversity or did not. 'If it did not, it was heretical from the very beginning; and, if it did, time should not alter its acceptability in the form of Ebionism.'

17. Meeks 1979–80, 117; cf. K. Berger's suspicion (1988b, 366) that the exegetical findings are sacrificed for the benefit of the system. Perrin 1984 also resorts to a rather vague solution: the unifying factor amidst diversity is 'the symbolic figure of Jesus' (423). This is really another way of establishing diversity, and it hardly excludes any known interpretation. For did not even the least 'orthodox' (Christian) Gnostics share 'the symbolic figure of Jesus' with the mainstream church? – For a thorough recent attempt to locate the theological unity in the continuity with the historical Jesus see Thüsing 1981.

18. Koester has here mitigated his earlier demand that the literature of the three first centuries be treated as an inseparable unit (1971, 273). For the problems involved in Koester's historiography see Lüdemann 1984, 118.

19. Cf. Koester's assessment of Bultmann's history-of-religions contribution (1985).

20. See Lüdemann 1984, 116.

21. The demand that a historian must not be content with accumulating 'objective statements about facts' but has to assess the 'theological purpose' and 'the intention of each and every document as part of an ongoing process' (1975, 8) by no means transcends the boundaries of a purely history-of-religions study; Koester actually refers to Baur's *Tendenzkritik*, which is 'not so wrong after all'. By contrast, the idea that the texts must be allowed to 'guide' us and 'critically judge' us and our thoughts (9) is at least so formulated that it suggests a normative biblical theology. Cf. Meeks 1982, 447.

22. Lüdemann 1984, 116, cf. 118.

23. Correctly Lüdemann 1984, 118.

24. See Malherbe 1984, 114.

25. Koester has a 'tendency to date canonical writings late and non-canonical ones early': Malherbe 1984, 114. Thus he dates the Pastorals in 120–160 and Luke's works in 125–135.

26. A similar interest is expressed by K. Berger 1988b, 370 (without reference to Koester's work).

27. Correctly observed by Malherbe 1984, 114.

28. It is condemned rather summarily by Baltzer 1975.

29. Petzke points out that this situation somewhat resembles the situation in which Christianity arose: then, too, Christianity was only one orientation system among many and it was relatively useless to appeal purely formally to *the* god or *the* scripture. Only in the Middle Ages did Christianity become the leading and, later on, the only system of orientation in Europe (5f.).

30. Even critical exegesis, including Bultmann, has fortified itself in an apologetic position. It has replaced the lost authority of the Bible with another entity, variously named, which is beyond the grasp of scientific argument: 'Word of God', 'action of God', 'the Gospel', 'die *Sache*', etc.

Analysis reveals the emptiness of such formulae (9–11). Even history-of-religions study has been pursued with the aim of saving the normative function of the Bible in that its 'unique' features have been absolutized. Yet any religious system, e.g. Islam or Stoicism, has its own unique traits (12).

On the 'heavily apologetic' character of Bultmann's endeavour cf. Georgi 1985, 81. On the impossibility of distilling a *'Sache'* out of the historical material cf. K. Berger 1977, 243, 249ff.

31. Luise Schottroff, another pupil of Braun, pleads for a practical task: biblical study ought to serve 'the liberation of all people into a life in fullness and justice' (1988, 255). Her horizon is that of faith (248) and hope (261) but not of the church, which is an institution open to severe criticism (256f.). The guild of biblical scholars is sternly criticized for legitimating existing power structures with their work. Cf. further Georgi 1985, 87: 'Is not the task of a critical theology, especially one of the New Testament and of the Bible at large, to uncover the suppressive manipulation which a so-called Christian culture, and in particular Christian power structures, have exercised on the tradition which has become ours?'

32. Petzke draws on Habermas and H. Albert in arguing over against Gadamer for a critical stance to tradition (6ff.).

33. The primacy of experience is also emphasized by Patte 1983 in his structural reading of Paul's letters. See above, pp. 134f.

34. For a more detailed evaluation of Johnson's position see above, pp. 127ff.

35. The new concentration on the 'story world' of, say, the Gospel of Mark hardly produces convincing results if it is pursued without taking account of Mark's 'real world'. Contrary to the claims of e.g. Rhoads and Michie (1982), Mark's story world is not a coherent self-contained unity. Rather, it contains tensions (e.g. in its depiction of the disciples) which are explicable only when attention is paid to Mark's real-world concerns. Regardless of whether or not these concerns can appropriately be called 'theological', surely some kind of religious or ideological convictions lie behind them. For criticisms of Rhoads and Michie see Räisänen 1989, ch. 1.

36. This model of three worlds is suggested and elaborated by Syreeni 1989.

Part Three: Outline of a Programme

1. Historical Interpretation: Principles

1. In my discussion 'the church' refers to any Christian denominations which have accepted critical exegesis to some degree.

2. On these different audiences see, although from a different point of view, Tracy 1981, ch. 1. The difference between 'exegesis at the Sorbonne' and 'exegesis in the church' is reflected on by Dreyfus 1975.

3. For a similar claim made for Old Testament theology see e.g. Dentan 1963, 96: Old Testament theology is 'part of the total organism of theological studies', the ultimate purpose of which is 'to prepare men for the Christian ministry' and to contribute 'to the general enlightenment of the Christian community with regard to the faith by which it lives'.

4. Strecker – Schnelle 1988, 159. The authors quote J. A. Bengel's exhortation: *'Te totum applica ad textum, rem totam applica ad te.'*

5. Cf. Barr 1980, 22f.

6. Cf. Dreyfus 1975, 324–8.

7. That is, if one is not financially dependent on acceptance by church authorities or, more subtly, tied to an academic programme exclusively committed to the education of clergy. Regarding the latter point cf. Morgan's comment: 'Until recently most biblical scholars have taught in contexts which required them to relate their rational work to the faith of their religious communities. This remains the case in German and Swiss university theological faculties geared to ministerial training, but elsewhere is now less common' (1988a, 34, cf. 134). It is one of Morgan's main points that this change of working milieu, due for instance to the establishment of Departments of Religion in the USA in secular universities which have no institutional relationship to the churches (1988a, 138), has profoundly affected the nature of biblical studies, bringing about their far-reaching secularization. That next to nothing of this is to be seen in the context of 'New Testament theology' is no doubt related to the fact that the latter is very much a German (and Swiss) affair. But it must not be forgotten that the foundation for an alternative vision was also laid in Germany (Wrede and the history-of-religions school).

8. Of course, in many churches there are both ministers and lay people who are willing to take a broad-minded view of the cognitive side of their religion; there is no hard-and-fast boundary between a church and the rest of society nor is it fair to speak of a unified church point of view. From the viewpoint of official church doctrine, and from that of the mass of believers, however, an exclusive dogmatic stance is a reality. Bowden (1988, xiv-xv) is not alone in observing that 'the level of theological and historical knowledge and insight has . . . fallen appallingly' in the churches in which a 'flood of anti-intellectualism . . . seems to be rushing up to engulf us all'.

9. Of course, abandonment of a church orientation in itself by no means guarantees that one's research is not affected by pressure from the outside. It is perfectly possible that it will be vitiated by political or commercial or even by ideologically anti-religious influences and that these influences will be even more harmful than church ones would have been. Whatever his frame of reference, the scholar must be on his guard to preserve his independence.

10. This decision has, of course, nothing to do with a desire to legitimate the existing social order of the society. Self-evidently, 'serving' means critical services.

11. To be sure the situation is more complicated, for even in a state university many, perhaps most, people study exegesis in order to become ministers in a church. This is certainly the case in my own country. In an exegetical class the teacher has to pay pedagogical or even therapeutic attention to the present mental and social situation of his pupils, and a wise pedagogue will probably try to avoid a head-on clash. In practice, then, compromises are hard to avoid. But it is imperative not to confuse pastoral strategy with ultimate aims. It is my experience, and that of some colleagues as well, that exegetical insights can be mediated in a more relaxed spirit in educated lay circles than among undergraduate theological students.

12. Cf. Fiorenza 1988 on the [hoped-for] public character of biblical study;

also Theissen 1979, 10f.

13. To give one instance, some years ago I participated in a meeting, called by the Archbishop of Finland, in which university theologians discussed the 'biblical question' with bishops and diocesan educators. I read a paper on unity and diversity in the New Testament, in which I presented James Dunn's work to the audience in some detail (not least because Dunn cannot be written off as a 'radical' by any church authority, but must be taken seriously by them precisely as an exegete with pronounced church concerns). I limited my discussion (mostly) to canonical texts, assumed that the New Testament is in some sense normative for the church and tried to drive home the question, 'What should the church learn from the undeniable theological diversity in this canon?' I did *not* suggest a direct answer (only the vague one that some kind of pluralism must follow), as I think that that is not the business of the exegete, but tried to specify some issues which would have to be faced if church leaders really take modern biblical study as seriously as they assert they are doing. (The paper is published in Finnish in *TAik* 91, 1986, 193–204; some of its contents are summarized above, pp. 81–3).

14. Cf. Küng 1987, xiii–xix, esp. xiv; Wilson 1982, 347ff.

15. Küng 1987, 441; see his chapter 'No World Peace Without Religious Peace' (440–3) as a whole. Cf. Kaufman, 1988, 4, 13f.

16. The problem lies 'in the tension between the precritical understanding of the Bible so deeply embedded in the Christian tradition and the demands of truth in the modern academic world': Bowden 1988, 3.

17. Cf. Kaufman 1981, 202: when talking to 'outsiders', are we interested in conversion or in 'open-ended dialogue on equal terms with other partners'?

18. See also Oeming's comments on Gerhard von Rad's 'inner tragedy' between the Scylla of historical-critical exegesis and the Charybdis of the pious confession which contributes to the vagueness of his central concepts (1985, 73). Oeming (128) feels that the tragedy reaches its consummation in Stuhlmacher.

19. J. T. Sanders 1975, 129, rightly notes (in an epilogue to a work characterized by largely 'negative' results regarding the applicability of New Testament ethics) that 'studies in controversial areas should not be undertaken – or published – only when they are affirmative!' He rightly refers to Albert Schweitzer's 'negative' classic (Schweitzer [3]1954).

20. On Galileo see Scholder 1966, 71–78.

21. For instance, some 90% of the Finnish population belong to the Lutheran church of the country; and even of the rest, many belong to one religious denomination or other. Such figures however, hardly give a correct idea of the actual (lack of) significance of confessional Christianity in the country. Cf. Bowden 1988, xv, on the situation in England ('the churches in England have never been numerically so weak'; 'recent statistics indicate an active membership in the Church of England of about 3% of the population').

22. Lindbeck 1984, 22.

23. Cf. Luz 1985, 19: half a century ago the classical reader, for whom commentaries were written, was the minister engaged in a scholarly preparation of his sermon. However, this situation no longer exists; times have changed even in the church.

24. Cf. Morgan's reference to 'a European butter mountain of research out of all proportion to its religious usefulness' (1988a, 117).

25. Again, it should be stressed that no hard-and-fast line can be drawn between a societal and an ecclesial way of framing the task. Even in a church context, clarification of the identity of the members (as distinct from preaching) is a most important task. Petzke (1975, 18) raises a pertinent question in asking whether the Christian religion is really irreversibly 'thrown upon this one form of proclamation (preaching) which arose in the social situation of antiquity'. Even in a church setting alternative forms of (group) communication may contain a greater promise. From an exegetical point of view the development of 'bibliodrama' commands great interest. Cf. Kiehn et al. 1987 (in particular the contributions of Laeuchli and Spiegel; Schramm's article on the relation between exegesis and bibliodrama draws on Stuhlmacher's hermeneutic and shares the problematical features of the latter); Laeuchli 1987.

26. Frye 1982, xviii.

27. Cf. Theissen 1979, 11.

28. Cf. Küng 1987, xix.

29. Cf. Schottroff's (1988, 248f.) remarks on Bultmann's and Braun's devaluing reading of Gnostic texts.

30. Cf. P. Berger's comments on the necessity of a global perspective (above, 124). Scroggs 1988, 26, who rejects a purely humanistic interpretation of the Bible comments: 'Here the sense of liberation is dizzying. Gone are the shackles of the Church once and for all. Gadamer's judgment that the text makes a truth claim can still be honoured and yet ignored, for the claim it makes is no more ultimate than that of the Quran or the Upanishads. Aesthetic appreciation has replaced the concern for a claim upon our lives.' But this is precisely the question: Why should the truth claim of the Qur'an be any less 'ultimate' than that of the Bible? Why is it only the truth-claim of our own tradition that ought to be 'honoured'?

31. A scholarly contest is at present going on in connection with my attempt to expose the weaknesses of Paul's arguments concerning the law (Räisänen 1987a). For a balanced discussion see Westerholm 1988.

32. Opinions will differ, of course, as to how much similarity is really possible, given the temporal and cultural gap (cf. Nineham 1976). On one view, the non-occurrence of the parousia alone has rendered the modern situation decisively different from that of the earliest Jesus movement (although not necessarily from that of subsequent generations). On an existentialist view the gap will seem smaller.

33. Morgan 1973, 3, justifiably criticizes Wrede's claim that the concepts of canon and inspiration belong inseparably together. He also rejects the claim that to recognize the concept of canon is to submit to the church and theological authorities of the early centuries; yet he allows Wrede's main point that 'the dogmatic category of the canon must not be allowed to influence a historical account of early Christianity'.

34. Stendahl, Robinson, Schlier (54, 74f.); emphatically also Perrin 1984, 415. See also Reicke 1953, 403–5; Pannenberg 1976, 375. Morgan (1977, 26off.) and Perrin (1984, 415) argue that *both* tasks should be adhered to, but in different connections; likewise Reicke 1953, 403.

35. Cf. K. Berger 1988a, 41: attempts to found 'biblical theology' in purely philological terms are ridiculous.

36. K. Berger 1987, 196, also wishes to include the 'positions of the opponents in New Testament congregations' in his overall picture. He suggests that some New Testament authors can be seen as the opponents of others: in his view, the opponents attacked by Colossians and the Pastorals are close to the position of the author of Revelation; the opponents assaulted in Jude and II Peter resemble the bearers of the Johannine epistles.

37. This orientation will have drastic results in a history of Israelite religion as contrasted with a 'normative' theology of the Old Testament. 'A history of religion would be as interested in the prophets which the biblical traditions now condemn as in those whom the traditions now canonize', Hayes-Prussner 1985, 267.

38. Regarding 'inspiration', this much was already claimed by Gabler (above, p. 4). Harnack correctly maintained against Barth that the concept of revelation is not a scientific concept (1962, 346).

However, even Bultmann freely used the concept of 'revelation'; cf. Bultmann 1984, ch. 4. On the other hand, Morgan 1987a, 166, observes that 'most biblical scholars today are silent about revelation' and this is because of 'genuine perplexity'. The observation is probably accurate as regards everyday exegesis, but it definitely does not pertain to syntheses of and general statements on 'New Testament theology' which display little perplexity on this score.

39. Under this heading, many issues will have to be dealt with which do not normally turn up when exegetes discuss 'revelation': e.g. dreams, visions and journeys to heaven.

40. E.g. Hasel 1982, 218, claims that 'the final aim of NT theology is to demonstrate the unity that binds together the various theologies and longitudinal themes, concepts, and motifs'. Cf. Strecker 1983, 118: 'New Testament theology' deals with the question of unity of the theology in the New Testament. Perrin 1984, 415: 'If we are to achieve a theology of the New Testament, we must first find a motif, a theme, a factor by means of which we can identify a unity within the diversity.'

41. K. Berger 1987, 188ff., does ask the question in a strictly historical framework (see above, 79). But then he does not in any way attempt to establish unity in terms of common theological convictions, but wishes to trace the ramification of the early Christian tradition. He finds a series of common elements which can be called 'characteristically Christian' (199); yet these elements have been interpreted in different ways in different cases.

42. Not surprisingly, many of the answers given are quite abstract (Dunn, Perrin, and even Schelkle: above, p. 55).

43. In my account of the history of 'New Testament theology' I had reason to note that in these syntheses an essential unity was often asserted without any attempt to explain the apparent diversity; cf. Gulin, Grant, Nikolainen. In the last two cases the discrepancy between the assertion of unity and the actual findings of the exegete was especially striking.

44. Kaftan (above, p. 28); cf. also Goppelt (above, p. 72). Cf. the apologetic use of the history of influence by Stuhlmacher (above, p. 81).

45. Cf. K. Berger 1977, 106.

46. Johnson 1986, 1–2, also thinks that the impact of the New Testament writings, 'disproportionate to their size or claims', justifies their separate study. But it is out of the question that, say, the Gospel of Mark has had an

impact on the basis of such literary merits as are discovered in it by Johnson (147–72) – supposing it had any impact at all between the second and the nineteenth century.

47. Quoted by Holtzmann 1911, II, 173 n. 4. Holtzmann states that nothing Paul wrote has had 'as interesting a history' as Rom. 13.1–7, in which politicians operating with religious motives have often found 'the contents of the whole Gospel, indeed of all religion' (173).

48. P. Berger 1969, 113, with reference to Max Weber. As a random example of ironic effects from outside the biblical area consider the history of the influence of Virgil's Fourth Eclogue (written in honour of Augustus), because of which Dante paid to Virgil the salute 'through you I became a poet, through you a Christian' (*Purgatorio* 22)!

49. Still another feature of the situation is that some non-Christian texts have exerted a greater influence on theology than many canonical ones, e.g. Plato's *Timaeus*.

50. This is seen by Petzke (above, p. 86). A new allocation of space is practised by Koester (above, p. 84).

51. Cf. Küng's justification of his concentration on ideas in the interreligious dialogue (1987, xix): 'In this process we must concentrate in the first instance on ideas, teachings, doctrines . . . without mistaking the fact that religion is more than ideas. And yet, religious practices are often not the factor that divides religions . . . but the ideas, teachings, dogmas, and everything that follows from them.' To be sure, one might argue that in the process in which Christianity emerged from Judaism and was eventually separated from the mother religion, precisely 'religious practices' (circumcision, table-fellowship) were a decisive dividing factor. But the most important thing after all, was not the practices as such, but the meaning accorded to them within the different systems of orientation.

52. Johnson, in giving his grounds for rejecting a historical model of interpretation, states that the historical model has been unable to deal with the religious contents of its sources 'except in a comparative, developmental, or theological fashion'. Historians have 'shied away . . . from asking what sort of religious experience gave rise to the Christian movement and motivated the writings that now interpret it' (1986, 11). But there is no reason why historical study which uses early Christian writings for purposes of reconstruction (rather than for a literary analysis) could not in principle focus on experience, and in fact the history-of-religions school did just that.

53. Barr 1980, 24.

54. I am here following Kari Syreeni's description of a controlled process of understanding in a Finnish article (*TAik* 93, 1988, 25f.). In some respects, this comes close to K. Berger's views (above, p. 78).

55. Fiorenza 1988, 14. Dentan 1963, 23, is right in contending that 'every subsequent attempt to obscure the distinction which Gabler made (sc. between biblical and dogmatic theology) has resulted only in confusion in both fields'.

56. Cf. Meeks' comment on Koester's way of combining a theological viewpoint with historical work (1982, 448): '. . . as a church theologian as well as a historian he is obliged to make some theologically critical judgments – about what ought to be as well as what has been. A less faithful or more cautious historian would have avoided the problem by leaving such

questions to the systematic theologian. Ironically that might have produced a history that would be more useful to the theologian, by avoiding certain confusions of categories . . . There is no direct line between was and ought.' Rudolph (1970, 184) has an analogous comment on the relation of comparative religion to theology: 'Only a "non-theological" science of religion is able to provide theology with unadulterated results of history-of-religions research that have not been filtered through theologizing or cryptotheological prejudices.' (The latter refers to the work of such scholars of religion as Heiler and van der Leeuw.)

57. Bultmann 1955, 251; Merk, 1972, passim.

58. Correctly Morgan 1977, 261.

59. Räisänen 1987a, 2; cf. xv–xvi with n. 18.

60. Räisänen 1987a, 264–9.

61. E.g. Schlier (above, p. 54) spells out the fact that faith postulates a necessary unity behind the historical diversity. This faith (or belief) is indeed manifest in recent 'New Testament theologies'. Only the syntheses born within the Bultmann school are not liable to forced harmonizing, although even these scholars emphasize the necessity of 'faith' on the part of the scholar.

62. For Richardson, Bultmann, a stern defender of a faith-approach in exegesis, is the arch-heretic (so is Barth, for that matter).

63. Cf. Strecker 1975, 25.

64. Baird 1971, 57.

65. Cf. Baird 1971, 57: 'If the historian of religions is ever to reach the goal of "understanding" other religions, belief must not be a desideratum. Otherwise one could only understand as many forms of religion as he could simultaneously believe.' Morgan points out that the assertion that unbelievers cannot understand religion and theology well enough to write its history is ungrounded and potentially obscurantist and can be challenged by plenty of counter-evidence from 'history of religions' study (1977, 250). Correctly also Cullmann 1967, 73; Theissen 1979, 11.

66. For a specimen of an outstanding contribution by a professedly (if posthumously!) non-believing scholar consider the work of Franz Overbeck.

67. Cf. Kaftan (above, pp. 27f.): whenever the interpreter's personal interest in the concern of the Bible lures him to read texts in a strained way this is detrimental. Witness the works of Richardson or Guthrie, and many others!

68. Contrast J. Weiss's careful distinction between what was central to Jesus himself and what is important to Weiss as a modern person (above, p. 23). Cullmann's criticism of the existentialist theologians (above, pp. 51f.) is also pertinent here.

69. The point is well made and illustrated with interesting examples by K. Berger 1988a, 168–170.

70. Even more so Schlatter's claim that the interpreter's own faith is the presupposition of true objectivity (above, p. 25)!

71. On Bultmann's view of Judaism see e.g. Sanders 1977, 43–7.

72. K. Berger 1988a, 144ff., argues convincingly that, contrary to a current view, no meaningful distinction can be made between 'explanation' and 'understanding' in textual work.

73. Cf. Dentan's claim (1963, 116) that the author of an Old Testament

theology should in some way share the Old Testament faith', or even 'the (!) biblical faith', in conjunction with his definition of Old Testament theology as a 'Christian theological discipline' (122). Westermann's *Elements* (1982) is still completely silent on Judaism! Cf. Levenson 1985, 1–2: 'The sad fact . . . is that the endeavour known as "Old Testament theology" has been, as its name suggests, an almost exclusively Gentile affair. Indeed, its evaluation of the central institutions of ancient Israel does not depart in substance from those provided by the premodern Christian tradition. It is as though the historical-critical methods have yet to take deep root. Pockets of old bias remain untouched.' For signs of a change cf. R. E. Clements, 1978 (unfortunately not available to me); Hayes-Prussner *Old Testament Theology* 1985, 251–2, 279.

74. Stendahl 1984, 22. Cf. Baird 1971, 59: it is our statements that are on trial and not the degree of empathy; Barr 1983, 112: 'What is generally meant, when people speak about presuppositions, is that they want deductive considerations . . .'

75. It is made by K. Berger 1988a, 186–8.

76. K. Berger 1988a, 187.

77. See K. Berger 1988a, 188.

78. Presumably consistency would further dictate the use of the Septuagint rather than the Hebrew Bible (cf. Hübner 1988, 155ff.).

79. It is appropriate to deal with 'early Christianity' as 'the most important Messianic sect of Judaism' (the subtitle of Rowland 1987).

80. Cf. M. Smith 1971; Barker 1987.

81. Cf. Lemche 1988.

82. Even Koester in his great work (1982) stopped in the mid-second century, although in his programmatic declaration (1971) he had required that the first three centuries be included in a history of early Christian literature.

83. Cf. Käsemann 1972/73, 243.

84. Cf. Perrin 1984, 417–19.

85. Thus also Schlier in his pointedly church-orientated reflections (above, p. 54); recently also the conservative theologian Morris.

86. Perrin 1984, 418.

87. Similarly Dreyfus 1975, 338f., 351f.

88. Recent studies (such as Uro 1987) have confirmed the view that a particular group with a distinct theological outlook is to be discerned behind 'Q' (which is not 'only what you make it').

Koester (above, p. 83) also treats e.g. the Synoptic apocalypse and the parable chapter Mark 4.1–34 as independent documents. Such a procedure is appropriate, if there are sufficient literary-critical indications to make the hypothesis of an independent source plausible (in this case, the Synoptic apocalypse has a higher claim to independent treatment than has Mark's collection of parables).

89. Correctly Strecker (above, p. 66); Morgan 1987b, 202f.

90. Strecker 1975, 29. His more dubious reasons include a reference to the outstanding position of Paul in the canon and to his significance for the church of the Reformation.

91. Cf. also Grant (above, p. 49). Burrows' 1946 thematic outline of biblical theology was not available to me. See on it Hayes-Prussner 1985, 192–5.

92. Cf. the reflections of the young Bultmann (1911/12, 436–7) in favour of

a thematic organization. Bultmann's reason then was that the aim of a theology of the New Testament is not to understand the person of Jesus or of Paul, but that which is characteristic of the new religion. Still, Bultmann also ponders the possibility of devoting a separate treatment to Jesus, Paul, and perhaps John, 'since in them stages of the historical development find their expression' (436). This, of course, is what Bultmann actually did decades later.

93. As noted above (78f.), K. Berger is currently working on a history of early Christian theology from a tradition-historical point of view.

94. Wrede pointed out that only a few individuals should be singled out of the mass of early Christians because of their intrinsic importance; his choice included Jesus, Paul, John and Ignatius. But if the history of influence is any guide, Matthew and Luke (the latter especially as the author of Acts) deserve special attention (more so than Ignatius), as does the author of the Pastoral letters (cf. Petzke). And perhaps Irenaeus should move up in the ranking list too?

95. This is stressed by Grant 1950, 22 (above, p. 49): to describe the rise of Christian doctrine satisfactorily one would probably need ten times more material than the five hundred pages of the New Testament!

96. Koester 1982 organizes the latter part of his work (chs. 10–12) geographically; K. Berger intends to follow a similar line even more intensively (1987, 197f.).

97. 'We cannot write a theology of Peter or James or even of Paul, for in no case do we have sufficient material, or even an indication that the writer is giving us what he sees as most important in Christian theology. They are all occasional writings. But these writings are theologically informed, and we do well to take seriously the ideas expressed or implied in them', Morris 1986, 11.

98. K. Berger (above, p. 79) may be overly optimistic in this regard.

99. For my own picture see Räisänen 1986, 242–306, where much literature is also given and various alternatives are discussed.

100. Consider Bultmann's discussion of pre-Pauline Hellenistic Christianity, largely gleaned from late sources.

101. So, in various ways, Koester (above, pp. 83f.) and Johnson (pp. 86f.).

102. Cf. Riesenfeld 1957, 1261. In Old Testament theology, Eichrodt's thematic structuring of his work had as its consequence that 'although he gave some lip service to historical development and historical change, the body of his discussion does not often pay attention to this historical perspective' (Hayes-Prussner 1985, 183).

103. For an example see my discussion of the various views of the law in Räisänen 1987a, ch. vi.

104. Nor with the creation, as Schelkle does.

105. Käsemann 1972/73, 243f., considers eschatology and christology as possible starting-points, opting for the latter.

106. Cf. Kaftan, Grant.

107. This course is taken by Rowland in his original and in many ways valuable text book *Christian Origins* (1987).

108. The late place allotted to christology stems from the understanding that Jesus was important above all because of his position as the eschatological bringer of salvation, but this belongs primarily to 'eschatology' and is to be discussed there. The subsequent elaboration of ideas

concerning Jesus' identity largely belong to a later, reflective stage.

109. Again, the position of the section presupposes a certain understanding of its contents: the radical view of the human condition, often taken to be Paul's decisive contribution, ought to be seen rather as a secondary ideological conclusion, an inference 'from the solution to the plight' (E. P. Sanders 1977, 474f., etc.).

110. Cf. Hellholm 1989 and the literature cited there; Rowland 1985.

111. Cf. Watson's question at the end of his study (1986, 180f.): can Paul 'still be seen as the bearer of a message with profound universal significance? Facing this question will mean that the permanent, normative value of Paul's theology will not simply be assumed, as is often the case at present. It must instead be discussed – and with genuine arguments . . .'. See also Wilson 1982, 347–51; J. T. Sanders 1975, 66.

112. So far only tenuously visible in Conzelmann's and Nikolainen's works.

113. See Malina 1983.

2. Historical Interpretation: A Model

1. On Schleirmacher see Gerrish 1984.

2. Schleiermacher 1958, 238, cf. 240.

3. It returned in due time. Discussing what he calls 'experiential-expressivism', Lindbeck 1984 can comment that it is 'pervasive in contemporary theology', albeit in a Christianized form that presupposes that 'the objectivities of at least biblical religions are not simply the expressive symbolizations of experience but have also another source in God's revelatory will' (31f.). It is all the more striking that programmatic syntheses centred on experience have been almost totally missing in biblical study since the 1920s.

4. On Otto's thought see Almond 1984.

5. Cf. the work of Grant (p. 48).

6. Notably 1970 and 1980. For discussions of Berger's theological contribution see the symposium on *The Heretical Imperative* in *Journal for the Scientific Study of Religion* 20, 1981, 181–96; Wuthnow et al. 1984; Hunter – Ainlay (ed.) 1986, esp. the articles by Wuthnow and Hammond.

7. Cf. Berger 1980, 59: 'The relativizations of modernity are irresistible if religion is taken as nothing but a body of theoretical propositions.'

8. The validity of this statement hinges on the criteria used to define a core experience. According to Hay 1988, polls indicate that the majority of Western adults have had a 'religious experience'; these would, in Berger's estimation, obviously fall into the category of fugitive intimations.

9. Berger distinguishes between the experience of the supernatural and the experience of the sacred, of which the former is the more fundamental. 'Originally, the sacred was a manifestation within the reality of the supernatural.' Subsequently, the sacred has been 'detached from its original supernatural matrix', so that even 'emancipated' modern man 'is capable of standing in such awe of mundane entities conceived as sacred . . . that the reality of ordinary life seems to him to have been breached' (42f.).

10. Berger has been criticized, not without reason, for privatizing religion: McCann 1981, 215f.

11. E.g. 1979, xv.

12. Eliade tries, in the last analysis, to fuse together religion and its study. Like Otto, he emphasizes eclectically a certain type of experience at the cost of others. His 'models of genuine existence' stem largely from India, non-literary cultures and folk belief. His account of the history of religions (1979–82), while instructive, is also highly selective. When Eliade deals with the history of Israelite religion, he never once refers to Deuteronomy or the Deuteronomic history (in which many find the centre of Old Testament theology). In his presentation of Paul, 'faith' is once briefly mentioned, while 'justification' never puts in an appearance.

For a sympathetic discussion of Eliade's contribution see e.g. Barbosa da Silva 1982. For a devastating critique of Eliade's interpretation of religion in archaic cultures see, however, Saliba 1976, 99–141.

13. In his search for 'signals of transcendence' Berger does at first pay considerable attention to everyday experience and behaviour, and to tragical events that raise 'Why?' questions on the fringes of everyday reality (1970, 52ff.). Gradually, however, everyday reality fades out of sight in his discussion of the essence of religion.

14. Eliade 1954, 102–12, does emphasize that Judaism (and consequently Christianity) differs from other religions in relation to history. Still, he regards even the Jewish attitude as fundamentally 'antihistorical'; a Jew endures history only in the hope that it will one day come to an end. But this is a misunderstanding (typical of Eliade's levelling of the differences between religious traditions). What a (typical) Jew hopes is that the course of history will one day be *changed*.

15. For an illuminating new study of religious experience see Batson-Ventis 1982. The authors follow James in focusing on 'the most dramatic and intense experiences' (56). But the existence of source-critical problems is obvious, as they include Luke's Paul (Acts 9), Augustine (on whom see Fredriksen 1986) and even Moses and his burning bush in their gallery of witnesses (57f.).

16. In the Old Testament some experiences of the prophets, notably the call vision of Isaiah, fall into this category.

17. Johnson, 100f., admits that the interpretation of the experienced power as the power of the *Holy Spirit* presupposes a certain linguistic tradition. That this is similarly the case with the interpretation of a certain experience as a resurrection experience does not become so clear to Johnson's reader.

18. See Marxsen 1968, 42f. As Jesus' followers shared an apocalyptic symbolic world with their environment, Johnson's assertion that their confession to the risen Lord was 'no less scandalous' in their world than in ours (108) is wrong. The confession may have been absurd to the ears of a Stoic or an Epicurean audience, but not at all in a Jewish environment. Cf. Stendahl 1984, 43, 198.

19. It is unfortunate that the English language lacks this means of differentiating between diverse 'experiences'.

20. Cf. Lindbeck's (1984) criticisms of what he calls the 'experiential-expressive model' of understanding religion in his ch. 2. Lindbeck argues instead for a 'cultural-linguistic' model which does not neglect the role of experience but inverts the order of inner and outer and derives the experience from the cultural-linguistic system (the symbolic world) rather

than vice versa. For the alleged unity of the inner experience of God see esp. 39–41. In many cases, different religions seem 'to produce fundamentally divergent depth experiences of what it is to be human' (41).

21. It has often been pointed out that Eliade's 'transhistorical' religious structures express an ontological (or theological, if you like) postulate and would belong to a second stage of work in historically orientated research; e.g. Baird 1971, 74–91.

22. Thus Schillebeeckx 1980 describes the theology of the New Testament as a theology of experiencing grace.

23. See Batson-Ventis 1982, esp. 56–96.

24. That the concept of 'religion' (in the singular!) is a metaphysical-theological abstraction is argued by Rudolph, e.g. 1967, 32. A historian does not know 'religion' in itself, only concrete religions (in the plural). W. C. Smith (e.g. 1964) goes even farther, emphasizing that even to talk of individual 'religions' amounts to operating with abstractions. What is called religion consists of an interplay between cumulative traditions and personal faith (I would rather say: of personal affirmation of a tradition).

25. P. Berger 1980, 30.

26. Cf. Geertz 1975, 140.

27. On the 'symbolic universe' see Berger-Luckmann 1967; P. Berger 1969, esp. 13–37; Johnson 1986, 11–18; Hargrove 1984. The word 'symbolic' refers to realities other than those of everyday experience (Berger-Luckmann 1967, 113). Other terms are used as well: 'system of orientation' (see Petzke 1975, 3); 'mythical universe' (Frye 1982, xviii: a body of assumptions and beliefs developed from man's existential concerns). (From Berger's and Luckmann's point of view, a 'mythical universe' is one particular type of symbolic universe.) Geertz's formulation is that 'man is an animal suspended in webs of significance he himself has spun' (1975, 5).

28. Johnson 1986, 13.

29. Wuthnow 1984, 124, discussing the contribution of Berger. See also Schillebeeckx 1980, 30–9. On the concept of 'experience' in general see e.g. Schäffer 1983, 47–118; Lange 1984.

30. Cf. Lindbeck 1984, 32–41, drawing on Chomsky and Geertz.

31. P. Berger 1969, 38.

32. The symbolic world may not in itself be coherent at all points, either. As it consists of layers from different periods of time, parts of it may well seem to critical reflection an 'inherited conglomerate' of which it is hard to make sense in rational terms. The term, coined by Gilbert Murray, was used by Dodds 1951, 179 (and elsewhere), to characterize e.g. Greek conceptions of the soul. 'A new belief-pattern very seldom effaces completely the pattern that was there before: either the old lives on as an element in the new – sometimes an unconfessed and half-conscious element – or else the two persist side by side, logically incompatible, but contemporaneously accepted by different individuals or even by the same individual.' Dodds goes on to say of the pictures of the soul that 'you could take some of them seriously, or more than one, or even all, since there was no Established Church to assure you that this was true and the other false'. But of course logically incompatible ideas are fully capable of persisting in the doctrine of such a church as well!

33. On this score Lindbeck 1984, who on the whole provides a healthy

corrective to a model like that of Berger or Eliade, seems to give an oversimplified account. According to him, religious change does not proceed from new experiences, but results 'from the interactions of a cultural-linguistic system with changing situations'. 'Religious experiences in the sense of feelings, sentiments, or emotions . . . result from the new conceptual patterns instead of being their source.' Thus, 'Luther did not invent his doctrine of justification by faith because he had a tower experience, but rather the tower experience was made possible by his discovering (or thinking he discovered) the doctrine in the Bible' (39), so that 'the core of Luther's reformatory breakthrough was an exegetical insight' (45 n. 21). 'Experience' seems to mean just the alleged religious core experience, i.e. feelings and the like, in Lindbeck's vocabulary. But in addition to *Erlebnisse, Erfahrungen* have also to be taken into account, and this leads to a more nuanced picture. We also have to ask why it was that Luther came to his novel 'exegetical insight'. Was this not due to a series of experiences that made him dissatisfied with previous interpretations?

34. On legitimation with special regard to Luke–Acts see Esler 1987, 16–23, and passim.

35. Of course the possibility of an experienced 'journey to heaven' is likely in some cases, but hardly in all.

36. It does not matter here that a great deal of the account must be ascribed to Luke's rewriting of history. No matter what the historical Peter did and thought, the point is that such a reconstruction made sense to Luke. Moreover, even though Peter's encounter with Cornelius (if it ever happened) was not such a turning-point as Luke claims it to have been, there must have been other cases in which a comparable 'experiential logic' was decisive.

37. Just consider Paul's claim that 'we are the (true) circumcision' in Phil. 3.2; or his assertion that circumcision or non-circumcision are irrelevant matters (I Cor. 7.19).

38. Nineham 1976, 184.

39. A similar explanation was given for the fall of Jerusalem in 70 CE. 'No generation in the history of Jewry has been so roundly, universally condemned by posterity as that of Yohanan ben Zakkai [both by Christians and by Jews] . . . This was supposed to be a sinning generation. – It was *not* a sinning generation, but one deeply faithful to the covenant and to the Scripture. . . , perhaps more so than many who have since condemned it. First-century Israelites sinned only by their failure. Had they overcome Rome, even in the circles of the rabbis they would have found high praise . . . Since they lost, later generations looked for their sins, for none could believe that the omnipotent God would permit his Temple to be destroyed for no reason. As after 586 BCE, so after 70 CE the alternative was this: "Either our fathers greatly sinned, or God is not just." The choice thus represented no choice at all', Neusner 1984, 20.

40. Cf. Johnson 1986, 50.

41. See Räisänen 1987b and 1988.

42. I am not suggesting that there was one 'Jewish' symbolic world shared by all Jews. Careful attention must be paid here to the actual diversity between different forms of Jewish religion.

43. Patte resorts to conventional systematization (albeit with unconven-

tional results) in order to harmonize Paul's different notions with one another (e.g. in Romans 9–11), above all on the level of ideas. While the experience of the believers is appropriately stressed, it is interpreted in a somewhat strange way as a repetition of Christ's experience (e.g. 134).

44. Moreover, contrary to Patte, it must be realized that even fundamental convictions can contradict each other logically. Patte disposes of contradictions in Paul by distinguishing between convictional logic and argumentative logic. Apparently contradictory statements occur when these two kinds of logic clash with each other. According to Patte there is no real contradiction if one statement belongs to the realm of convictional logic and the other one to that of argumentative logic. But this is too easy a way out of Paul's difficulties. Paul can have 'conflicting convictions' (which surface e.g. in Romans 9–11, as I have argued: see above, n. 41). And surely he would have thought that even his convictions make sense in argumentative terms.

45. It seems that Patte would read things *vice versa* at this point!

46. These include the notion of biblical inerrancy held by numerous Christians, or the view of many Muslims that Muhammad was totally ignorant of Jesus or Abraham when the revelation came to him. But they also include the much more sophisticated Christian theological idea of revelation through history which is inevitably affected by profane historical criticism of the 'acts of God' described in the Bible (Exodus, the sack of Jericho, etc.). Cf. Gilkey 1961.

47. In this sense it is incorrect to claim that the New Testament writings 'must be approached as much as possible on their own terms' (Johnson 1986, 5). It is simply not the case that (scholarly) readers must 'adjust their questions' to the texts; on the contrary, *all* sorts of questions are allowed and desirable to get as full a picture as possible.

48. Cf. Theissen 1979, 14f.; P. Berger 1980, 82: the compelling force of the experiences of the first Christians necessarily made them feel that there is no salvation except in Christ (Acts 4.12). But again Berger wisely emphasizes the distinction between experience and its interpretation. 'No hierophanic experience must be taken in isolation, as if there had never been any other', for the experience of the sacred intoxicates. The religious experiences of mankind neutralize themselves, as it were, on the level of interpretation; no *single* experience can be provided with such emphasis as the person in question claims. Yet Berger's emphasis on experience is here, too, one-sided. For undoubtedly one reason why the first Christians ascribed global significance to their experiences was the fact that their symbolic world encouraged them to *expect* events with a global significance in the first place. Cf. Nineham 1976, 188.

Even Johnson (1986, 93) comments that the first Christians behaved 'as though the North American colonies in 1690 declared themselves to be a world political power' and asks, 'Were the first Christians megalomaniacal?' The answer he gives is no answer: 'The claims of the first Christians were based on their experience.'

49. For a refreshing exception see Wilson 1982, 349f., who explicitly takes up the concern of Ernst Troeltsch and of the history-of-religions school.

It is sobering to reflect on the impact of Muslim or Mormon experience as well. Shipps 1985, 45, refers both to the resurrection of Jesus and to the translation of the Book of Mormon – both are instances which are only supported by a testimony of believers – when she writes: '. . . the story of a tradition's beginning rests on a paradoxical event that has proved anomalous enough to sustain the weight of supernatural explanation across a long period of time'. In the Book of Mormon, its coming forth was presented 'as the pre-eminent event toward which all history had been tending, at least since the Resurrection, and perhaps since the division of Israel's monarchy . . .' (73).

50. For recent theological criticisms of the exclusive claims of biblical writers see Knitter 1985, 171–204. He tries to outline a 'theocentric, non-normative christology'. On the apocalyptic cultural context of the absolute claims in the New Testament see 182–4. See further the very important collection of articles in Hick – Knitter 1988.

3. Actualizing Interpretation

1. Morgan 1977, 264.

2. Cf. Ebeling 1963, 94, 96. It would be best, however, to abandon the confused term 'biblical theology' altogether.

3. Cf. K. Berger 1977, 261: an exegete only has the right of veto, for he is not capable of positively confirming the legitimacy of the reception of the texts in new situations.

4. The expression is used by Rudolph 1967, 33, in connection with the relation of the science of religion to philosophy of religion and theology.

5. We can ask with Barr (1980, 25), 'how much would the study of an ancient thinker like Plato have been impoverished if throughout the ages scholars had confined themselves to expounding the text and its internal semantic linkages and had rigorously excluded from their minds the question, "Is Plato right?"'

6. This basic agreement over method does not, however, imply an acceptance of the contents of Pannenberg's personal theological construction, i.e. his theology of history. My own position is closer to Kaufman's.

7. Cf. Kaufman's proposal that the criterion of 'humanization' be used in the assessment of theological beliefs (1981, 182ff.).

8. In Scandinavian countries systematic theologians like Bring and Nygren have long struggled to establish a methodology which is acceptable in other humanistic disciplines as well. Jeffner 1981, 9f., notes that in a Swedish university 'theology' now is mostly equivalent to a scientific study of religion without religious commitment. These efforts should not be disqualified (as they sometimes are) as timid attempts to gain a right to exist in the wonderful world of the academy. Rather, they reflect an honest concern to avoid special pleading.

9. Theissen 1979, 12ff. Cf. Kaufman 1981, 101f.

10. It is not quite clear to me whether Pannenberg would accept a two-stage working programme for an exegete, but unless he does, the task imposed on exegesis seems simply too formidable (and the same is true of church history). Pannenberg wants the exegete to question the historical texts to find out 'whether and how far the religious conceptions documented in these texts were adequate to the experience of reality of their period, how far therefore they were able to describe the divine activity they

claimed to have taken place as a manifestation of the all-determining reality' (382). How could one do that at the stage of a historical approach?

In the science of religion, at least, Pannenberg distinguishes between ancillary disciplines (psychology, sociology and even phenomenology of religion) and the real 'science of religion' which uses these materials in the service of checking truth-claims (363f., 368f.; I would rather call such a discipline philosophy of religion). It might be possible, in this framework, to conceive of historical exegesis as an analogue, say, to phenomenology of religion.

11. In this, Pannenberg comes close to Wrede (1897, 18, on 'revelation') and Troeltsch. Cf. Morgan's contention (1977, 265): all theology must stand the test of historical criticism; what is historically false cannot be theologically true. This is correct, if it is one's aim to build theology on a historical basis. But if one makes no such claim, then one should also be free to exploit 'non-historical' theologumena (Strauss!). It will then be possible e.g. to commit oneself to some of the values found in biblical stories, and draw on the stories as evocative pictorial presentations, whatever the relation of the stories to actual history may be.

12. Cf. Pannenberg, e.g. 1976, 259f., 315–26.

13. Kaufman 1981, 179f.

14. Cf. Eissfeldt's position *vis-à-vis* 'Old Testament theology' (above, p. 181n.2).

15. Kaufman 1981, 273f.

16. For a judicious discussion of Jesus' ethics from the latter point of view see R. Robinson 1964, 140–55. Robinson indicates which of the precepts of Jesus should be accepted and which of them rejected, and why, cf. Bowden 1988, 107. In my understanding and terminology, Robinson presents a nuanced 'theological', i.e. actualizing and normative, interpretation, though from an atheistic point of view. It should be noted that on the level of historical interpretation his views of Jesus' ethics come very close to those of T. W. Manson, whom he calls one of Jesus' 'most judicious twentieth-century followers' and a 'learned and responsible exponent' (144, 142).

17. It is in the nature of the matter, moreover, that what counts as commitment to the Christian tradition for one person, is experienced by another as its abandonment – consider the discussion of Bultmann's and especially Braun's decisions.

18. Fiorenza 1988, 15f.; cf. Georgi 1985, 87.

19. E.g. as regards one's attitude to Israeli politics. A particularly American version at the moment is a critical evaluation of political fundamentalism. 'Since literalist biblical fundamentalism asserts the public claims and values of biblical texts' which it uses to feed 'antidemocratic authoritarianism' and to foster 'personal prejudice', biblical scholarship is called to make its research available to a wider public. Fiorenza 1988, 16.

20. Cf. Pannenberg 1976, 353. An exception to confirm the rule is Gerd Theissen's bold attempt to 'interpret biblical faith with the help of evolutionary categories' (1984, xi), i.e. in the broadest possible framework. His thesis is that culture in general, and religion in particular, is 'a rebellion against the principle of selection'; the Bible is an outstanding witness to this rebellion (49f.). The argument, however, that Jesus represents

a 'mutation' of human existence, love being the 'new feature' (86f.) carries little conviction. Was love (or solidarity with the weak, as Theissen defines it) unknown to humanity before Christ?

21. Cf. e.g. the works of Barr (1980, 1983) and Bowden (1988; the latter's thoughts I find even more congenial).

22. Cf. most recently Dunn 1987, 22: 'The exciting potential of the dialogue of New Testament theology is that at its best it enables the New Testament theologian both to hear the message of his texts with first-century ears and to explain or re-express that message with twentieth century lips.' When the exegete has immersed himself in the historical context and entered into the meaning of his text, he may 'hope to find that he himself has become the hermeneutic bridge which spans the centuries and cultures and allows the impact of these writings to be experienced once again . . .'

23. Morgan 1987a, 164, aptly comments on the 'ambitious schemes which fused historical criticism and theological interpretation': 'From Vatke and Baur in the 1830s to Bultmann and von Rad and their respective followers, liberal scholars have been as keen as their conservative counterparts to draw their theology more directly from their biblical interpretation than Gabler envisaged.'

24. See e.g. Hick – Knitter 1988. In the history of 'New Testament theology', one way of paving the way for present-day decisions with historical material has been the attempt to sort out what seems novel or unique in the New Testament as compared with other sources. See already Holtzmann 1911, I, xiv-xv (above, 10). But uniqueness is no guarantee whatsoever of superiority or truth, nor does lack of novelty testify to inferiority. There are unique features in any religious classic; just consider the Qur'an or the Book of Mormon. On the other hand, it is well known that the novelty of at least the elements of Jesus' message can be disputed. On the issue cf. Petzke 1975, 12.

INDEX OF MODERN AUTHORS

Ainley, S. C., 195
Albert, H., 186
Albertz, M., *49f.*, 116
Almond, P. C., 195

Baird, R. D., 192f., 197
Baltzer, K., 185
Barbosa da Silva, A., 196
Barker, M., 193
Barr, J., 110, 187, 191, 193, 200, 202
Barth, K., xii, xiv, 31, *35–7*, 43, 50, 90, 111, 157, 167f., 190, 192
Batson, C. D., 196f.
Bauer, G. L., 156, 158
Bauer, W., 81, 159
Baumgärtel, F., 181
Baur, F. C., xiv, 7, *8–9*, 30, 70, 124, 158f., 163, 169, 185, 202
Bengel, J. A., 186
Berger, K., *78f.*, 156, 158, 164, 169f., 174–6, 179, 181, 184–6, 189–94, 200
Berger, P., xv, *124f.*, 128f., 134, 168, 189, 191, 195–9
Best, E., 184
Best, T. F., 184
Beutler, J., 179
Beyschlag, W., 17, 156, 162
Block, P., 175f.
Boers, H., xi, 156f., 159, 162f., 165f., 169, 177
Bonsirven, J., 174
Bousset, W., xiii, 18, *21f.*, 31, 42, 84, 114, 160f., 164
Bouttier, M., 178
Bowden, J., 187f., 201f.
Braun, D., 173

Braun, H., *62–4*, 82, 85f., 118, 139f., 174, 177f., 186, 189, 201
Bring, R., 200
Brown, R. E., 184
Brückner, M., 159–61, 164–6
Büchsel, F., 44, 47, 170
Bultmann, R., ix–x, xiii–xv, 26, 31, *36–42*, 43, 54, 61f., 64–6, 68, 70, 75f., 78, 82–4, 89f., 93, 97, 102, 111, 115f., 119f., 140, 157, 159f., 163, 165–70, 172, 176f., 179, 182, 185f., 189f., 192–4, 201f.
Burrows, M., 193

Carlyle, T., 164
Catchpole, D., 176
Ceuppens, F., 174
Childs, B., 184
Chomsky, N., 197
Clavier, H., 183
Clements, R. E., 193
Conzelmann, H., 58, 62, *64–6*, 75, 89, 93, 97, 116, 173f., 177f., 182, 195
Cullmann, O., *51–3*, 71, 75, 171–3, 180, 192

Dahl, N. A., 169f.
Deissmann, A., 159, 161
Dentan, R. C., 186, 191f.
Dewailly, L-M., 175f.
Dodds, E. R., 197
Dreyfus, F., 186f., 193
Dunn, J. D. G., xv, *81–3*, 118, 157f., 165, 184f., 188, 190, 202

Ebeling, G., 200
Eichrodt, W., 181, 194

Eissfeldt, O., *181f.*, 201
Eldredge, L., 157
Eliade, M., 87, 123f., *125*, 128, 196–8
Esler, P. F., 198
Evang, M., 168

Fascher, E., 172
Feine, P., 24, *27*, 47, 166
Fiorenza, E. S., *86*, 140, 187, 191, 201
Fredriksen, P., 196
Frei, H., 157f.
Fries, J., 164
Frye, N., 189, 197
Fuller, R. H., 176

Gabler, J. P., xiii–xv, *3–5*, 6–10, 13, 17, 30, 37, 43, 46, 64, 74–6, 85, 89, 109, 112, 137, 141, 156f., 177, 182, 190f., 202
Galileo, 97, 188
Geertz, C., 197
Georgi, D., 165, 170, 184, 186, 201
Gerrish, B. A., 195
Gese, H., 80, 183
Gilkey, L., 199
Goppelt, L., 62, *71–3*, 107, 156, 170f., 173, 176f., 179–82, 190
Grant, F. C., *48f.*, 58, 132, 172, 184, 190, 193–5
Grässer, E., 168, 184
Greimas, A., 124, 134
Gulin, E. G., *45–8*, 57f., 166, 171f., 184, 190
Gunkel, H., 161
Guthrie, D., *60*, 184, 192
Güttgemanns, E., 173, 175, 177

Habermas, J., 186
Hahn, G. L., 158
Halse, P., 175f.
Hammond, P. E., 195
Hargrove, B., 197
Harnack, A. von, 35, 167, 190
Harrington, W., 174
Harris, H., 157f.
Hasel, G. F., 156, 160, 165, 169, 171, 174, 176, 179, 181, 190
Haufe, G., 174f., 179
Hay, D., 195

Hayes, J. H., 190, 193f.
Hegel, G. W. F., 6–9, 158f.
Heidegger, M., 41, 170
Heiler, F., 192
Hellholm, D., 195
Hiers, R. H., 164
Hick, J., 200, 202
Hodgson, P. C., 159
von Hofmann, J. C. K., 71, 166
Holland, D. L., 164
Holtz, T., 180
Holtzmann, H. J., xiii–xiv, *9–12*, 13–14, 16, 30, 46, 159–64, 168f., 191, 202
Hübner, H., 183, 193
Hunter, J. D., 195
Hurtado, L., 184

James, W., 126, 196
Jaspert, B., 168
Jeffner, A., 200
Jeremias, J., 180
Johnson, L. T., xv, *86f.*, 95, 124, *127f.*, 190f., 194, 196–9
Jülicher, A., 35, 37, 167f.

Kaftan, J., xiii, *27–9*, 47, 71, 164, 166f., 190, 192, 194
Kalusche, M., 183
Kant, I., 158
Käsemann, E., 56, 62, *67f.*, 82, 93f., 165, 177f., 193f.
Kaufman, G. D., *138f.*, 188, 200f.
Keck, L. E., 53, 174, 183
Kieffer, R., *58f.*, 175–7
Kiehn, A., 189
Klein, G., 173
Knitter, P. F., 200, 202
Knoch, O., 175
Koester, H., xv, 76, *83f.*, 101, 113, 182, 185, 191, 193f.
Kraus, H-J., 157, 159, 163, 165, 167, 182f.
Krüger, G., 161
Kubo, S., 185
Kümmel, W. G., 62, *68–71*, 72, 76, 82, 102, 107, 156, 160, 163, 166f., 174, 177, 179–81, 184
Küng, H., 188f., 191

Ladd, G. E., *59f.*, 171, 176

Laeuchli, S., 189
Lange, D., 197
van der Leeuw, G., 123, 192
Lemche, N. P., 193
Lemcio, E. E., 184
Levenson, J. D., 193
Lindbeck, G. A., 188, 195–8
Lindemann, A., 178–80
Locke, J., 3
Lohse, E., 62, *68*, 177, 179
Luckmann, T., xv, 129, 197
Lüdemann, G., 18, 160, 163, 182, 185
Luz, U., 188

Malherbe, A., 185
Malina, B. J., 195
Manson, T. W., 201
Marshall, I. H., 157
Marxsen, W., 196
McCann, D. P., 195
Meeks, W., 83, 179, 184f., 191
Meinertz, M., 174
Merk, O., 156–8, 160, 165, 167, 169–72, 174, 177, 183, 192
Michie, D., 186
Moltmann, J., 167
Morgan, R., xi, 18, *76f.*, 140, 156–9, 161–3, 165f., 168–70, 177, 179, 182, 187, 189f., 192, 200–2
Morris, L., *60f.*, 66, 116, 176f., 193f.
Murray, G., 197
Müller, K., 160f.
Müller, M., 164

Neill, S., 179
Neusner, J., 198
Nikolainen, A. T., *57f.*, 175, 184, 190, 195
Nineham, D. E., 189, 198f.
Nygren, A., 200

Oeming, M., 173, 183f., 188
Otto, R., 87, *123f.*, 195f.
Overbeck, F., 192

Painter, J., 168
Pannenberg, W., *138f.*, 189, 200f.
Patte, D., 124, *134f.*, 186, 198f.

Perrin, N., 169f., 185, 189f., 193
Petzke, G., xv, *85f.*, 87, 95, 98, 139, 185f., 189, 191, 194, 197, 202
Piper, O. A., 171
Prussner, F. C., 190, 193f.

von Rad, G., 52, 156, 173, 181, 188, 202
Räisänen, H., 109, 162, 169, 176, 183, 186, 189, 192, 194, 198f.
von Ranke, L., 104
Regner, F., 164
Reicke, B., 179, 189
von Reventlow, H. Graf, 183
Rhoads, D., 88, 186
Richardson, A., *53*, 111, 116, 174, 183, 192
Riesenfeld, H., *56f.*, 175, 194
Ritschl, A., 9, 22f.
Robinson, J. M., *75f.*, 86, 90, 162, 174, 182, 189
Robinson, R., 201
Rollmann, H., 162
Rowland, C., 193–5
Rudolph, K., 164, 192, 197, 200

Saebo, M., 157
Saliba, J., 196
Sandberger, J. F., 158
Sanders, E. P., 156, 164, 180, 192, 195
Sanders, J. T., 177, 188, 195
Sandys-Wunsch, J., 157
Schäffer, W., 197
Schelkle, K. H., *55*, 116, 174f., 180, 190, 194
Schelling, F., 158
Schillebeeckx, E., 197
Schlatter, A., xii, *24–7*, 36, 47, 71, 76, 80, 165–7, 192
Schlaudraff, K-H., 172f.
Schleiermacher, F. D. E., 14, *122f.*, 125, 195
Schlier, H., *53f.*, 59, 80, 100f., 113, 115, 189, 192f.
Schmithals, W., 168
Schnackenburg, R., *54*, 174
Schnelle, U., 162, 186
Scholder, K., 158, 188
Schottroff, L., 186, 189
Schramm, T., 189

Schweitzer, A., 97, 112, 156–8, 160,
    164, 168, 188
Scott, E. F., 172
Scroggs, R., **87f.**, 189
Shipps, J., 199
Smend, R., 156f.
Smith, M., 156, 193
Smith, W. C., 197
Spiegel, Y., 189
Stauffer, E., **44f.**, 75, 89, 116, 171
Stendahl, K., **74f.**, 77, 90, 107, 110,
    167, 171, 174, 189, 193, 196
Strauss, D. F., xiv, **6–8**, 23, 30, 37,
    43, 69, 76, 85, 97, 140, 157f., 182,
    201
Strecker, G., 17, **66**, 116, 161–3, 178,
    184, 186, 190, 192f.
Stuhlmacher, P., **80f.**, 86, 97, 113,
    124, 157, 161, 163, 165, 168, 177,
    183f., 188–90
Syreeni, K., 186, 191

Theissen, G., 138, 188f., 192, 199–
    201
Thüsing, W., 185
Tiele, C. P., 164
Tracy, D., 186
Troeltsch, E., 163, 199, 201
Tuckett, C. M., 193

Uro, R., 193

Vatke, W., 202
Ventis, V. L., 196f.
Verheule, A. F., 163f.

Watson, F., 195
Weber, M., 125, 191
Weinel, H., xiii, 18, **20f.**, 22, 30,
    163f., 167, 171
Weiss, B., 17, 156, 161f., 165
Weiss, J., xiii, 16, 18, 22–4, 30f., 40,
    42, 48, 93, 112, 158, 164f., 192
Wernle, P., xiii, **18–20**, 22, 24, 29f.,
    162f., 168f.
Westerholm, S., 162, 189
Westermann, C., 193
Wiles, M., 184
Wilson, S. G., 188, 195, 199
Windisch, H., 161, 163f., 166
Wrede, W., xiii–xv, **13–18**, 20–2, 24,
    28, 30f., 42, 54, 57, 59–61, 67, 69,
    74–6, 78, 83, 85, 89f., 93, 95, 98,
    100f., 105f., 114, 120, 137, 159–
    63, 165f., 168, 176–8, 187, 189,
    194, 201
Wuthnow, R., 195, 197

Zahn, T., **43f.**, 71, 115, 170, 180

9332